Family Tightrope

Family Tightrope

THE CHANGING LIVES OF
VIETNAMESE AMERICANS

Nazli Kibria

PRINCETON UNIVERSITY PRESS

PRINCETON, NEW JERSEY

The author gratefully acknowledges permission
to reproduce the following poems:
"Tomorrow I Will Be Home" by Cao Tan (epigraph to
chapter 5) and "The First Day of School" by Truong Anh Thuy
(epigraph to chapter 6), both from *War and Exile:
A Vietnamese Anthology*, ed. Nguyen Ngoc Bich
(Springfield, Va.: Vietnam PEN Abroad, 1989);
"Written Aboard a Boat on the Way Back to
Mount Con" by Nguyen Trai (epigraph to chapter 3),
from *The Heritage of Vietnamese Poetry*,
ed. and trans. Huynh Sanh Thong (New Haven:
Yale University Press, 1979); and "The Tale of Kieu"
by Nguyen Du (epigraph to chapter 4), from
The Tale of Kieu, trans. Huynh Sanh Thong
(New Haven: Yale University Press, 1983).

Library of Congress Cataloging-in-Publication Data

Kibria, Nazli
Family tightrope : the changing lives of
Vietnamese Americans / Nazli Kibria
p. cm.
ISBN 0-691-03260 — ISBN 0-691-02115-5 (pbk.)
1. Vietnamese American Families.
2. Vietnamese Americans—Social conditions.
I. Title.
E184.V53k53 1993
305.895'92073—dc20 93-18777

FOR MY PARENTS

Contents

Acknowledgments   ix

CHAPTER ONE
Assimilation, Adaptation, and Immigrant Life   3

CHAPTER TWO
The Study and the Setting   24

CHAPTER THREE
Vietnamese Roots   38

CHAPTER FOUR
Patchworking: Households in the Economy   73

CHAPTER FIVE
The Family Tightrope: Gender Relations   108

CHAPTER SIX
Generation Gaps   144

CHAPTER SEVEN
The Changing Contours of Vietnamese American Family Life   167

Bibliography   173

Index   181

Acknowledgments

RESEARCHING AND WRITING THIS BOOK has been much like a journey for me. And like many journeys, it is one in which numerous people have helped me along the way. My greatest debt is to the Vietnamese Americans whose voices and experiences resound within this book but whose names I cannot acknowledge due to the necessity for anonymity. This book would not have been possible without their cooperation and support.

As my dissertation advisor, Renée Fox sensitively and wisely helped to navigate me through the intricacies of the fieldwork process. I benefited a great deal from her skills and experience as an ethnographer. Fred Block provided critical feedback and encouragement during both the fieldwork and writing of the study. Steve Gold, Rubén Rumbaut, Barrie Thorne, and Diane Wolf took time out from their busy schedules to make extensive comments on the entire manuscript. Willy De Cramer, James Freeman, Pierrette Hondagneu-Sotelo, Jonathan Imber, Eun Mee Kim, Jon Miller, Ewa Morawska, and Christine White provided important feedback on various chapters. For helping me to translate interviews and for teaching me about Vietnamese culture, history, and language, I thank Hoang Hau, Huong Le, Lan Nguyen, Dinh Pham, and Binh Pham.

Greg Brooks's friendship has helped me get through every stage of this project. From listening to me "let off steam" about my work to editing portions of the manuscript, his support has helped to ease some of the burdens and loneliness of the research and writing process. I also thank Susie Chow and Dinh Pham for always believing in me, and Eun Mee Kim for helping me to stay sane in the final months of writing.

Last but not least, I thank James Allen Littlefield, who has lived with "the book" for many years and has advised me on all computer-related aspects of it. I thank him for his unflagging support of this project throughout its duration. But most of all, I thank him for helping me to build a family life that is both nurturing and empowering.

Family Tightrope

Assimilation, Adaptation, and Immigrant Life

BINH[1] WAS BORN in 1933 in North Vietnam, in the province of Binh Ninh, in a village that was heavily Catholic. Of his eleven brothers and sisters, only two were alive today, the rest having died from either illness or the effects of war. Binh's father had told him that their family had lived in the village for at least three generations, and until his grandparents' generation, they had been village notables (*lý trưởng*). When Binh was ten years old, his father had gone south to work on a rubber plantation owned by the French. His father had inherited a hectare and a half of land, from which he sold one hectare to pay for his passage to the south as well as that of his wife and two of their youngest children. Binh did not accompany his parents but remained in the village under the care of his maternal grandmother and attended school for about eight years.

In 1953 Binh joined the French armed forces, who were engaged in battle against nationalist Vietnamese forces for control of Vietnam. In 1954, following the Geneva Treaty and the subsequent partition of the country, Binh and other family members moved to the south, fearing religious and economic persecution from the Northern regime. Binh remained in the armed forces. A couple of years after the move to the south he got married: "My father sent me a telegram saying my mother died, and so I went there for the funeral. I found out that it was a lie and they wanted me to marry. That time I didn't have any success, so I didn't want to get married. I was twenty-three or twenty-four at the time. But my father told me, 'you are mature now, you should marry, otherwise you will hang around and do bad things.' So I got married; someone matched me with my wife, Van."

Binh began his career in the army in the south in the rank of first corporal (*hạ sĩ*). In 1973, his last year of military service, he was a warrant officer (*thượng sĩ*). During his years in the military, Binh moved constantly, although most of his transfers were within Central Vietnam. In order to supplement his income, his wife, Van, engaged in small-scale

---

[1] All names have been changed in order to protect the anonymity of informants.

trading activities, and she eventually opened a small variety store. By 1972, with the help of his wife, Binh had managed to accumulate enough money to buy two buses. He described life in the south in the 1960s and 1970s to be economically "comfortable and easy." Although they did not have a car or many luxury items, he and his family (which included his six children) never had to worry about money at that time.

But things changed in 1975. The government collectivized his buses, and it became more and more difficult to make ends meet. Binh worried about the economic future of his sons and about the possibility that they would be drafted into the army to fight against Cambodia. These considerations, as well as others, played into his decision to leave Vietnam: "I came here [the United States] for freedom. In Vietnam I had enough to live, but I wasn't free. For instance, I had money in the bank but if I wanted to spend it I had to send them an application letter telling them why I wanted to withdraw it, and they could still forbid it. They didn't forbid religion, but if the priest wanted to do the worship he had to do it only at certain times and places. That's why I left, for freedom and for my children to have education. The best thing about life in America is that we're free to do what we want, but the worst thing is that the culture and customs make people rotten."

In 1981, Binh left Vietnam with three of his sons. His wife did not want to leave, and it was also necessary that someone remain behind to look after their aged parents. Binh planned to send money back for the remainder of his family to escape after he had been in the United States for about a year. The boat journey out of Vietnam to Thailand took three days, during which time they were robbed twice by Thai pirates. After about six months, Binh and his sons arrived in Philadelphia, sponsored by a social service agency.

For about ten months after arriving in the United States, Binh drew on the financial support available to newly arrived refugees. After this he began a part-time janitorial position that paid minimum wage. But then a back injury that he incurred in a serious car accident prevented him from working for several months. All three of Binh's sons were in school, and one was soon to enter college. The family managed to live on the cash public assistance they received as well as on the income from the sons' after-school jobs. Binh tried to find another job, but he felt tired and frustrated. He spent his time talking with friends in the neighborhood as well as doing the laundry and cooking for the household. He had never prepared food in his life before. When his sons complained about his cooking, he told them that they would have to make do with whatever food he prepared until they married and there were women around to do the cooking.

Binh had felt sad and dispirited since arriving in the United States. It had proven to be much more difficult to bring his wife and remaining children over to the United States than he had anticipated. He did not want to "die alone" in the United States, and he felt that he would like to return to Vietnam some day. What troubled him most about life here was the change in his sons. They no longer respected him or listened to him. They had quickly become Americanized. Sometimes he tried to discipline them, but this was difficult because U.S. society was "on their side."

Lien was born in Saigon in 1966, the second-youngest in a family of twelve brothers and sisters. She described her family:

> We lived in a big house, and my paternal grandfather and grandmother lived next door to us. All around us, near us, we had relatives. . . . aunts, uncles. Not my maternal grandparents, though, because they lived in the countryside and they also died when I was very young.
>
> When I was small, my father was in the army and my mother had a small store [*tiệm tạp hóa*]. I think we were rich in Vietnam at that time, because we lived in a nice house and we had a housekeeper. I never did any work; I was so spoiled, when someone asked me to do something, I cried and then I didn't have to do it. I think it's because my grandmother lived next door. I spent most of my time with my grandmother. And she used to say, "you're so spoiled, no one will want to marry you." I said I didn't care about that. I was always very independent.

In 1975 life changed for Lien and her family. Her father and a brother were sent to one of the reeducation camps that had been set up by the new government for the members of the old regime. Her mother's business also suffered because of the new government's policies toward private businesses. Eventually her mother closed her store because the high taxes no longer made it a profitable venture. In order to make ends meet, Lien's mother and sisters began to sew clothes and sell them at the market.

In 1977, one of Lien's elder brothers escaped from Vietnam by boat and eventually resettled in the United States. Lien was in school at this time. But she felt increasingly restless and depressed, in part because the return of her father from the reeducation camp had been followed by a period of great tension and unhappiness between her mother and father. After hearing of her brother's successful escape, she began thinking about following him. At first, Lien's parents refused the request. But they eventually gave in, persuaded by the idea that life in the United States would be much better for her, a child of the former regime, than it could ever be in Vietnam. Also, her parents planned to try to follow her later— although this plan never materialized, partly because of the serious illness that Lien's mother developed shortly after Lien's departure from Vietnam.

Lien left the country under the guardianship of an aunt who was a close friend of her mother. After five nights at sea, they arrived in Hong Kong, where they were to spend the next eight months. Lien, her aunt, and her aunt's three children eventually resettled in Hawaii. Lien described Hawaii as a beautiful place, one to which she often dreamed of returning someday. About two months after arriving in Hawaii, Lien's aunt remarried, to a Chinese-American man she had met there. At this time, Lien decided to leave Hawaii, both because she felt uncomfortable with her aunt's new husband and, more important, because her older brother, who had resettled in Philadelphia, had sent her a letter asking her to join him there.

After arriving in Philadelphia, Lien moved into her brother's one-room apartment. He worked as a cook in a restaurant while she went to school. The next year was a painful one for Lien as her brother began to beat her up every day when she returned home from school. After about a year of putting up with her brother's physical abuse, Lien made the decision to leave her brother and live with some friends. She was encouraged to do so by an Asian American teacher at her school with whom she had become close friends. Her friends' parents treated her like a daughter and adopted her into the family. Lien felt happy under their care, and she was also proud of the excellent grades that she was receiving at school. But a few months later, Lien dropped out of school to marry a Vietnamese American she had met at school. She and her new husband then moved into an apartment that they shared with three of her husband's brothers.

Binh and Lien are two of the Vietnamese refugees I became acquainted with from 1983 to 1985, when I conducted research among recently arrived Vietnamese refugees in an inner-city area of Philadelphia. Through in-depth interviews and participant observation in household and community settings, I sought to understand how these newcomers were experiencing their initial years of life in the United States. The two life histories that I have summarized here hint at the myriad and often dramatic quality of the life changes that have accompanied Vietnamese migration and settlement in the United States. This book explores one dimension of these changes: shifts in family life.

In recent years, many popular media reports have described Vietnamese Americans as among the latest representatives of the quintessentially American immigrant success story. News stories describe how, in a short period of time, the group has managed to overcome poverty by dint of hard work and effort. As *Time Magazine* put it, after describing the economic accomplishments of a Vietnamese immigrant fisherman in Texas, "A decade after their arrival in America, the onetime refugees are becoming solid members of the Sunbelt's middle class."[2]

Popular media reports further suggest that what is responsible for the alleged miraculous economic progress of Vietnamese Americans is the cultural quality of their family life. That is, like other Asian Americans, within the stable, traditional, and hierarchical confines of their families, the Vietnamese are taught the cultural values that are integral to their success. Thus Ellen Hume, in a newspaper article describing the group, comments: "What explains their success? The values they come with—a dedication to family, education and thrift—are cited as the main reason by people who have observed the refugees."[3] (1985). The invoking of family life as an explanation for immigrant economic progress has also been fostered by the statements of neoconservatives and New Right spokespersons, who in recent years have used "'the family' . . . in explaining away the differential success or failure of ethnic minority groups, including Asian Americans" (Hamamoto 1992, 35).

But to what extent does this image of stability, cultural continuity, and internal consensus reflect the reality of Vietnamese American family life? Contrary to the media images that I have described, the families that I studied were not the unchanging and uncompromisingly traditional and Confucian entities that they are often made out to be. Rather, I found family life to be an arena of considerable conflict and flux. I saw and heard women, men, and children struggling to reconstruct and redefine the structure and meaning of family life. This book unravels and describes that reconstruction process.

The notion that migration has left Vietnamese American family life

[2] From an article titled "Finding Niches in a New Land," in the Special Immigrants Issue of *Time Magazine* (July 8, 1985): 24–101. For another report see "Asian-Americans: A Model Minority," *Newsweek* (December 6, 1982) 40–51.

[3] From: "Vietnam's Legacy: Indochinese Refugees Prosper in U.S., Drawing on Survival Skills, Special Values," *Wall Street Journal* (March 21, 1985).

unscathed is belied by the tremendous disruption wrought on the family groups and networks of Vietnamese refugees by the move to the United States. Although separation from kin is perhaps a universal aspect of the immigrant experience, the circumstances that have surrounded the Vietnamese migration have made the extent and depth of these separations extremely sharp for the group. For example, it is far from uncommon to find young Vietnamese children in the United States without their parents, or Vietnamese husbands without their wives. Responding to these losses, Vietnamese Americans worked hard to rebuild family ties in the United States. They did this by shifting and expanding the criteria for inclusion in the family circle. Thus, for example, friends and distant relatives who had been marginal members of the family circle in Vietnam became part of the active circle of kin relations in the United States. In short, migration to the United States had, in significant ways, altered the substance of family ties for the group.

In addition to altering family boundaries, migration to the United States had also challenged the traditional gender and generational hierarchies of Vietnamese family life. Crucial to understanding these challenges are the social and economic losses that Vietnamese refugee men had suffered in the transition to life in the United States. In pre-1975 South Vietnam, my male informants had been members of the middle class. But once in the United States, they found themselves in an environment in which their occupational opportunities were limited, and they were often treated with disdain as "foreigners" and subordinates in the racial hierarchy of U.S. society. Because of the men's losses, the status of Vietnamese immigrant men and women (in terms of relative control of social and economic resources) had approached a situation of greater equality than in the past. This decline in men's economic and social resources was also responsible for the greater generational equality in families and, concomitantly, a rise in blatant and visible conflicts between the generations in family contexts.

The rise in women's access to resources, relative to that of men, was a source of tension and change in the relations of men and women in Vietnamese American families. But contrary to what one might expect, Vietnamese American women did not simply react to this situation of greater equality by attempting to restructure family life along more egalitarian lines. Rather, I found women to be deeply ambivalent about changes in family life, particularly those that would signify crucial departures from the traditional family system. I found women struggling to reconcile and incorporate their new resources into the framework of Vietnamese kinship traditions. They walked an ideological tightrope, struggling to use their new resources to their advantage but not in ways that significantly altered or threatened the traditional family system. Vietnamese American women valued the traditional Vietnamese family system for its ethic of collectivism and cooperation, in contrast to what they described as the "selfishness" of U.S. families and culture. They also spoke with approval of the ties of obligation that bound Vietnamese men and children to their families, as well as the tremendous authority assigned to parents in the traditional Vietnamese family system. These were both aspects of Vietnamese family traditions that women felt were vital and valuable, and sorely missing from U.S. family life.

Of course, my informants' attitudes and feelings about Vietnamese family traditions were far from uniform and in fact varied a great deal, particularly according to age and family circumstances. Younger informants' (in their early twenties or younger) feelings about the traditional Vietnamese family system were certainly more conflicted than that of their elders. Nonetheless, few younger informants were willing or eager simply to discard Vietnamese family traditions. I found that for the young, Vietnamese family traditions entered into their efforts to come to terms with their cultural identity, to understand and define what it meant "to be Vietnamese" in the United States. Vietnamese American young explicitly identified what they saw to be the distinctive features of Vietnamese family life as essential to what set them apart in U.S. society, what "made them Vietnamese." Their efforts to redefine family life were informed by concern and anxiety about how to carve out a cultural place for themselves in the United States, a place that would give meaning to their racial-ethnic[4] status. More generally, for Vietnamese Americans, both young and old, the traditional Vietnamese family system, particularly its cooperative and collectivist elements and manifestations, was a source of cultural pride and self-esteem.

The value that Vietnamese Americans placed on the traditional Vietnamese family system also arose from the fact of its close relationship to the economic practices of Vietnamese Americans, or the ways in which they survived and reached for the attainment of middle-class status in the United States. Much as they had done prior to migration, Vietnamese immigrants relied on a collectivist household economy, one in which indi-

---

[4] I use the term *racial-ethnic* to convey what Amott and Matthaei (1991) have described as "the contradictory nature of racial theories and practices, in particular the fact that those people seen as belonging to a particular 'race' often lack a shared set of distinctive physical characteristics, but rather share a common ethnicity or culture" (p. 17).

vidual resources were shared and pooled to cope with the demands and vicissitudes of the economic environment faced in the United States. These collectivist household economies were organized around Vietnamese kinship traditions, drawing on them for structure, support, and legitimation. Thus Vietnamese Americans strove to preserve the traditional Vietnamese family system partly because of its significance to their economic lives and future.

The picture of Vietnamese American family life that I paint in this book is, of course, one that is bounded by time. Perhaps the best way to see it is as a snapshot of the Vietnamese American experience. Indeed, my data constantly reminded me of the dynamic quality of Vietnamese American family patterns, and the ongoing nature of change. There are, however, reasons to believe that the initial years following resettlement do hold some special insights for those who are concerned with the immigrant experience. It is when immigrants first arrive in the new country that the social and cultural challenges posed by migration may be experienced in an exceptionally sharp fashion because of the novelty of the new society and the pressures associated with beginning a new life. It is at this time that immigrants may begin to feel most poignantly, the tremendous and far-reaching consequences of having made the migration journey. Immigrants' reflections about how their social worlds have changed as a result of migration are likely to have an immediacy and sharpness in the early years of settlement. It is precisely the "newness" of the immigrant and the sense of disjuncture that he or she experiences that make a study of the initial years valuable in its ability to provide a clear picture of how migration challenges prior realities and how immigrants understand and respond to the new realities of their lives.

VIETNAMESE IN THE UNITED STATES

The flow of Vietnamese refugees into the United States began in April 1975, with the fall of the U.S.-backed South Vietnamese government and the reunification of the country under the Communist leadership of North Vietnam. At this time, about 130,000 Vietnamese were flown into the United States, as part of an evacuation effort to aid the employees and associates of the United States government who were in Vietnam. However, in a largely unanticipated trend, the outflow of people from Vietnam was to continue after the 1975 evacuation. From 1975 to 1985, nearly half a million Vietnamese settled in the United States, making them one of the largest Asian-origin populations in the country.[5] Given current growth rates, in the future the Vietnamese are expected to be a significant presence, particularly in California and Texas.[6]

Despite the increasingly sizable presence of the Vietnamese population in the United States, studies of the group are as yet of limited scope. For the most part, existing works are concerned with either the economic situation or the mental health of the group. Available research also usually fails to differentiate among the various Southeast Asian nationalities and groups (e.g., Vietnamese, Cambodian, Lao, Hmong, ethnic Chinese), treating them instead as a single category of analysis.[7] Yet the social, cultural, and historical gulfs between these groups are vast. For example, Southeast Asians speak different languages and their degree of urbanization and exposure to Western culture prior to arrival in the United States has been varied. There is a dearth of research that considers the specific experiences of the groups in terms of their particularities and also goes beyond the exploration of employment patterns to more detailed, contextual accounts of their experiences in a variety of life spheres.

Within the larger history of immigration to the United States, Vietnamese Americans are aptly seen as part of what has been described as "the new immigration" following the Immigration Act of 1965 (Gold 1992, 7). This act set in motion a flow of immigration into the United States that has been, in many ways, distinct from previous flows. Whereas prior to 1965, most immigrants were white and of European extraction, since 1965 they have been mostly nonwhite and from Third World countries. Furthermore, reflecting the greater diversity of their social and economic backgrounds in comparison to previous waves of immigrants, post-1965

[5] The 1990 census reported 614,547 Vietnamese in the United States, a number that was about 100,000 persons short of actual admissions from Vietnam from 1975 to 1990. A possible explanation for this discrepancy is the self-reported identification in the 1990 census of many Vietnamese as "Chinese" due to the significant presence of Chinese-Vietnamese persons among Vietnamese refugees to the United States (Rumbaut, personal communication).

[6] The 1990 census showed California to be home to 45.6 percent of the Vietnamese population in the United States, with Texas following at 11.3 percent. For information on fertility rates among Southeast Asian refugees see Rumbaut and Weeks (1986).

[7] The treatment by researchers of Southeast Asians as a group reflects the similar treatment and legal status accorded to them by the U.S. government. Related to this is the fact that one of the major sources of statistical information on Southeast Asian refugees in the United States are the annual reports to Congress prepared by the Office of Refugee Resettlement. In these reports, which are often used by social scientists in their analyses, information is presented on Southeast Asians as a group.

11

immigrants have entered into an extremely varied range of occupations and sectors of the United States economy (Massey 1981; Portes and Rumbaut 1990, 7).

Besides their economic status, another source of diversity among contemporary immigrants is government classification of their legal status. Of those who legally enter, some are treated as "immigrants," and others, such as Vietnamese Americans, as "political refugees." Those who are classified as refugees have been judged by the United States government to have left their homelands due to political, religious, or other forms of persecution, in contrast to immigrants who have *chosen* to emigrate. As Steve Gold (1992, ix–x) observes, the refugee/immigrant distinction, although by no means a completely invalid one, has been somewhat overplayed in the refugee literature, which has often treated the two groups of people as completely distinct in their experience. In reality, the motivations for migration often involve a complex mixture of political, economic, and other factors, and the official labels imposed are "not a matter of personal choice" (Portes and Rumbaut 1990, 23). In other words, it is quite possible for an immigrant to be driven by persecution to leave his or her homeland and yet be classified by the United States government as an "immigrant" rather than a "refugee." Given these complexities, I suggest that it is useful to consider refugees as a type of immigrant rather than as a group that is completely divorced from the concerns and experiences of the larger immigrant population. It is certainly true that the experience of the refugee often differs from that of the immigrant, particularly in terms of the conditions of departure from the homeland, which are often far more constrained. At the same time, there is considerable overlap in experience between the two groups.

But clearly, refugees and immigrants do differ in the type of reception that is accorded them by the United States government. For example, unlike immigrants, those who are classified as refugees are eligible for government assistance. Stimulated in part by the growing Southeast Asian entry into the country in the late 1970s, the United States government has created an elaborate "structure of refuge" to deal with refugees (Rumbaut 1989a).[8] This structure of refuge, involving a complex configuration of policies guiding entry and settlement, has included special government-funded programs designed to aid adjustment. Thus refugees have access to the welfare system (Aid to Families with Dependent Children, Supple-

---

[8] The Refugee Act of 1980, stimulated in part by the increased flow of Southeast Asian refugees, formalized and supplemented the ad hoc, nationality-specific refugee resettlement system that existed prior to this time.

12

mental Security Income, Medicaid, food stamps) on the same means-tested basis as citizens. For a period of time following arrival,[9] there are also special Federal programs (Refugee Cash Assistance and Refugee Medical Assistance) for those refugees who are income-eligible but do not meet the other criteria of AFDC and Medicaid. The vast majority of immigrants in the United States, both in the past and today, have not had access to such government aid programs. Thus because the Vietnamese have entered the United States as political refugees, government policies and programs have played a fairly important part in shaping their initial years of resettlement. The effects of the structure of refuge on Vietnamese American life are among the questions to be explored in this book.

The eligibility of refugees for government assistance has perhaps contributed to the rather lukewarm reception that U.S. society has accorded Vietnamese refugees. In a series of Gallup polls conducted in 1979, more than 60 percent of those surveyed indicated that they opposed the admission of Vietnamese refugees into the country (Stern 1981). Besides the fact that they have served as a somewhat painful reminder of the long and fateful U.S. military involvement in the Vietnam war, the resettlement of Southeast Asians has occurred at a time of widespread hostility toward racial-ethnic groups. Vietnamese Americans entering the country during the late 1970s and early to mid-1980s faced a social and political climate of conservatism and "backlash" to the political gains of minorities forged in the previous decade. In an analysis of these trends, Omi and Winant suggest (1986, 109–13) that the major economic dislocations of the 1970s and 1980s made much of U.S. society increasingly resistant to and resentful of providing economic benefits to the "underprivileged." These public sentiments were reflected in the election of Ronald Reagan and in the widespread support and partial success of his efforts to dismantle Federal programs for the poor—efforts that particularly affected minorities (Palmer and Sawhill 1984). The economic recession of the early 1980s and the Federal cutbacks in programs for the poor intensified the poverty caused by the long-term economic stagnation plaguing many urban areas since the 1960s (Wilson 1987, 39–41). In many instances, Vietnamese Americans found themselves perceived as new and unwelcome competitors for scarce jobs and public resources. It was in the con-

---

[9] In accordance with the 1980 Refugee Act, states received Federal reimbursement for assistance to refugees through RCA and RMA programs, for a period of thirty-six months following their arrival in the United States. In 1982, the period of reimbursement was changed to eighteen months, and in 1988 it was further reduced to twelve months (Office of Refugee Resettlement 1989, 36).

text of these considerable economic pressures that tensions between racial-ethnic groups, often involving Vietnamese refugees, began erupting in urban areas throughout the country in the early to mid-1980s.[10]

Resentment toward Vietnamese refugees was perhaps further fueled by the tendency of the popular media to portray the group as a "model minority." In reality, the economic "progress" of Vietnamese Americans has been extremely uneven. Available evidence does show that by the mid-1980s, those Vietnamese immigrants who had arrived as part of the 1975 evacuation had achieved parity in their household income levels with the general U.S. population (Office of Refugee Resettlement 1988, 147). But succeeding waves of Vietnamese refugees, who have been from less privileged backgrounds than the 1975 cohort, have had less economic success (see Gold 1992, 64). A 1984 survey of Vietnamese refugees in San Diego found 22.4 percent of respondents to be unemployed and 61.3 percent to have incomes below the poverty level. Of those who were employed, 29.2 percent indicated that they received no fringe benefits at work, and 48.7 percent said that there was no possibility for promotion at their jobs (Rumbaut 1989b, 152).

FROM ASSIMILATION TO ADAPTATION: PERSPECTIVES ON IMMIGRANT LIFE

Reflections on the immigrant experience almost invariably touch on family life, an arena in which central and contradictory elements of the immigrant experience converge in powerful ways. The immigrant experience is often one in which old loyalties and relations are simultaneously strengthened and challenged in the face of new social forces. These conflicting processes of change and continuity are powerfully reflected in immigrants' familial experiences. Traditional family arrangements may be threatened by migration but also reinforced as immigrants turn to their families for help and support in their efforts to build a new life.

The scholarly literature on immigrant life in the United States has often treated these synchronous and intertwined processes of transformation and persistence as separable and distinct rather than as integrated aspects of the immigrant experience. Thus some scholars have focused on the

---

[10] For example, see "Slaying of Boy Stuns Refugee Family," *New York Times* (January 2, 1984); and "Severe Beating of Asian Shakes a School," *Philadelphia Inquirer* (November 6, 1983). Also see Takaki (1989, 480–86).

disruptions that settlement in the United States brings to the immigrant's traditional way of life, whereas others have been concerned with how immigrant institutions help the immigrant to cope with and adapt to U.S. life. Although both these perspectives hold an important place in the social science literature,[11] the past two decades have witnessed a growing focus on the latter concern. In short, there has been gravitation from a concern with how immigrant institutions change to an interest in how these institutions help immigrants to adapt to the "host" society.

The Assimilation Vision

The assimilation perspective[12] has been a dominant paradigm in U.S. scholarship on immigrant life (Gordon 1964; Park and Burgess 1969). Born out of the influential Chicago School of Sociology in the 1930s, under the leadership of Robert Park, assimilation theory suggested that immigrant groups were inevitably to move from attachment to "traditional" immigrant identities and culture toward integration into the "modern" mainstream of U.S. life. In other words, immigrant groups gradually became "Americanized," shedding their loyalties and connections with the immigrant culture and becoming assimilated into the melting pot of the United States. Assimilation theorists did not deny that in the early years, immigrant institutions and loyalties could prove useful to immigrants (Lal 1985). But the theoretical assumptions of these scholars led them to view the survival of and dependence on immigrant institutions as very much a temporary phase, because of the powerful and inevitable quality of assimilation. There were differences of opinion about the exact outcome of assimilation. It could result in "Anglo-conformity," or the complete melding of the immigrant into the majority culture of the United States. Alternatively, in the process of assimilating, immigrants could preserve elements of their own culture within that of the dominant culture. But whether the outcome was "Anglo-conformity" or "cultural pluralism," there was agreement about the centrality of assimilation processes to the immigrant experience.

[11] The concern with assimilation remains important in the empirical literature, which examines the degree of assimilation of various groups and the causal factors that drive the assimilation process (Hirschman 1983; Lieberson 1978; Massey 1981).

[12] My definition of the assimilationist model or what Omi and Winant (1986) call "ethnicity-based theory" includes its subvariations, including "cultural pluralism" and "Anglo-conformity."

15

So far as immigrant family life is concerned, the assimilationist model suggested a gradual movement toward a more "modern" family structure. In making this claim, the model was supported by modernization theorists who argued that industrialization resulted in decisive and inevitable changes in family life. In one of the most influential statements of this perspective, *World Revolution and Family Patterns* (1963), William Goode argued that industrialization set in motion processes that replaced extended and structurally complex family systems with the "conjugal family," nuclear and more egalitarian in its internal relations.[13] Scholars of immigrant life extended Goode's analysis to understand the evolution of family life among immigrant groups. Thus in studies of turn-of-the-century European immigrants in the United States, social scientists wrote of how the traditional, patriarchal, extended family evaporated as immigrants were torn from their peasant world and thrust into the industrial city. Because migration was such a disruptive experience, in the years following settlement there was much disorganization and pathology in the family—as expressed, for example, in high rates of marital separation and child delinquency (Handlin 1951; Warner and Srole 1945). Eventually, however, immigrant family patterns would become more stable as they became more "Americanized," or as assimilation into "modern" family patterns began to take place.

Among the modernizing transformations that were expected of immigrant families, perhaps the most fundamental was a movement toward greater generational and gender equality in families. Previously disenfranchised groups in the family—women and children—gained economic freedom due to the opportunities for wage employment in the industrialized society of the United States. Also relevant to the breakdown of the patriarchal family order was the more egalitarian quality of U.S. cultural values and patterns in contrast to immigrant ones. Thus, although they sometimes portrayed immigrant women as resisting change, those working in the assimilation tradition argued that "Americanization" brought greater equality in the relations of men and women (see Deutsch 1987, 719–20). In other words, because the immigrant culture was "traditional" and hierarchical, as immigrant groups assimilated into U.S. culture, women and children experienced growing freedom from the shackles of tradition and patriarchal authority.

---

[13] Other characteristics of Goode's "conjugal family" were autonomous mate selection, an absence of bride price, and a bilateral mode of determining kinship (1963).

Ethnicity and Households as Vehicles of Adaptation

In the popular U.S. imagination, the assimilation vision remains the dominant paradigm for understanding the dynamics and progress of immigrant life. Its power and strength have stemmed not only from its explanatory powers but also from its ideological appeal. The vision of the United States as an open society, a melting pot into which immigrant groups enter and then successfully integrate, has proven to be remarkably powerful and sustained.

However, in recent decades, social scientists have subjected the assimilationist model to a series of sharp and wide-ranging attacks (see Hirschman 1983; Morawska 1985). Omi and Winant (1986) point out that the model assumes that race is not a central or persistent feature of modern societies, and thus neglects the part played by racial dynamics in assimilation processes. Other criticisms are that the dichotomous and unitary concepts of "traditional" and "modern" are deeply problematic ways of understanding societies and social change. At the very least, it is too unrealistic and simple to assume a continuous and progressive unilinear movement from traditional values and behaviors to modern ones. Instead, scholars have argued that modernization processes are uneven; traditional values and social forms may co-exist in relative harmony with more modern ones:

> Attacked by multiple theoretical and empirical critiques, dichotomous, linear-polar conceptions of tradition and modernity have been discarded. The *becoming* of urban industrial society is now interpreted as an uneven and multifaceted development in which, dependent on particular historical circumstances, old and new elements and aggregations, often ill fitting and inconsistent, come to exist in varying blends and combinations. (Morawska 1985, 7)

Both reflecting and reinforcing the demise of the modernization perspective, the field of family studies has also become less inclined to interpret changes in family life as a movement from "traditional" to "modern." Increasingly, Goode's "logic of industrialization" and its proposed relationship to the family has been questioned, as studies show the relationship between families and industrialization to be far less inevitable, linear, and rigid than previously conceived (Lee 1987, 63). In other words, industrialization does not necessarily generate the kinds of changes in family life that Goode outlined, such as a shift to a nuclear

17

family structure that is more egalitarian in its internal relations. Harevan's (1982) historical study of factory workers, for example, shows how exposure to the industrial workplace reinforced rather than destroyed the extended kin ties of workers.

In fact, scholars of immigrant life have become increasingly concerned not with processes of change in immigrant life but rather with the persistence and the adaptive role of immigrant ties and institutions. There has been a discovery and even a celebration of the strength and resilience of immigrant institutions and their roles in facilitating the economic survival and adaptation of their members in the new society. I suggest that this trend can be understood in part as a counterreaction to the assimilation model's tendency to denigrate immigrant institutions, to conceive them as backward, outmoded, and dysfunctional. The interest in adaptation also grows out of a concern for assigning agency to immigrants, in contrast to the assimilation model's view of immigrants as being passively "acted on" by the forces of change (Kivisto 1990, 463).

In a variety of ways, current social science research and thinking about immigrant life reflects these concerns. On an empirical level, there has emerged a large body of work on diverse immigrant groups, ranging from European immigrants at the turn of the century to Cuban, Mexican, and Korean immigrants in the contemporary United States, that documents the salience of immigrant ties and institutions to economic adjustment (Min 1988; Morawska 1985; Portes and Bach 1985). For example, ethnic economic enclaves—concentrations of businesses owned and operated by co-ethnics—have been identified as potentially critical to the economic adaptation of many immigrants, providing them with jobs, training, and opportunities for advancement. More generally, immigrant ties may be "sources of information about outside employment, sources of jobs inside the community, and sources of credit and support for entrepreneurial ventures" (Portes and Rumbaut 1990, 88).

Theoretical perspectives on ethnicity have also shifted in recent years. The term "ethnic group" is generally understood by social scientists to refer to a group that shares a collective identity, based on the group's perception of a common culture or shared national origins. The root origins of ethnicity or ethnic identity are, however, a matter of some debate. Many scholars working in the assimilationist framework saw ethnic ties to be inherent or primordially rooted, stemming from a common heredity or sense of group origins. Scholars today, however, have moved to a situational view of ethnicity, one that sees ethnicity as socially generated and constructed (Okamura 1981). The situational perspective emphasizes the dynamic qualities of ethnic affiliation and boundaries, and the *active* role of the ethnic group in generating and providing meaning to ethnic group membership. In this framework, the external structural conditions encountered by the immigrant group following migration play a more-or-less crucial part in shaping the strength and character of ethnic identity and institutions. In other words, ethnicity is, in part, a reactive response of the immigrant group to the conditions they encounter. It may be understood as a strategic resource that is activated by the group in their efforts to survive and to achieve in the new society. In short, ethnicity is not "given" but rather something that the ethnic group actively and selectively constructs in response to the circumstances it faces.

So far as immigrant familial institutions is concerned, much of the current scholarship in this area focuses specifically on the household, which is defined as a co-residential unit into which resources are brought together and organized to meet the needs of household members. The immigrant household is viewed as a strategic arena, a social site within which members collectively construct strategies that will help them to survive and realize collective goals (Dinerman 1978; Massey et al. 1987; Perez 1986). With its focus on the construction of strategies, this approach appeals to the growing need to assign agency to immigrants. It is an approach that also allows immigrant familial institutions to be seen not as obsolescent and irrelevant but as adaptive social forms that are strategically used by immigrants to realize their goals.

In this general shift in focus that I am describing, from assimilation to adaptation, perspectives on gender divisions within immigrant life have also shifted. The assimilationist assumption that migration fosters women's emancipation has been dismissed, bolstered by growing evidence that migration, like economic development, may not be beneficial for women. Women in the midst of such social changes may actually lose their traditional sources of support and power. In the domestic sphere, for example, immigrant women may lose the power and authority they used to have over children. Women may also lose economic resources when migration or economic development diminishes their access to and control over production processes (Beneria and Sen 1981; Deutsch 1986).

Indeed, recent scholarship on immigrant women emphasizes not the liberating consequences of migration for women but the disadvantaged status held by many immigrant women within the majority society. Terms such as *multiple jeopardy* and *triple oppression* increasingly

19

dominate discussions of immigrant women's and, more generally, racial-ethnic women's experience (Brettell and Simon 1986, 10; King 1988). These terms refer to the multiple disadvantages experienced by these groups of women, as racial-ethnic minorities, as women, and as inhabitants of the lower rungs of the social class ladder. This emphasis on racial-ethnic women's oppression within the majority society has been accompanied by an altered view of the relationship of women to immigrant ties and institutions. Feminist scholars have suggested that immigrant institutions are not just arenas of patriarchal oppression but also sites of resistance, or vehicles by which groups struggle to survive (Caulfield 1974; Glenn 1986; Thornton-Dill 1988). Evelyn Nakano Glenn, for example, describes the racial-ethnic family as a "bulwark against the atomizing effects of poverty and legal and political constraints" (1991, 194–95). While immigrant women may struggle against the oppression they experience as women *within* immigrant institutions, the oppression they experience from the majority society as members of a racial-ethnic group may generate needs and loyalties of a more immediate and pressing nature. Thus immigrant women may remain attached to and indeed support traditional (i.e., premigration) family structures. This is due not simply to their entrenched cultural beliefs or conservativism but also to the benefits that women gain from retaining these structures, given the multiplicity of disadvantages they face in social and economic realms outside the ethnic community. In other words, for women, immigrant institutions are ways of coping and adapting to the new society, and this consideration may override their concern with gender inequalities within these institutions.

To summarize, a focus on the adaptive role of immigrant institutions appears as a significant point of convergence in current social science scholarship on immigrant life. Although insightful in many respects, this singular emphasis on adaptation neglects the essentially conflicted character of immigrant life. I suggest that recognition of the enduring and positive value of immigrant institutions must be balanced by a consideration of change and conflict within them.

CONFLICT AND CHANGE IN IMMIGRANT LIFE

An emphasis on the notion of adaptation, central to the literature on the immigrant experience, has led to a neglect of the divisions and conflicts of immigrant life. To see immigrant institutions only as vehicles of adaptation and resistance to oppression by the majority society implies a uniformity of experience and interest within immigrant groups. But to what extent is this true? For example, do all members participate and benefit in the same way from immigrant institutions? It seems essential to explore the divisions of immigrant life and the ways in which members may gain very different kinds of benefits and rewards from immigrant institutions.[14]

The current tendency to ignore or downplay the internal fissures of immigrant life is perhaps best exemplified by the literature on household strategies. Here it is simply assumed that the household is a unified social group, constructing strategies in a manner that is consensual and democratic and benefits all members equally. The construction and implementation of strategies is unmarred by conflict, resistance, and noncompliance among household members. As feminist scholars have pointed out, these assumptions of democracy, altruism, and consensus reflect an idealized view of the household—one in which age and gender do not create basic distinctions in family experience and interests (Benería and Roldán 1987; Thorne 1982; Wolf 1990).

Immigrant institutions are not only internally divided but also fluid and shifting in their organization and dynamics. Central to understanding processes of change in immigrant institutions are the social and economic conditions encountered by the immigrant group in the "host" society. Scholars of ethnicity have called attention to the important role played by external structural forces in determining the strength of ethnicity and the forms in which it is expressed (Nagel and Olzak 1982; Yancey, Ericksen, and Juliani 1976). For example, when immigrant groups encounter hostility or are excluded from participation in the economic mainstream, ethnic solidarities may become particularly strong. It is not simply shared culture or origins that foster ethnicity but also the circumstances and constraints the immigrant group faces in the new society.

In comparison to current scholarship on ethnicity, discussions of immigrant familial institutions have been less attentive to the effects of structural conditions in shaping them (Zinn 1990). Perhaps because so much of research has focused on the part played by the immigrant family in *facilitating adaptation* to the "host" society, there has been a neglect of how "host" society conditions shape the organization and dynamics of immigrant family life. The focus on cultural determinants has been particularly sharp in discussions of Asian American families (Glenn 1983).

[14] Some current research on the dynamics of ethnic enclave economies has begun to explore this point, by looking at how men and women derive different material rewards from work in the ethnic enclave economy (Zhou and Logan 1989).

Whereas research on the family life of African Americans has highlighted the impact of structural conditions (Gutman 1976; Stack 1974), Asian American families have been widely perceived in cultural terms.

In contrast to such cultural explanations, I suggest that immigrant families must be analyzed in relation to the external structural conditions encountered by immigrants in the "host" society. These structural conditions provide the fundamental parameters—the opportunities and constraints—within which immigrants must construct their family life. Immigrants' responses to these structural conditions are, however, affected by the cultural baggage, or experience and understandings about the world, that they bring with them to the new society. Thus for example, with respect to familial institutions, I suggest that immigrants draw on premigration family experiences and ideologies in their efforts to construct families within the structural context of the new society. The ideologies on which immigrants draw are, however, not static or "given" but shifting and emergent. These ideologies are also multidimensional, composed of intersecting and often contradictory elements. Too often, discussions of immigrant life paint a monolithic and one-dimensional picture of the premigration culture of immigrants, in an effort to trace in a simple manner the effects of this culture on the group's life after migration.

Besides this interplay of structural conditions with immigrant culture, I suggest that the internal divisions of immigrant life are central to the dynamics of change in immigrant communities. The differing interests of immigrant group members mean that they will disagree and thus negotiate over the shape of immigrant institutions. For example, young and old members of the immigrant group may feel differently about the appropriate organization of community institutions. The processes by which these community institutions emerge and develop will reflect this division, as young and old immigrants struggle with one another to shape community institutions in the ways that they desire. Similarly, gender conflicts and negotiation are critical to understanding the development of immigrant familial institutions. Immigrant families are simultaneously sites of adaptation for men and women, and arenas of conflict and struggle between men and women. The development of immigrant families as well as other institutions is a gendered process. Women and men clash over the reshaping of these institutions, attempting to fashion them in ways that enhance their interests, both as members of the immigrant group and as men or women. I suggest that the struggle between men and women to shape immigrant institutions will vary in its strength and visibility, depending on the balance of power between women and men in the immigrant group. This balance of power is deeply shaped by the immigrant men's and women's comparative access to and control over economic, political, and social resources in the dominant society (Blood and Wolfe 1960; Blumberg 1991). Particularly when migration is concurrent with a drastic shift in the resources of women and men relative to each other, the gender-based struggle to control immigrant institutions may become especially blatant.

OVERVIEW OF THE BOOK

In the following chapter ("The Study and the Setting") I provide information on the particular setting of the study, my research methods, and the social background of my informants. Chapter 3 ("Vietnamese Roots") explores the historical and cultural roots of the Vietnamese American experience, piecing together information from secondary sources and the life histories of informants. I pay special attention to the lives of urban pre-1975 middle-class South Vietnamese and their traditions and experiences of family life and gender relations. Chapter 4 ("Patchworking: Households in the Economy") explores Vietnamese American responses to the economic conditions of life in the United States, focusing on the part played by household structure and ideologies of family life in mediating these responses. Chapter 5 ("The Family Tightrope: Gender Relations) looks at how migration shifted the relative resources of men and women in favor of women, thus changing the gender balance of power. I look at the consequences of the shift in the gender balance of power for men's and women's experience of family life. Chapter 6 ("Generation Gaps") explores another migration-induced shift in the balance of power in Vietnamese American families, that between the generations. I analyze the familial experiences and attitudes of the young, paying close attention to the effects of differentiation in age and family circumstances.

The Study and the Setting

THE SETTING

DAO AND TINH lived on the first floor of an old yellow rowhouse that had a large front porch filled with broken electrical appliances, including TVs and refrigerators. The neighborhood was a residential one, and the inhabitants were mainly African American. Dao and Tinh did have two Vietnamese American neighbors—one lived above them and another next door. About five blocks away from the rowhouses there were a number of small shops and businesses. There was a newly opened Vietnamese American dentist's office and, close by, an all-night convenience store run by Asian Indians. There was also a pharmacy, a pizza and hoagie shop, and a laundromat. Farther down the street were two Asian food stores; one of them was run by a Chinese family from Vietnam, and the other by an ethnic Vietnamese refugee family.

Nga and Vinh lived about seven blocks from the area described above, on the second floor of an apartment building overlooking a busy street. No other Vietnamese Americans lived in the building, which seemed to house people from an assortment of backgrounds, including a few college students. Across the street and a couple of blocks down from the building was a small cluster of businesses. There was a used clothing store, a laudromat, a pizza shop, and a TV repair shop. There were several ethnic businesses—on one side of the area was an Ethiopian restaurant, and on the other a Laotian grocery store. Also present were a Vietnamese restaurant, a jewelry store, and a hairdressing shop run by Chinese Vietnamese.

Nguyet and Phong lived about five blocks from this area in a large apartment building near a Korean American church. On the front door of the building, in bright orange paint, was prominently scrawled: "Fuck all Americans who live here." The building was large and partially abandoned. Many of the building's inhabitants were Cambodian refugees. Trash and broken glass were strewn in the halls, whose walls were marked with graffiti.

This study was conducted in an inner-city area of Philadelphia during 1983–85. In many ways, Philadelphia in the early 1980s exemplified, in a heightened way, the economic and social problems facing Vietnamese Americans throughout the country at this time. In 1980, both the poverty and unemployment rates in Philadelphia were far higher than the national rates.[1] The economic problems of the city were only exacerbated by the national economic recession of the early 1980s.

Although neighborhoods and areas of Vietnamese American concentration were present in the city, the total number of Vietnamese Americans was quite small.[2] Unlike the large Vietnamese immigrant settlements in Southern California or Virginia, the one in Philadelphia was neither highly visible nor clearly bounded, and it did not have a core geographical center. As the initial fieldnote excerpt suggests, the prevalent pattern was of small clusters of Vietnamese American settlement rather than dominance over a large area. Frequently, these clusters of settlement were situated next to those of other Southeast Asian refugee groups. In fact, the overall racial-ethnic composition of the site of the study was diverse, including blacks, Koreans, Indians, Chinese, and Ethiopians as well as the various Southeast Asian refugee groups. The ethnic diversity of the area came into public attention in 1983–84, when there were a number of well-publicized clashes among various groups.[3] The conflicts led the Philadelphia City's Commission on Human Relations to hold public investigatory hearings in which residents were invited to air their concerns. Among other things, the hearings revealed a sharp sense of competition among area residents for scarce jobs and public resources (Philadelphia Commission on Human Relations 1984). Southeast Asian refugees for example, were often perceived by other residents to be receiving special favorable treatment from the government, due to their eligibility for refugee aid and assistance programs.

Because of these intergroup hostilities as well as the high crime rate and poor schools in the area, my informants did not consider this part of the

[1] The 1980 census shows unemployment rates in Philadelphia to be 11.4 percent compared to the national figure of 6.6 percent. There was a poverty rate of 20.6 percent in the city, compared to 11.4 percent for the country (Philadelphia City Planning Commission 1984).

[2] The Philadelphia Commission on Human Relations (1984) provides an estimate of six thousand Vietnamese Americans within the city limits. However, most of the social workers and Vietnamese American community leaders interviewed felt that the actual number was higher (eight to ten thousand).

[3] Local newspaper articles during the period included the following: "Koreans Are Arming Themselves" (*Philadelphia Daily News* [September 6, 1981]); "School Security Boosted: University City High Hit by Racial Violence" (*Philadelphia Daily News* [November 11, 1983]); and "Beating of Hmong Decried" (*Philadelphia Inquirer* [September 6, 1984]).

25

city to be a particularly desirable place to live. Most had been resettled in this part of the city by social service agencies that had found these neighborhoods to be convenient and inexpensive places in which to house recent arrivals. The participants in my study continued to live in the area for largely economic reasons. The rents were cheap and the area was close to public transportation routes and the downtown neighborhoods where many service and informal sector jobs were located. Thus those Vietnamese Americans who lived in this part of the city tended to be recent arrivals in the United States whose limited economic and social resources made it difficult for them to move elsewhere. Those of my informants who eventually purchased their own homes inevitably did so in other parts of the city.

In addition to the somewhat scattered residential patterns, the Philadelphia Vietnamese refugee community also lacked political cohesion. There were numerous competing Vietnamese ethnic associations in the city that claimed to represent the community. But they lacked widespread legitimacy—a situation that resembled what has been noted in studies of Vietnamese refugee communities in other parts of the United States (Finnan and Cooperstein 1983; Gold 1992, 221). Thus when I began collecting data for my study in 1983, I faced a confusing array of numerous Vietnamese associations, leaders, and political cliques all of which existed in a situation of tense rivalry and competition with one another. The absence of a strong and cohesive Vietnamese community organization in the area was also frequently noted by outside observers of the community. In the following, a social service agency worker who had been involved in the resettlement of Southeast Asian refugees since 1975 talked of the highly factionalized character of the Vietnamese refugee community:

[How would you describe the Vietnamese community here?] I don't think I would describe it at all. I don't have a clear sense of it—even though I've been working with refugees since 1975 and I can tell you a lot about the Cambodian community and the Hmong community; both of them have very strong communities. But the Vietnamese . . . I can give you a list of maybe ten or fifteen men who are considered by us as the leadership or representatives of the community. But it's not a very organized kind of thing. I doubt that most Vietnamese actually have any contact with these guys.

Certainly none of the many Vietnamese ethnic associations in the city seemed to hold much legitimacy in the eyes of my informants, who expressed little interest in participating in their activities. In part, their unwillingness to participate in the organizations reflected a deep, histori-cally rooted suspicion of formal government. French colonization fol-lowed by the long years of war, and finally a period of Communist rule, had engendered widespread antipathy toward political institutions. As a participant-observer, for example, I was almost invariably initially "screened" through intense questioning about my background for possi-ble connections to the United States government or any social service agency. It was only in the absence of such connections that the partici-pants of the study were willing to talk openly to me.

Besides this suspicion of anything that smacked of "government," my informants were also wary of the leaders of the ethnic associations, many of whom were drawn from the 1975 wave of Vietnamese refugees to the United States. In contrast to the middle-class backgrounds of my infor-mants, much of the 1975 cohort was from the elite sectors of pre-1975 South Vietnamese society. This difference in social class background was a source of considerable distance and even hostility between the leader-ship of the associations and my informants, who often spoke with disdain about the corrupt character of the former South Vietnamese elite (cf. Gold 1992, 120).

My informants' involvement with religious organizations, although more extensive than that with ethnic organizations, was also quite lim-ited. Four out of the twelve households I studied contained members who belonged to the Catholic Church, and of these persons about three-quar-ters attended church regularly. But the majority of the study-participants, who were not Catholic, had little to do with formal religious bodies and their activities.

In the absence of clear geographical boundaries as well as powerful community organizations, the ethnic community life of Vietnamese Americans had a localistic quality. That is, my informants' contacts with fellow ethnics were centered around the specific clusters of Vietnamese American settlement in which they lived. However, informal social net-works, based on ties of kinship and friendship, did connect them to other Vietnamese Americans living in different neighborhoods. As I will de-scribe in later chapters, these informal social networks functioned as powerful conduits of resources and information among Vietnamese Americans in the area.

The particular characteristics of the study setting that I have described, such as its economically impoverished character and the absence of a clear-cut Vietnamese ethnic territorial turf, are of course vital to under-standing and assessing the findings that I report in the chapters that follow. However, as a case study, the value of this book lies not in its ability to capture the experience of all Vietnamese Americans at all times but in clarifying and illuminating the dynamic interaction between the specific social context and the lives of those I studied. Through this detailed, contextual analysis I hope to generate insights into *processes* of change in immigrant family life and gender relations (Stoecker 1991). That is, I attempt to shed light on the social forces that generate such change and on the manner in which those who are involved understand, respond, and shape these transformations.

METHODS

A red paper heart dangled outside the door of apartment 202. This was my second visit to the home of Ha, a Vietnamese immigrant woman in her thirties who had arrived in the United States three years ago with her husband and three children. The front door of the two-room apartment opened into a largish room. At the far end was a television, a videocassette recorder, and a single bed. There was another bed on the other side of the room, as well as a couch and a small kitchen table. The walls were decorated with two calendars from local grocery stores, posters of Vietnamese singers, and scenes from San Francisco and Los Angeles, as well as many black and white photographs of relatives. On the left side of the room there was an ancestral altar—a shelf with two photographs, incense sticks, and bowls. Ha was in the kitchen, which was a small area that opened up from the right side of the room.

My initial contacts with the participants of the study occurred in a variety of ways. I had been acquainted for some time with a Vietnamese immigrant family who owned and operated a restaurant. Luckily, members of this family were willing to help me locate other Vietnamese refugees by introducing me to friends and relatives in the neighborhood. Also, a Vietnamese American teacher took me on a number of visits to the homes of his students. A few other contacts were made with the help of a Vietnamese American minister who provided informal social services to new Vietnamese arrivals in the neighborhood.

After the introductions, I began a series of home visits to five households who had expressed a willingness to participate in the study. At first I visited the households occasionally, once every week or so. During these initial visits I talked with household members informally. After this, I visited each of the five households frequently for about a week. At this stage, I showed up at the household almost every day (at different times of the day) and spent four to five hours there. During these periods I observed, listened to, and chatted with household members. Sometimes I gave impromptu English lessons, helped with children's homework, and interpreted bills and letters. At other times I was coached in Vietnamese, as the informants were aware that I was taking Vietnamese language lessons at this time. Following this period of intensive observation, I continued visiting the five households, but less frequently. I was often invited to weddings, birthday parties, and other social events organized by the households.

At the next stage, I expanded both my methods and my sample. With the help of already-established relationships with Vietnamese Americans who lived in the area, I was able to expand the household study group from five to twelve households. I began to visit the seven households I had added to the study, although my observations of the later households were less intensive than those of my initial five. I also began to conduct in-depth interviews with various members of the twelve households, whom I selected to include as wide a range of age and gender variation as possible. By mid-1985, I had conducted thirty-one interviews, with fifteen women and sixteen men. The interviews were unstructured, usually taking the form of a life history. I asked respondents to talk about their lives, starting from their childhood, and I told them that I was particularly interested in their experiences of family life. I often probed for further information and asked questions about topics of particular interest to me. However, I encouraged the interviewees to speak freely and to steer the interview toward issues that were of importance to them. When the respondent was willing, I tape-recorded the interviews. Many, but not all, of the interviews took place with the help of Vietnamese language interpreters who were unacquainted, prior to the interview, with the household in which the interview was taking place.

The third component of the data collection process focused on community structure and activities.[4] I interviewed eleven Vietnamese American community leaders and social service agency workers in the city about the organizations in which they were involved and the relationship of these organizations to the Vietnamese American population in the city. Besides this, I also spent time just "hanging out" in the neighborhoods of study, in an attempt to gain a better understanding of the informal community life of Vietnamese Americans in the area and of the relationship of com-

[4] For clarity, I present these various components of the research separately and in chronological order, although in reality they often overlapped in time.

munity life to household organization and dynamics. Eventually, I focused my time on three central meeting places—a restaurant, a grocery store, and a hairdresser—all neighborhood businesses run by Vietnamese Americans. Sometimes I took fieldnotes while sitting at these places, but more often I wrote down my observations after returning home.

The actual process of data collection, as well as the quality of the materials that I gathered, were all influenced in crucial ways by my personal and social characteristics. One of the most important of these characteristics was my Bangladeshi ethnicity. After the first few months of fieldwork, I found myself being introduced around to other Vietnamese Americans as the "Indian girl" who was "interested in Vietnamese people." Although at first I insisted on correcting these introductions from "Indian" to "Bangladeshi," I eventually accepted the appellation of Indian. I realized that the Indian label made it somewhat easier for my informants to situate me culturally in their minds. Some Vietnamese Americans felt that they were quite familiar with Indian culture due to their prior contacts with Indians who had lived in South Vietnam. As a result of this exposure to Indians, they felt a certain familiarity with my background and so were perhaps more comfortable with my presence than they might otherwise have felt:

> It is my second visit to Kim's place. They are just finishing lunch but Kim insists that I join them. As she goes into the kitchen to get a bowl, her sister-in-law says, "You eat rice in your country, right? I know, because some Indian people live in my town in Vietnam. They eat rice with their hands. You do that too, right? Vietnamese people, they eat rice. Sometimes noodles, but more rice."
>
> When Kim brings me the bowl of rice, I put a spoonful of *nước mắm* (hot fish sauce) on it. Watching me, Kim says, "Oh yes, the Indian people, they like hot food, just like the Vietnamese people. That's good, you can eat with us anytime. I don't have to worry about whether you like our food."

The sense of familiarity that Vietnamese Americans felt with my cultural background had, I believe, some important effects on the information I was able to obtain on family life. I was seen as someone from a "traditional" society, one in which family loyalties were strong and respect for the elderly a prominent value, in contrast to U.S. society. This perception perhaps influenced the ease and candor with which informants spoke of the family conflicts that had been engendered for them by the migration process and of their efforts to come to terms with the traditional Vietnamese family system. Conversely, my cultural background made me especially sensitive to the experience of living in such close-knit and hierarchical family structures.

Because of my Indian subcontinental origins, Vietnamese Americans also perceived me as someone who shared, to some extent, their experience of being foreigners and outsiders in U.S. society. There were several occasions on which I was closely questioned about how I, as someone who was "not American," was treated by my classmates and teachers. And toward the end of my graduate student career, when I began to express anxiety about my prospects in the academic job market that I was about to face, I was startled (and not particularly reassured) when several Vietnamese Americans told me that I should expect it to be very difficult to find a good job. This was because I, unlike my classmates, did not "look like an American."

But although my ethnic background placed me closer in certain respects to the experiences of Vietnamese Americans, it simultaneously clearly marked me as an outsider. When I began the study, I had little knowledge of Vietnamese culture, history, and language. Both the participants of the study and I were highly aware that many aspects of their lives, in both the past and the present, were completely unfamiliar and alien to me. In many ways my outsider status was highlighted by my stumbling attempts to speak Vietnamese, which began when I started to take Vietnamese language lessons two months after beginning fieldwork. But my attempts to speak Vietnamese, although a source of conversation and constant jokes, did ultimately serve to further my acceptance in the community.

Besides my ethnic background, my status as an aspiring teacher or educator also had important effects on the fieldwork process. In Vietnamese culture, teaching has traditionally carried high status and prestige. More generally, my status as a university student who would presumably enter into a good, well-paying job in the future meant that I was seen and received as someone who was respectable and relatively trustworthy. I was also someone who was quite knowledgeable about U.S. culture and social institutions. In fact, because of my "expertise" in U.S. life, I was often asked by women to interpret various bureaucratic procedures and documents, such as utility bills and children's report cards, for them. In general, I was seen as a trusted source of information about the often confusing procedures and regulations of U.S. social institutions.

In addition to being a source of information about U.S. life, I was also, appropriately enough, considered as a "student" of Vietnamese Americans and, more generally, of Vietnamese culture and language. Almost immediately following the initial introductions, I told the participants of the study that I hoped to study their lives through observation and interviews. I explained that besides writing a doctoral dissertation, I would be writing papers and possibly a book on what I had found out about their lives. I assured them that I would not use their names in anything that I wrote, and I would do everything else possible to ensure their anonymity. During at least the first few months of fieldwork, the initial reactions to my pronouncements were disbelief and a certain amusement. But at a certain point—when I did not disappear but persisted on "hanging around"—Vietnamese Americans began to take my aims more seriously. They began to see me as a serious student of Vietnamese American life. As this perception developed, I also found that many people that I came to know made a point of reporting to me any events or situations that they felt would be of interest. For example, when the police intervened in a domestic conflict between a father and son, several women and teenagers telephoned me over the next few days to tell me about the incident.

The fact that I was female also had critical effects on the fieldwork process. For one thing, it meant that I had much easier access to female than male informants. My age (early twenties) also meant that some women, particularly those who were elderly, related to me in a maternal fashion, questioning me about my health and my marriage prospects. With other women, I played the role of confidante. This was a role that I was well suited to assuming, because of both my intense curiosity about their lives and my status as an outsider in the community. As an outsider, I was less likely to gossip and to pass strong judgments on their activities and experiences.

Although in general I was far more successful in establishing close relations with women than with men, I was eventually able to achieve good rapport with many young Vietnamese American men. For the most part, older Vietnamese American men retained a posture of distance and formality toward me throughout the course of the study, although they greeted me warmly during my visits to their homes and agreed to be interviewed for the study. But with younger Vietnamese American men, I often played—as I did with women—the role of confidante. I was someone who had developed a reputation for not gossiping. And particularly when, as was often the case, young men talked to me of the dilemmas of their love lives, I was someone who had no obvious stake in the outcomes of the situations they described. At the same time, I was often at least somewhat familiar with their concerns, as well as with the particular situations and relationships in which they were enmeshed. With the young men, as with the other Vietnamese immigrants that I came to know, I was simultaneously an insider and an outsider—a position that shaped the study in profound ways.

CHARACTERISTICS OF THE SAMPLE

The people I studied were in many ways a diverse group. But they also had similarities, stemming partly from the fact that I did not generate my sample through a random process. For one thing, those who were willing to be involved in the study tended to have more advanced English language skills than others in the community. Thus it is possible that, as a group, they were somewhat more assimilated into the majority U.S. culture than others. Second, as I have mentioned, the expansion of my sample of households took place through a process of "snowballing" whereby I was "passed along" in the community. And so many of those I interviewed and observed were members of the same social networks. Third, with the exception of two households, all those I studied contained adult women, despite the numerical preponderance of men over women in the Vietnamese American community. This was due to issues of both rapport and propriety; it would have been unacceptable for me, as a woman, to make regular visits to households in which no women were present.

Although these factors largely determined the sample, I also used certain criteria to shape the sample's boundaries. First of all, the participants of the study were all ethnic Vietnamese rather than Chinese persons from Vietnam.[5] The decision to exclude the Chinese-Vietnamese arose from the distinctiveness of their social and cultural background as well as from the historical hostility between this group and the ethnic Vietnamese.[6] Second, all the households were located in a certain section of the city— in fact, in close proximity to each other.

The end result, I believe, was a sample that shared some important

[5] All twelve households both considered themselves and were considered by others in the community as ethnic Vietnamese, although a few of them contained members who claimed Chinese ancestry.

[6] The place of the Chinese-Vietnamese in Vietnam is a complex one. Although portions of the group had integrated into the dominant Vietnamese society, by and large they had retained their distinct cultural identity. They had played a central role in rice trading in Vietnam and were often resented by ethnic Vietnamese for their economic power (see Peters et al. 1983).

TABLE 1
Interview Sample, Showing
Years of Arrival

Year of Arrival	Number of Persons
1978	1
1979	5
1980	6
1981	9
1982	6
1983	4
Total	31

characteristics. As table 1 indicates, at the time of the study, the interviewees were recent arrivals in the United States. It is worth noting that none of the informants were from the first wave of Vietnamese refugees in 1975, many of whom had been part of the social and economic elite of South Vietnamese society. In general, all were undergoing an initial period of adjustment to U.S. society, a period in which their economic resources were quite limited.

In other ways, the sample was a varied group. For example, as table 2 indicates, the twelve households differed in size and in number of children. The smallest household contained three people, whereas the largest had nineteen.

Table 2 also reveals that the households were diverse in their membership composition. Whereas four of the twelve households were composed of a male-female couple and their children, the remainder contained a variety of kinfolk and friends. Below are descriptions of the size, gender, and kinship composition of the eight households that were not synomymous with a nuclear family situation.

Six persons: a couple, the man's three brothers, and a male friend.
Eight persons: a couple and their three children, the woman's cousin, the woman's brother, and a male friend.
Three persons: two brothers and a sister.
Nineteen persons: a couple with seven children. Three of the children are married and have a total of six children. There are also three sons and one daughter who are unmarried, as well as a female friend of the daughter.

TABLE 2
Interview Sample, Showing Number of Members per Household

Household Number	Women	Men	Children	Total
1	1	5	0	6
2	1	4	3	8
3	1	2	0	3
4	6	7	6	19
5	3	4	0	7
6	0	5	0	5
7	2	2	6	10
8	0	2	1	3
9	1	1	3	5
10	1	1	3	5
11	1	1	1	3
12	1	1	3	5
Total	18	35	26	79

Seven persons: a woman, her three sons, two daughters, and one son-in-law.

Five persons: five men with no kinship ties.

Ten persons: a couple and their five children, the woman's nephew, and his wife and child.

Three persons: a man and his two sons.

The thirty-one household members who were interviewed ranged in age from eighteen to fifty-eight years (see table 3). Notable in the sample and in the community in general was the high proportion of young single men in their twenties. There were also fewer women than men in the older age groups.

The participants of the study were overwhelmingly from urban backgrounds, although many of the adults had spent some portion of their lives in rural areas. Tables 4 and 5 provide further information on the social and educational background of those interviewed.

On average, the women had fewer years of education than the men. Most of the men had received some secondary school education. Only two of the women interviewed had been homemakers in Vietnam. Other women had been involved in family business or informal trading, although participation in these activites was usually sporadic. For men, the most common occupational arena was the South Vietnamese military.

CHAPTER TWO

TABLE 3
Interview Sample, Showing Years of Age

Years of Age	Women	Men	Total
16–20	3	2	5
21–25	2	4	6
26–30	3	3	6
31–35	5	1	6
36–40	0	2	2
41–45	0	2	2
46 and above	2	2	4
Total	15	16	31

TABLE 4
Interview Sample, Showing Years of Education

Years of Education	Women	Men	Total
5 or less	4	0	4
6–8	3	4	7
9–12	7	10	17
13 or more	1	2	3
Total	15	16	31

TABLE 5
Interview Sample, Showing Occupation
before 1975

Occupation before 1975	Women	Men
Homemaker	2	0
Student	4	6
Military	0	7
Family business	3	2
Small-scale trading	4	0
Employee	2	1
Total	15	16

Here they tended to occupy the middle-ranking positions, ranging from corporal to lieutenant. A significant proportion (ten out of thrity-one) of those interviewed had been young and attending school before 1975 in Vietnam. It is notable that many of the younger men who had arrived in the United States alone had fathers who had occupied fairly high positions in the military or government bureaucracy before 1975. However, in general terms, the participants of the study were from the pre-1975 urban middle class of South Vietnamese society.

Vietnamese Roots

> Ten wandering years—a rootless tumbleweed.
> My homesick heart flaps like a wind-lashed flag.
> To my old village I've gone back in dream.
> With tears of blood I'll wash the family graves.
> *(Nguyen Trai, "Written Aboard a Boat on the*
> *Way Back to Mount Con")*

EXILE FROM THE HOMELAND is a common theme in the writings of the fifteenth-century Vietnamese poet and nationalist Nguyen Trai. The presence of the exile motif in so much Vietnamese literature reflects the turbulence of Vietnamese history, especially in the contemporary era, a time in which migration and separation from home have been far from uncommon experiences for Vietnamese.

For the Vietnamese refugees that I studied, their migration to the United States was not the first but rather one of several relocations experienced by themselves or their families in recent times. In this chapter I explore these relocations, as well as other aspects of the Vietnamese experience that help to shed light on Vietnamese responses to the process of migration and settlement in the United States. What follows, however, should be taken as an extremely selective rather than exhaustive or complete account of Vietnamese history and culture. My emphasis is on the lives of the urban middle class in South Vietnam, because the origins of my informants lay within this social stratum. I also focus particularly on family life and gender relations.

TRADITIONAL VIETNAMESE LIFE

Historical Influences and Events: Colonization and War

Vietnamese society has been deeply shaped by the Chinese, who invaded Vietnam in 111 B.C. and ruled the country for a thousand years. The long era of Chinese rule was not, however, passively accepted by the Vietnamese, who launched numerous efforts to assert their national independence. One of the most famous revolts against Chinese domination occurred in A.D. 40 and was led by the famous Trung sisters who organized a general insurrection against the Chinese. They reigned for three years before Chinese rule was restored.

The years of Chinese rule deeply affected Vietnamese society. Although the depth of Sinicization actually experienced by Vietnam is a matter of some controversy, there is little doubt that the Chinese had a crucial impact:

> [The] later Chinese governors of Nam Viet undertook a policy of assimilation. The people adopted the Chinese concept that the emperor is the son of heaven, intermediary between the people and heaven, and the supreme judge and grand pontiff. Chinese books, literature and writing were introduced to the Vietnamese, and the Sinophiles formed a class of literati. No less important were the teaching of Chinese culture and traditions, and of social and religious ceremonies and technical education in land cultivation. With equal zeal, Chinese administrators tried to change the feudal government of Nam Viet into a model of a Chinese province. (Nguyen Xuan Dao 1958, 10)

Confucianism, Taoism, and Mahayana Buddhism were all introduced to Vietnam through the Chinese. Combined with older indigenous beliefs and practices, the Three Teachings coalesced to form the core of the Vietnamese religious-cultural tradition. The relative importance of the three traditions varied across different regions and social strata. Especially in the south, Taoism and Buddhism were more important than Confucianism in the daily life of the peasant population (Tai 1983, 20–23). In fact, the relative weakness of Confucianism in the south was often of concern to Vietnamese rulers, given the important part played by Confucianism in legitimating the authority of the governing class. According to the hierarchical model of society prescribed by Confucianism, a relationship of inequality prevailed between ruler and subject as well as between father and son, husband and wife, and elder and younger brother. In exchange for its absolute authority over the masses, the ruling class took on the responsibility of attuning the human world to cosmic forces through proper rituals and ethical action.

Vietnam wrested itself from Chinese control in A.D. 939. What followed was a succession of dynastic rulers who governed in relative peace and stability for four centuries. But the fifteenth century saw another phase of Chinese occupation (1406–28) as well as growing economic and political unrest. The period of civil wars that ensued energized Vietnamese efforts to expand territory south of the Red River Delta. This movement to the south, which was to continue for centuries, had some enduring consequences for Vietnamese society. One of these is the cultural disparity between the northern and southern regions of the country, which persists to the present day:

> Once the various territories had been conquered, Vietnamese migrants would move into and settle these areas. Here, they often intermarried with Chams and Khmer, and even when they did not, they were exposed to the different social and cultural patterns of these Indianized peoples. These contacts tended to result in some compromising of the dominant Chinese-derived tradition, at least among the peasantry. Many of the cultural differences between northern and southern Vietnamese can be traced to such compromises. (Keyes 1979, 13–184)

By 1883, France had gained control over Vietnam after two centuries of trading and Catholic missionary activity in the area. The period of French rule is marked by great disruptions in Vietnamese society (see Ngo Vinh Long 1973). There was growing landlessness and poverty among the peasantry. The colonial regime reaped benefits from the expansion of rice export and coal, mineral, and rubber production in the country. Yet the prosperity was not felt by most Vietnamese, as the French continued to pursue policies of "high taxation and exasperating monopolies, of unproductive public works and opposition to Vietnam's industrialization" (Buttinger 1968, 11). The colonial period also saw the growth of a semi-feudal class of landowners and a French-educated elite among the Vietnamese. Also important were the divisive effects of French policies, which sought to solidify and deepen the traditional regional divisions (especially between the north and the south) in the country (Marr 1971, 79).

Vietnam endured a period of Japanese occupation during the Second World War. When the occupation ended in 1945, the Viet Minh (Vietnam Independence League) gained control and declared Vietnam's independence from the French. In 1946, war broke out between the returning French and the Viet Minh, a nationalist political coalition. With the armistice of 1954, France withdrew militarily from the conflict. What followed was the consolidation of Viet Minh power in the north and the declaration of the State of Vietnam by opposing political forces supported by the French in the south. With the support of the northern regime, the National Liberation Front (often referred to by urban southerners as the VC or Viet Cong) began a campaign against the South Vietnamese government. As conflicts escalated between the two regimes, the United

States, with military and political support for the South Vietnamese government, began its long and fateful entry into the war.

Under the French, and in the long period of war that followed French rule, the political and legal organization of Vietnamese rural society changed. The village holds great significance for an understanding of traditional Vietnamese life and so warrants discussion.

Village Life

Throughout Vietnam, the village center has traditionally been marked by a communal temple (*đình*). The communal temple served as a meeting place for the Council of Notables (*hội đồng nhân sĩ*), the traditional body of leadership in Vietnamese villages. The Council was a group of men chosen and also internally ranked according to traditional status criteria: age, education, and, in some cases, wealth. The Council elected a village headman (*lý trưởng*) who acted as an intermediary for the village with the state, supervising public works and village finances, including the collection of taxes. The highest-ranking member of the Council also led ceremonies at the village communal temple to honor the village guardian spirit.

The Council of Notables usually maintained links with village inhabitants through selected representatives of smaller groups within the village. In fact, most Vietnamese villages consisted of clusters of households that were sometimes treated as hamlets (*ấp*).[1] Ties of kinship connected households in the hamlets or in the even smaller clusters of settlement within hamlets (Hickey 1964). Much of the daily social life of village inhabitants revolved around the informal kin-centered networks running through the hamlets, which were an important source of mutual aid. For example, households collectively performed the tasks involved in rice cultivation, such as the transplanting of young rice shoots and the harvesting of crops. And families without land would often organize themselves into groups to contract themselves out to farmers. Coastal fishing entailed careful group organization and cooperating, and boat crews often consisted of neighbors or kinfolk (Donoghue 1962; Hendry 1964).

Besides cooperating in work tasks, those who needed financial loans usually turned to relatives and friends. Other options for those who

[1] The density or separation between hamlets varied across different regions of the country, with the density being far less in the south because of its more sparse settlement. Hamlet size also varied a great deal (Woodruff 1961).

needed a money loan were to approach local moneylenders or to form a rotating credit club (*hụi*). Such clubs were both a mutual aid society and a gambling game. All members agreed to pay a certain amount of money over a period of time, and the initiator received money from the others during the first meeting. After this, members made bids on the amount of interest they were willing to pay for use of the funds. The highest bidder received the loan for that month. At the end of the operation of a club, all members would have both contributed and received money, the exact amount depending on the skill and luck of the bidder. Such rotating credit clubs were most common among merchants (including women) because they had regular sources of income from shopkeeping and petty commerce (Nguyen Van Vinh 1949).

Modern Vietnamese history is marked by the gradual disintegration of the traditional political and legal organization of village life. Under French rule, the traditional autonomy of the village from the state was considerably reduced, particularly in the south. Village legal authority was transferred to district and regional French courts. By 1927 all appointments to the village council required the approval of the province chief who was appointed by the French. Because of these changes, village leadership gradually lost its traditional authority and status:

> Local notables were compelled to collect a fixed amount of tax revenues for the state, and were closely watched for any breaches in law and order. Budgeting was centralized and taken out of the hands of the village, and oral custom lost its force in running everyday affairs. Formerly in office as a result of social and political relationships within the village, village notables increasingly responded to outside pressures. In exchange for their loyalty, the colonial government offered notables unprecedented opportunities for expanding their personal fortunes and promoting their self-aggrandizement. (Werner 1981, 6)

French rule ended in 1954 but the traditional village political order was never to be restored. Indeed, the encroachment of the state into rural life was to continue and gain momentum over the years. In South Vietnam after 1954, the war with North Vietnam and subsequent concerns about security deeply shaped government policies toward village organization. For example, in an attempt to exercise close supervision and control over the people, the South Vietnamese government incorporated villages, hamlets, and family groups into a formal hierarchical administrative structure. Each unit in the administrative ladder exercised some control and responsibility for the one beneath it. However, the new, highly centralized structures failed to gain widespread legitimacy—a fact that was used by the revolutionary forces to gain support among South Vietnamese villagers (see Race 1972). In short, traditional political structures crumbled in the wake of the social turmoils of the era, but there were no new institutions that could effectively fill the vacuum. What did survive were kinship ties, which, amid the transformations that came to rock much of Vietnamese society, were to be an enduring source of community.

Family Life

The character of the traditional Vietnamese family system suggests that it was shaped by a variety of cultural traditions. Among these traditions was Confucianism, which molded the inner core of family life, proffering a set of ideal standards and structures for kin relations. But the realities of kinship in traditional Vietnamese society deviated from Confucianism in important ways, suggesting the presence of alternative traditions of kinship. The varied and pliant qualities of the Vietnamese family system have, I suggest, been important to its ability to adapt to changing circumstances and yet maintain its traditional character in important respects.

One of the most enduring legacies of Confucianism in Vietnam is the almost universally practiced ancestral cult,[2] an important element in the ideological makeup of the traditional Vietnamese family system. The ancestral cult is based upon the belief that after death one's "vital principles" survive. A number of these "principles," by attaching themselves to the ancestral tablets, assume the form of ancestral spirits. When the ancestral spirits are neglected or the appropriate filial duties are not fulfilled, the spirits may punish the offender and his or her family. Conversely, correct behavior is believed to bring good fortune through the rewards of the ancestral spirits. The ancestral cult provides important affirmation for the conception of the family as an entity that looms larger than the individual, stretching through time into both the past and the future. This conception of family is key to understanding the basic organization of traditional Vietnamese kinship, which was modeled on the Chinese system.

The traditional Vietnamese kinship system was structured around the patrilineal common descent group (*họ* or *tộc*), composed of several nuclear families who were the descendants of a common male ancestor. The

[2] Keyes (1979, 196) notes that the ancestral cult was somewhat less important among the Vietnamese elite, as they were skeptical of its premises. Nonetheless, the elite recognized its importance for maintaining order among the rebellion-prone Vietnamese peasantry.

43

họ emphasized hierarchy and solidarity. Each had a ritual head (*tộc trưởng*) who was the senior male in the direct line of descent from the focal ancestor. The ritual head was responsible for maintaining the lineage property and the tombs of ancestors and for making entries in the family genealogies. He also had the general responsibility of seeing to the welfare of *họ* members, arbitrating their disputes, and counseling them when necessary. Ideally, each branch of the patrilineage and each nuclear family also had a male head who played a comparable role. Prescribed residence for sons was patrilocal: that is, after marriage, sons were expected to live in the household or general vicinity of their parents. After marriage, women joined the household and *họ* of their husband. The eldest son, the successor to the role of the family head, inherited the family cult land, which was used for ancestral rites.

While these Confucianist structures shaped the basic parameters of the Vietnamese kinship system, they did not completely determine it. Hy Van Luong has suggested (1984, 300) that along with the Confucian model of kinship, there is "an alternative, coexisting and intertwined model of and for kinship relations in the Vietnamese sociocultural system." The presence of this alternative model is apparent in the many ways in which Vietnamese kinship differed from the prescribed Confucian structures. This alternative model defines the *họ* in broad terms to include bilateral and distant kin and is in general less rigid and male-dominated than the Confucian model. For example, in contrast to what one might expect given the official Confucian ideology, in reality, Vietnamese women still maintained connections with their natal *họ* after marriage and participated in its rituals and activities. Also, unlike their Chinese counterparts, women in Vietnam had rights to the paternal inheritance, a fact that served further to strengthen women's ties to their families of origin.

Despite the differences between them, the two models or traditions of kinship that Luong describe appear not as competing and separable but as integrated aspects of the traditional Vietnamese family system. However, changing circumstances could shift the relative importance of the two models of kinship in people's lives. As I will later describe, it was the more fluid and flexible model of kinship that rose to the surface in response to disruptions to the traditional fabric of Vietnamese rural society. Thus the presence of these diverse traditions gave the traditional Vietnamese kinship system an adaptable quality. It was a resilient system rather than a brittle one that was unable to cope with change. This quality of resilience enabled the kinship system to be a critical part of the practices by which Vietnamese coped with the upheavals that have gripped South Vietnamese society in recent times.

Women's Status

The complexity and diversity of kinship traditions in Vietnam have sometimes been taken as evidence of the relative equality of men and women
in traditional Vietnamese society. It is true that the position of women in
Vietnam had a somewhat distinctive cast, particularly since Vietnamese
women clearly had more options and resources than Chinese women, a
group to whom they are often compared. Despite this, the basic subordination of women in traditional Vietnamese life is difficult to dispute. The
oppression of women was firmly embedded across kinship, political,
legal, and economic institutions. In the formal political arena, for example, women were completely absent: the village notables were an exclusively male group, as were the heads of hamlets and family groups.

Confucian ideology, which shaped Vietnamese family life in critical
ways, was predicated on the dominance of men over women. Women
were expected to be married at a young age, after which they entered the
household of their husband's father. Young brides were subservient to
both men and older women in the household and had little domestic
status until they produced sons. For the young bride, her relationship
with her mother-in-law was perhaps the most onerous of all, as suggested
by the abundance of Vietnamese folk tales describing the harsh treatment
of the wife by her mother-in-law (Marr 1976, 373). The subordinate position of Vietnamese women in their families was strengthened by Confucian tenets. According to the "three submissions," a woman was ordered
to obey first her father, then her husband, and finally her eldest son. Ideal
feminine behavior was conceived in terms of the "four virtues": to be a
good housewife, to have a beautiful appearance, to speak well and softly,
and to be of good character. These ideals legitimated the subordination of
women by upholding passivity and submission to male authority, as well
as restrictions on women's sexuality.

Traditional Vietnamese legal codes were heavily influenced by Confucian ideas and so served to institutionalize further the subservience of
women. An important exception was the Le Code of the fifteenth and
sixteenth centuries, which went against Confucian principles by sanction-
ing equal property rights for men and women and protecting women
against certain forms of coercion by men.[3] Nonetheless, even in the Le
Code, women were assigned a lesser status than men, as evidenced, for
example, by the law that a husband could unilaterally divorce or repudi-

[3] For example, Nguyen Ngoc Huy and Ta Van Tai (1987) note that in contrast to previous codes, the Le Code did not allow a husband to sell or marry off his wife.

ate his wife, a privilege not extended to women (Nguyen Ngoc Huy and Ta Van Tai 1987, 80). Traditional legal codes also sanctioned polygamy, which was held as a mark of affluence and prestige and was usually practiced by the wealthy. Second-rank wives and particularly concubines had few rights under the law, and they "were usually treated very poorly, akin to indentured servants, so that there existed a class of women inferior even to other women" (Marr 1976, 373).

In rural life, women also had less economic power than men, although they were vitally involved in the task of rice cultivation, from which most Vietnamese made a living. The saying "men plow, women transplant, the buffalo pulls the harvest" reflects the traditional gender division of labor in the process of rice cultivation. Women not only played an important part in rice cultivation but also did most of the household work. Women were responsible for childcare and housework and for taking care of household gardens and livestock. One of the older women refugees that I interviewed, originally from a rural area in the north, described the arduous work of rural women: "Women at that time had a lot of work with no name (*việc không có tên*). Women worked from morning 'til night, because they grew vegetables and chickens, and they took care of the children and cooked. I, myself, I was young but I had a difficult life. I took care of my nephews and nieces and I threshed rice."

Besides the various kinds of household work described above, women were also involved in petty commerce and family businesses as part of their domestic caretaking activities. Women sold woven goods, vegetables, and fruit at the village market to supplement household income, and in fishing families, women were often involved in selling the fish. Women's income-generating activities became particularly prominent in those families in which men were intent on passing the mandarin examinations. In these cases, the woman often assumed complete responsibility for the family's economic needs, as her husband toiled away at the sacred books: "The scholar preparing for mandarin examinations, taken up by his readings of sacred books in preparation for his future role as 'Father and Mother of the People,' literally sponged on his wife. The latter tilled the fields, carried out a small trade, worked the loom, did the household chores, raised the children, toiled and moiled while her husband did absolutely nothing" (Mai Thi Tu 1966, 13).

Despite their involvement in a range of economic activities, women's economic participation was widely seen as secondary and peripheral to that of men, who were viewed as the primary breadwinners in rural society. This is revealed by the words of a male informant in his late fifties, from the south. He told me that women did not work, but then went on to contradict himself by describing women's involvement in rice cultivation: "In the countryside the man was the boss because the men had to work hard to make money for the family and most of the women did nothing. The men did things like plowing and harvesting and the women would plant the rice and weed."

Men's economic dominance was reinforced by their authority over the allocation and disposal of economic resources. Women often kept the household money and regulated everyday expenditures, a pattern that was perhaps strengthened by the Confucian disdain for commerce, as reflected in the saying "a man would not measure the fish sauce (*nước mắm*) and count the cloves of garlic." However, I did find evidence to suggest that men controlled discretionary income and that, in general, men had the final say over economic decisions. This was suggested to me by a woman who had grown up in rural South Vietnam: "In the house where I grew up, my grandmother kept the money. . . . my grandfather was dead at that time. But her son was the one who decided how to spend the money. Once my uncle wanted to sell some land. My grandmother didn't want to do that but she let him go ahead because the men were the bosses at that time; they decided the important things."

Thus despite the heavy involvement of rural Vietnamese women in economic activities, their control over economic resources was limited. David Marr provides a succinct summary of the complexities of Vietnamese women's relationship to the economic realm in traditional rural society:

> What the majority of Vietnamese women lacked was not involvement in economic production . . . Rather, they lacked control of the means of production, they were excluded from key decision-making, their work was considered less valuable, and their occupational alternatives to laboring in the fields and at home were more circumscribed than the case for men. If they wished to exercise power, it had to be via their menfolk. Perhaps the entire relationship was summed up in the adage: "A man's property is his wife's work." (1981, 197–98)

Although the fundamentally patriarchal character of traditional Vietnamese society is difficult to dispute, gender relations were not without their complexity. Within the overarching umbrella of the patriarchal structures of Vietnamese life, there were paths by which women could cultivate their own interests, a fact that strengthened the loyalty of women to the patriarchal structures. As I have argued with respect to the kinship system, the complexities of women's status in Vietnam gave traditional patterns of gender relations a certain resilience, an ability to adapt to change that was later to prove important.

What were the avenues of power and reward for women in traditional Vietnam? As scholars of the Chinese family have noted (Johnson 1983; Wolf 1972), the isolation and subordination suffered by young women after marriage in the household of their husband's father was made more tolerable by the expectation that in their old age, they too would come to hold considerable power in the household. The power that women could eventually hope to wield in the home was expressed by the popular reference to the woman of the home as the "Chief of the Interior" (*nội tướng*). While this was a term that emphasized the great power that some women had in their household, it was also a phrase that helped to define this power as being limited to the "interior"—the home.

Further tempering the oppression of Vietnamese women was the fact that most were not quite as isolated from the support and resources of their natal families as was suggested by the Confucian model.[4] The legal rights of Vietnamese women to a share of the paternal inheritance (unlike in China) served perhaps to strengthen the bonds and influence of women with their families of origin after marriage. Women's rights to inheritance as well as their involvement in family bookkeeping and petty commerce also suggest that women were not devoid of access to economic resources. Also, although women were excluded from formal positions of power in the village, they were able to exert some influence in their communities through the social networks of kin and friends. Via the gossip generated in these networks, women could collectively exert social pressures on village inhabitants (cf. Wolf 1972). Thus these informal social networks were potential means by which women could protect themselves against the excesses of the patriarchal family system.

A final point that must be raised concerns the effects of social class and regional background on women's status. The lesser influence of Confucian beliefs in the south meant that the status and activities of women in that region were less rigid and asymmetrical than in the north. Also, for the poorer social strata in Vietnam, the ability to put Confucian ideals into practice was limited by economic circumstances (Mai Thi Tu 1966, 16). The ideal of female passivity, for example, was belied by the heavy labor that peasant women were compelled to undertake. The upper social

---

[4] In his research in Khanh Hau, a village in South Vietnam, Hickey (1964, 93–94) found that although patrilineal ties dominated, bilateral kin were part of social networks that ran through hamlets and sometimes across villages.

strata, however, had greater ability to rigidly define and circumscribe the activities of women. This was described to me by a male informant in his recollection of village life in the north in the 1940s: "Especially the families who had a lot of land, they lived in a feudal (*phong kiên*) way. When the husband was eating the wife would stand and fan him. They were like maids."

In general, the greater ability of the upper class to put Confucian ideals of family life into practice meant that these ideals held wide value for Vietnamese, who associated them with respectability and high social status. And so, for the South Vietnamese middle class that was to emerge in the 1950s through the 1970s, Confucian ideals of family life continued to hold meaning and significance.

FROM VILLAGE TO CITY: THE URBAN MIDDLE CLASS

The 1950s to 1970s was a time of great upheaval in South Vietnam, as war and urbanization transformed the society in deep-seated ways. The 1954 partition of the country following the Geneva Treaty marked the beginning of a large-scale movement to urban areas and, with it, the disruption of traditional kinship and community life for many Vietnamese. The rural-urban migration of the era may be roughly divided into two phases. In the first phase, the 1954 partition of the country generated an exodus from the north, particularly of Catholics, as well as others who feared Viet Minh reprisals because of their association with the French presence. Some, though not all, of those who moved from the north resettled in the urban areas of the south. Binh, originally from Phat Diem, a Catholic region in the north, explained the decision of his family to move south:

> In 1954, after the Geneva Treaty, the whole family went south. Because in the north, even during the time I was small, the priests told us that the VC followed the Russians, so they were Communists. Communism means that no one can have their own property; the government would keep everything and the people would only go to work and the government would supply them with rice. And the Communists don't believe in God; in that way there's no freedom. When we first went to the south we lived on the camp settlements (*trại định cư*) given by the Diem government.[5]

[5] In 1954 the Diem government set up an assistance program for the refugees from the north, in which they were resettled and given temporary material assistance.

49

Among my informants there were also a few who took advantage of the flow of people to move to the south for better economic opportunities or to escape from repressive family situations. For example, one of my women informants left her village in the north with a friend in order to escape an unwanted marriage that had been arranged by her father:

> The reason I left for the south was that my father wanted me to marry someone who was not Catholic. Before she died, my mother told my maternal grandmother, "let her marry a Catholic man." But my father promised me to that man who wasn't Catholic. My father was a Chinese medicine doctor (*đông y sĩ*). He liked that man [who wanted to marry me] because that man was also a Chinese doctor and his father owned a store. So my father wanted me to marry him. That man even came and stayed at our house a few months for *làm rể*.[6]

Also relevant is the image of opportunity and less social rigidity that the south seems to have held for some northerners. A male informant in his early thirties who had grown up in Saigon explained the decision of his father to move south:

> My father was like an adventurer. To my understanding, for people in the north, going to the south was very romantic at that time. When there were many people leaving, he went to Haiphong and took the boat with other people going south. My father dared to leave everything; he left my grandmother and the family property to go to the south. But his older brother stayed in the north to take care of the family.

The southward migration of this time was also spurred by the disruptions wrought on the traditional social order that were due to the Japanese occupation and the struggle against the French presence that followed. With the Viet Minh launch for independence a good portion of the countryside became directly involved in the military conflict. Involvement in the war was often unavoidable, as revealed by a man originally from the north, who explains why he began fighting in the war in 1953:

> That time I stayed at home and in the daytime the French came and forced me to fix the road. At night when the French went back to their base the Viet Minh came and forced me to dig the road. So I had to do something. I wasn't thinking anything patriotic; the side that supplied me with enough

---

[6] This refers to a traditional practice whereby the prospective bridegroom would live in the home of his future in-laws and work for them for a period of time.

food and clothes, I would follow. I didn't think about the country. During the time the Viet Minh forced me at night to dig the road, I saw that they didn't have enough food to eat; each meal was under two bowls of rice and they ate it with vegetables only. When they got wounded they carried the wounded nine to ten kilometers to the clinic and there they just did some first aid. Son-of-a-bitch! (*Con mẹ nó!*) The side that gave me more food and clothes, I decided to join.

The French–Viet Minh struggle set into motion a process of widespread militarization that was to become an enduring aspect of South Vietnamese life. The militarization is an important backdrop to the southward migration of the era in two senses. First, for those who had fought in support of the French, the movement to the south was spurred by fear of Viet Minh reprisals. Second, the French–Viet Minh war, which took place on the heels of the social disruptions generated by French colonial policies, worked to loosen further the social bonds tying rural inhabitants to the countryside.

A second phase of migration took place after 1954. This rural-urban movement was of greater magnitude and perhaps more unexpected than the 1954 migration. From the 1950s to the 1970s, South Vietnam moved from being a largely rural society to a highly urbanized one, so that by 1975, 35 percent or more of the population lived in the cities (see Beresford 1988, 57; Keyes 1979, 300).[7] Cities such as Danang, Nha Trang, and Can Tho grew enormously. In 1945 the population of Saigon was estimated to be 500,000, whereas in 1975 it had swollen to about four million (Beresford 1988, 57). The war had much to do with this rapid urban explosion.

The most obvious effect of the war was that it simply drove people to leave the dangers of the war-torn rural areas for the relative safety of the cities. The massive bombings and defoliation of land, combined with the displacement of people into the "agrovilles" and "strategic hamlets" created by the South Vietnamese government to reduce enemy infiltration, all contributed to the rural exodus.[8] The overwhelmingly urban backgrounds of my informants had often grown out of their families' search in the 1950s and 1960s for an escape from the destruction and uncertainty

[7] Kolko (1985, 202) asserts that by 1971, three-quarters of the urban residents were not native to the city.

[8] Kolko writes: "The most conservative estimates are that at least half of the peasants were pushed into refugee camps or urban settings one or more times, many repeatedly" (ibid., 201).

51

that was tearing apart the countryside. We see this in the account of an informant who explains why his father had left his native village during the late 1950s:

> I grew up in a small town near a city called Cam Ranh. My paternal grand-parents came from another province in the middle of Vietnam, called Binh Dinh. They were farmers. When I was very small, my father decided it wasn't safe there [in Binh Dinh] because of the war, so we moved down to a small town near Cam Ranh. My father didn't have land in the new place for farming, so he decided to buy a store and start a new life doing business.

For the rural refugees from the war, the attractiveness of the cities was further enhanced by the expansion of certain sectors of the urban economy that took place during this time. As a number of analysts have noted, the economies of the urban areas of South Vietnam were heavily tied to the necessities generated by the war effort itself. In the 1960s and 1970s, the cities of South Vietnam saw a rapid expansion of service and commercial sectors that were deeply tied to the war and to the United States military and economic presence:

> Urbanization in South Vietnam has been much more a function of the war than of economic development . . . In essence the war produced an economic boom as a rapid increase in the demand for labor occurred at the military bases and ports and in the various facilities providing services to South Vietnamese, American, and other servicemen fighting in the war. Although some war-created jobs, such as those of mechanics, carpenters, stenographers, and so on, were skilled or semiskilled, many more were unskilled. Women became prostitutes or servants or street hawkers whereas men became cyclo drivers, road construction laborers, and petty traders. (Keyes 1979, 209)

Foreign aid intensified the somewhat artificial character of the urbanization process in South Vietnam. The conditions attached to U.S. economic aid compelled South Vietnam to use the aid funds to import goods from the United States. The South Vietnamese market was flooded with imported goods, which included food as well as luxury consumer items. The disadvantage of this situation was that the productive capacity of the South Vietnamese economy stagnated, and the country's industrial production and exports fell (Beresford 1988, 147–48).

For the rural migrants of this era, the cities presented conflicting economic possibilities. On the one hand, life was not easy for most Vietnamese in the cities. Unemployment was high, and the swelling of the urban population had created a serious shortage of housing, water, and other facilities (Beresford 1988, 57). At the same time, the cities held open the potential for acquiring luxury consumer items and of making a lucrative living from the service economy. Urban life in the south was particularly attractive for the emerging middle class, who were beneficiaries of the more positive side of the urban growth process. The economic appeal of urban living in the south during this era is revealed in the following words of a man who had lived near Saigon but was originally from a fishing town in Central Vietnam:

> Life in Saigon was very good. I think people from the south, from the Mekong Delta, are nice people, different from people in Hue. In the south the economic situation was very good. In the south people made four hundred and spent four hundred; that was the way that people lived. Even the men who drove the cyclo, they worked five days and spent two days spending the money with their family. The market price was so low for things, you could buy beer and Coke for just a few *dong*;[9] everything was cheap. And the quality of things was good . . . like the cigarettes. But after 1975 the price of cigarettes went up and the quality was like garbage.

Perhaps the major factor driving urbanization for my informants was involvement in the army. The process of militarization in the years prior to 1954 was to continue and gain momentum in the 1960s and 1970s, during which time the South Vietnamese government imposed a military draft. Especially during the years of the Thieu regime (1967–75), the number of people employed by the military and the government rose sharply (Kolko 1985, 213, 234). Of the twelve households that composed my core sample, most contained people who were from military backgrounds, either through their own involvement or through that of their father or husband. Army involvement tended to spur settlement in urban areas. The following segment from the life history of Toan, born in 1943, and originally from a rural fishing village, illustrates how urbanization was tied to military service:

> I joined the army in 1960. The reason I joined was that I was so bored with my life, and I saw my brothers who were forced to join the army. If I was forced to join I would get only eighty dong, but if I went by myself I would get more. After joining, I studied at the school for noncommissioned offi-

[9] There have been wide fluctuations in the value of the *dong*, or Vietnamese piaster, in recent times. For example, the 1962 piaster-dollar exchange rate on the free market was ninety-seven, and in 1974 it was seven hundred (Trullinger 1980, 14).

cers (*Đồng Đế*) for two years. After graduating I was a warrant officer (*thượng sĩ*). First I was stationed at Vung Tau, then Bien Hoa. I lived in Saigon from about 1968. For a few years after I got married my wife and children lived in the countryside; they lived with my parents so my wife could take care of my parents, who were old. But after my wife had the second child, she and the children moved to Saigon to live with me.

Joining the army not only led to urban living but was also, for some, a gateway into the middle class. For those men fortuitous enough to find themselves in the right place at the right time, the military offered a particularly steep path of upward mobility:

> When I first joined the army in the north I was a plain soldier. But when we went south a lot of soldiers deserted, and after this, there were only a few drivers left. When I was based in Hanoi I got two licenses, one for a smaller car and one for a truck. That time Lieutenant General Nguyen Van Vinh wanted to encourage people who had two licenses to join him. So I jumped from plain soldier to first-class corporal. I got a higher salary. For a plain soldier it was twelve hundred *đồng* and for a corporal it was twenty-five hundred *đồng*.
>
> In 1957–58 in the south there were a lot of people in the army who were of high rank but not well trained. The Diem government wanted to train these people, so we went to training sessions called rank adjustment. At that time there were people who couldn't read but were high ranking. I requested to go to training school for noncommissioned officers.

Thus out of the turmoils of war and urbanization there emerged an urban middle class in South Vietnam. In general, the rural forbearers of my informants were from the well-to-do[10] but not the economically elite sectors of rural society. The economic and educational resources that they did have at their disposal placed them (and their progeny) in a particularly good position to take advantage of the expansion of middle-level positions in the army and government bureaucracy that took place in South Vietnam at this time (see Beresford 1988, 57) and to join the ranks of the emerging urban middle class. But the urban middle class occupied a somewhat peculiar position in South Vietnam, one that was both privileged and marginalized. Although they were a group occupying a social and economic position above the large numbers of unskilled, often uneducated rural refugees in the cities, they were also excluded from the upper

[10] My interview data suggest that the majority were from small business and landowning rather than tenant farming backgrounds.

levels of economic and political power. In many ways, as Charles F. Keyes observes, (1979, 309) "the war never seriously threatened the class structure that had been inherited from the colonial period." Positions of high power and prestige in the political and economic structure continued to be controlled by a small group, including the French-educated elite and the Chinese, who for generations had dominated much of the wholesale trading and banking in the south. However, urban middle-class parents often hoped that educational achievements would enable their children to break into elite society in the future.

URBAN MIDDLE-CLASS LIFE IN THE PRE-COMMUNIST YEARS

Family Life

In assessing the character of family life for the urban middle class in the decades before Communist rule, one point that stands out is the tremendous importance of familial ties and loyalties in the lives of the urban migrants. My evidence suggests that although traditional kinship structures underwent much change in the urbanization process, family ties nonetheless remained the most important source of community, providing support for coping with the turmoils of the era. For one thing, despite the general prosperity of this era for the middle class, there was a widespread underlying feeling of material insecurity. The sharp economic inequalities of South Vietnamese society served to remind people constantly of the dire consequences of downward class mobility. The specter of poverty was all the more daunting given the underdeveloped structure of social welfare and assistance in South Vietnam. In this context, the value of kinship ties lay partly in the fact that they could be counted on in difficult times, as the following words of a male informant, a former army officer, suggest: "When my sister's husband died, she and her children came to live with us. My sister's husband had been in the army, but she didn't get much money from them after he died. So she came to live with us and she got a job as a secretary at an American company. After a few years, when her youngest child was about seven, she moved to her own house, but it was close by."

Kinship ties functioned not only as an economic safety net but also as a source of loans and business capital. Kin sometimes pooled resources and opened joint business ventures: "My parents had a bicycle repair shop in Can Tho. Actually, it belonged to them and two uncles and one aunt. They owned it together; they all gave money to start the business, and some of them worked there. I think my paternal grandfather gave a lot of the money, because when he sold the land he had in the countryside he got some money from that."

As suggested by this account, despite the disruptions to familial relations caused by the urban migration, the middle-class families in the cities tended to retain their extended character. Over half of those I interviewed indicated that in Vietnam they had lived in households composed of kin beyond the nuclear family. And even when extended family had not lived in the same house, they had often lived nearby. Thus in their accounts of life in Vietnam, many of my informants talked of how contacts with relatives were daily and frequent. Furthermore, these relatives were from both maternal and paternal sides of their families.

In fact, these middle-class urban inhabitants tended to see the family group as a broad and inclusive entity, instead of equating it with the patrilineal common descent group. The emphasis on the more fluid model of kinship arose at least in part because of war and urbanization—events that had seriously eroded, in manifold ways, the ability to attain the more rigidly defined Confucianist family structure. For one thing, the social turmoil of the era simply scattered and separated kin, thus making it difficult to define kinship boundaries in an extremely rigorous fashion. Family members sometimes fought on different sides of the war. Urban dwellers lost touch with their rural relatives (cf. Freeman 1989, 155–56). For urban inhabitants, there was also a loss of contact with ancestral graves and land, which further contributed to the disbandment of the patrilineal common descent group. In the face of these many changes, the more flexible dimensions of Vietnamese kinship traditions rose to the surface. Only to a limited degree, however, did the movement away from the ideal Confucianist system mark the emergence of a more egalitarian family life. In many ways, the conditions of urban middle-class life strengthened parental authority and male dominance—two central tenets of Confucian familial ideology.

Women's Status

The structure and dynamics of the patrilineal extended household were at the core of men's dominance over women in traditional Vietnam. Thus one may well speculate that the inequality of women receded as this type of household structure crumbled. Undoubtedly, for the middle-class families who are the subject of this study, war and urbanization tempered gender inequality in important ways. But I argue that male dominance remained entrenched in the economic and social institutions of urban middle-class life in the decades before 1975.

Crucial to the subordination of the women in the cities was the continued economic prominence of men in the family. As I have described, movement into the urban middle class was often tied to the entry of men into the military or government bureaucracy. Men remained the primary breadwinners—a fact that helped to reinforce male dominance. Related to this is the fact that economic expansion in urban South Vietnam during the 1950s to 1970s had affected men and women somewhat differently. The economy remained segmented by gender. In the burgeoning middle-level segments of the army and government bureaucracy, the more lucrative and prestigious jobs were held by men rather than women. However, the small business and especially the service sectors of the urban economy relied heavily on the labor of women. In fact, the upheavals of the war had generated a class of women who eked out a marginal existence from work in these sectors.[11] While they were not part of this impoverished group, urban middle-class women also worked in small business and service jobs.

Among my female informants, I found three types of income-generating work to have been prevalent in Vietnam. The first of these was *buôn bán*, or trading.[12] Some women indicated that they had at least periodically engaged in trading to supplement the household income. This form of trading generally involved buying wholesale goods and selling them in the market, or selling homemade products in the market. The peculiar qualities of the South Vietnamese urban economy—the abundance of luxury consumer items and foreign goods, combined with the plentiful discretionary income of certain segments of the population—often made such trading quite lucrative.

Despite their profitability, women's trading activities were rarely considered to be anything more than supplemental to the income of men in the household. In part, this perception was tied to the peculiar qualities of *buôn bán*. First of all, this type of trading tended to be seasonal and gen-

[11] For example, by 1975, there were an estimated half a million women engaged in prostitution (see Nyland 1981).

[12] The heavy involvement of women in trading activities is supported by survey data on the occupational background (in Vietnam) of Vietnamese refugees in the United States. Haines (1989, 9–10) cites 1983 survey data showing 60.8 percent of women in the sample indicating that they had been involved in sales or clerical jobs in Vietnam, compared to 34.3 percent of the men.

erate an uncertain amount of return. Second, such work was highly integrated into the day-to-day tasks of taking care of the household and thus
had an invisible quality. Some of these qualities were revealed to me by
one of my younger male informants, in response to questions about his
mother's employment in Vietnam: "My mother didn't work, but sometimes she did some business, when we needed some extra money. She sold
some food to the American cafeteria at the dorm for soldiers. She and her
sister made the food at home and took it over there. The food was American cakes and desserts that she learned how to make from a friend."

It is also worth noting that the trading activities of the women in the
cities were not without rural precedent: women had also engaged in
small-scale commerce in village society. The following words of a woman
informant captures the traditional, seasonal, and secondary character of
women's commercial trading activities:

> My husband was a corporal (*hạ sĩ*). After I got married I followed him to
> different places and I did trading, sometimes right in the post. When I was
> young and living in the countryside I had done trading with my aunt, so I
> was used to it. It was also easy for me because my daughter helped me and
> I didn't go there every day. What I did was buy radios and watches and sell
> them in the market. Sometimes I sold *bánh dầy* (rice cakes). My husband's
> pay was twelve hundred *đồng* a month, and that wasn't enough for the
> family, especially because he gambled. But with the money I made we could
> live well and send money to his mother.

Besides small-scale trading, women were also frequently involved in
more regularized types of family businesses. Most common among my
informants were small variety stores (*tiệm tạp hóa*) and restaurants.
Sometimes women owned and operated these businesses independently
of men in the family. In other cases, especially when the businesses were
large or the main source of income for the family, women ran the businesses in conjunction with men. In such cases, the degree of influence
wielded by women in the operation of the business varied across families.
In some cases, women performed the everyday tasks of running the business, especially selling, while major decisions were left to the men. But in
other cases, women played a more prominent role:

> My parents owned a store, and we sold different things. My father also did
> some farming. My mother is the one who ran the store, actually. I think my
> mother was the smart one because she ran the business better; everyone
> knew that. Sometimes my father would try to take charge, and he would

make some mistakes and my mother yelled at him. Usually after that they had a big fight; they would throw things around the house.

A small number of my women informants had worked in white-collar clerical jobs, usually for foreign companies or for the South Vietnamese government. Two of the women interviewed had been office secretaries— one at a government office, the other at an electrical company before her marriage. The mother of one of my young male informants had been a clerical worker at a U.S. insurance company before 1975. In general, the women who had been in such jobs had more years of education than the others in my sample. The social class status of their households had also been higher, as suggested by the fact that their husbands or fathers were in the upper ranks of the government or military forces.

Almost all of the adult women I interviewed indicated that they had been involved in the types of income-generating activities that I have just described for at least some portion of their lives in Vietnam. Despite this involvement, when first questioned about whether they had "worked" in Vietnam, some of the women told me that they had not done so—a response that points to the hidden, supplemental, and seasonal characteristics of women's work compared to that of men. The primary status accorded men's jobs stemmed not just from the greater income generated but also from the fact that it was usually the man's job that was a source and symbol of social status for the members of the household, a mark of their place in the middle class.

For all these reasons, women remained dependent on men and committed to ensuring men's ties to their families. In Vietnam, women had been fearful of male desertion of their families and the loss of economic and social resources that desertion signified. According to the women I interviewed, the potential for male desertion had been high, given that the army demanded long periods of separation of men from their families. The army milieu also promoted "loose" sexual behavior among men, as described to me by one woman:

> To tell you the truth, men became corrupt in the army, and especially him [her husband]—he was a driver. He said that every man is like that, needs someone to help him when he's away from the family. I followed my husband to Phu Quoc and to Rach Gia. Sometimes it was not convenient to do that, because his mother was living with us at that time and she was old. But I decided it was better because when men are alone in the army they become rotten, they take other women. And life for my children would be much harder without a father to help them.

The potential loss of men's economic contributions to the household was particularly troublesome given the sharp economic inequalities of South Vietnamese society at this time. In addition, the possibilities of remarriage for women were somewhat limited, because the war had created an unbalanced sex ratio in the cities, with women outnumbering men (Sully 1971, 79).

In short, the quality and basis of men's dominance shifted in the process of integration into urban life. But male dominance did not disintegrate, buoyed up as it was by the segregated character of modern South Vietnamese economic and social institutions. The disruptions of the war, urbanization and incipient Westernization had undoubtedly tempered some of the rigidity of the traditional prescriptions surrounding women's behavior and the relations of men and women. But traditional gender ideologies legitimating the subordination of women continued to be a part of urban middle-class life at this time. One expression of the continued power and dominance of men over women in urban middle-class life was the apparently high frequency of wife beating in families. Duyen, a women in her early twenties who had grown up in a well-to-do family in Saigon, spoke about this at some length:

Vietnamese women are brought up to obey the husband. So in Vietnam when the man beat her up for some reason or even for no reason, she accepted it. It was very, very common in Vietnam; don't believe anyone who tells you it wasn't. When it happened, no one thought it was their business to interfere, and I'm sure most people here don't want to talk about it. It happened in my family—not a lot, but sometimes. When my father got angry he beat up my mother, and she just accepted it. It was kind of strange because my mother was a really active woman, she had her own business, made her own money, she was really smart. But when it came to my father beating her up, she did nothing.

Another informant, a man, also talked of his father beating his mother. He also described his somewhat curious method of intervening in such situations:

My mother pampered me very much. I still remember my mother crying every time when my father beat up my mother. And I didn't accept it. When that happened my elder brothers were crying, but not me. I would use a knife and chop things in the house. My father was afraid that he would have to spend money fixing up the house, so he would stop. Before in Vietnam, if a husband got mad he would beat his wife; that's the way it was. My brothers would sit and cry, but I would break things. If I didn't do that then my father would keep beating her forever. My father respected me because I was obstinate.

The Young: The Urbanites

For the younger generation of my informants—those who entered adulthood during or after the 1975 takeover—memories of Vietnam were primarily of life in the cities, because few had had sustained contact with rural society. Their lifestyles and experiences were in many ways quite different from those of their parents and rural forebears. And yet, particularly with regard to family life, their experiences show important elements of continuity with the past.

A striking aspect of the family reminiscences of the younger generation was the important role played by extended family members in their lives. Relatives, especially grandmothers, participated heavily in child-rearing. Sometimes, as in the following case, children lived in the household of their grandparents for some portion of their childhood.

After I was born, I lived with my maternal grandmother. I lived with her 'til I was ten years old, then my parents took me home. [Why did you live with her and not your parents?] The reason I lived with my grandmother was that I loved her very much. I stayed with her from when I was very young; I never lived with my parents before, so I just didn't want to stay with them. When my parents came to take me I just cried and cried, so they said okay. I saw my mother every day, though; she visited me every afternoon. Sometimes she brought me cookies.

When grandmothers were not as directly involved in child-rearing as in the preceding case, they often nonetheless played an important emotional role in children's lives. Quite typical among my informants was the response of Huong, a woman in her late twenties, when asked about her closest family relationships in Vietnam: "The person I was closest to in my family was my paternal grandmother. She lived just next door to us, and I spent most of my time with her. I was her favorite grandchild, so I was very spoiled. I didn't want to do any work, and when I wanted to buy something I just aked her for the money. All my brothers and sisters teased me because I was her favorite."

In contrast to such memories were those related to relationships with fathers. In many accounts, fathers appeared as more physically and emotionally distant to their children than mothers. The father was also the main authority figure in the family, the one to mete out punishments (usually physical) for the most severe transgressions. Punishments often resulted from inadequate performance at school, disrespectful behavior toward elders, and, for boys, staying out late. As James Freeman has noted (1989, 52–55), the youngest child held a favored status in the family and so was sometimes exempt from physical punishment.

The general impression, however, that was conveyed by the younger generation of my informants was that life in Vietnam before 1975 had been filled with ease and pleasure. Undoubtedly, such recollections were heavily tinged with nostalgia. Nonetheless, it is true that before 1975, these children of the urban middle class grew up enjoying the prosperity of their parents. They felt secure in their economic and social status, assured that the resources of their parents would enable them to gain a foothold in the middle or perhaps upper ranks of South Vietnamese society. Family economic resources, for example, assured one of access to formal education. The urban middle class valued educational attainment for the prestige that it brought and for its ability to secure a place in the professions, or at least a high position in the government bureaucracy or military. However, educational achievement was not easy in South Vietnam, which had a French-influenced system of education that required students to take a series of competitive national exams. The student's performance in these exams determined the course and nature of his or her educational career. The first exam took place after five years of primary schooling, and its results determined qualification for registered public schools. The vast majority who were not able to qualify for entrance into these schools relied on familial financial support to enroll in private schools that would enable them to continue their formal education (Dorais, Pilon-Le, and Nguyen Huy 1987, 61). But even for those middle-class children who were disinclined toward academic studies, there were other avenues for the achievement of socioeconomic mobility. Children could expect to take over lucrative family businesses: "By the time I was older, my father's store was very big, maybe the biggest in town. So my parents wanted me to run the store after they were too old and unable to run it. They wanted me get a good education, but they didn't expect me to be a doctor or engineer. They thought I could have a comfortable and good life running the stores."

Thus for the urban middle-class young, economic support from their families remained extremely important to their socioeconomic attainment, a situation that bolstered the economic dependence of the young on their families. This dependence was reflected in the fact that parents and other elder kin continued to play a central part in the marriage decisions of their children, although marriages were no longer arranged by parents with the same regularity as they had been in the past.[13] Among the urban middle class, dating was acceptable; however, it was carefully monitored by families and was usually taken as a prelude to engagement and marriage. Tang, a male informant in his midtwenties, described his dating experience in Vietnam: "I went out with a girl in Vietnam for a few years. We met in high school. Our families were happy about it because we had the same kind of family, educated and well off. Dating was different in Vietnam; you had to go to meet the family and then ask if you could take her out. And I went out with her for five years, but I never touched her. I held her hand sometimes and we kissed once, that's all."

The information I gathered suggests that women's premarital virginity continued to be valued.[14] Restrictions on the sexuality of unmarried women were considered to be important to the reputation of the women and their families. In a certain sense, the emphasis on the sexual purity of women was strengthened by the widespread and visible prostitution in the urban areas of the south at this time. As mentioned previously, the war had generated a class of women in the cities who had out of economic desperation turned to prostitution and other jobs that serviced the United States military presence. For the middle class, these women symbolized the pollution of the war and foreign presence as well as the threat of poverty. Thus the ability to maintain the pure sexual reputation of young women in the family was important for the middle class as a means to distinguish themselves from the lower social strata in the cities. The symbolic contrast posed by "fallen" poorer women was suggested by Huong, who had grown up in Saigon:

> You know, in Vietnam, if a woman had an American boyfriend, it was bad not just for that woman but also for the rest of the family; everyone looked

[13] A study of Vietnamese refugees in Quebec City, Canada, found that arranged marriages had taken place only among informants aged forty years or older. But even for younger informants, "the choice of a spouse was not free from family control. In five cases out of ten, the future husband or wife was first introduced to the informant by his brother or sister" (Dorais, Pilon-Le, and Nguyen Huy 1987, 63).

[14] Several of my younger informants indicated that before 1975, premarital sex was not unheard of, particularly among college students. It is of course extremely difficult to gauge the actual extent of premarital sexual activity in urban South Vietnam before 1975. However, it does seem fair to say that premarital sexual activity, especially for women, was frowned upon by the middle and upper strata of South Vietnamese society.

down on that family. The woman had to leave her parents' house because they would disown her. Myself, I don't think it's fair to blame the women, because there were women who were so poor they needed money to help their families, and that's why they started sleeping and living with American men. And there were also women whose husbands beat them up and they wanted to leave them. But when I was in Vietnam I remember my mother and aunt talking about these women, saying that they were really bad. They said no woman in our family was ever like that; they were proud about that. Because our family was very strict about dating. My older sister, she wasn't allowed to go out at all.

The "Fall" of Saigon: 1975 and Its Aftermath

Vietnam entered a new political era in April 1975, when North Vietnamese forces captured Saigon. The event had tremendous significance for the Vietnamese in my study. In about half of the study households, men were forcibly sent to "reeducation camps" (*trại cải tạo*) created by the new government to indoctrinate and punish those associated with the former regime. Conditions in the camps were extremely harsh, and prisoners were often made to perform heavy labor (Freeman 1989; Nguyen Van Canh 1985). Some South Vietnamese were also pressured to relocate to NEZs (New Economic Zones)—tracts of land that had been abandoned or damaged by the war. The NEZs were devised by the government as a means of coping with the economic problems of the south, in particular to reduce the swollen population of the southern cities and to increase the land under cultivation. But conditions in the NEZs were difficult, particularly for urban dwellers who had little previous experience with farming.

Even for those who were not forced into "reeducation camps" or NEZs, the 1975 takeover had many repercussions. With the withdrawal of United States troops in 1973, the South Vietnamese economy had plunged into a recession. The demobilization of the South Vietnamese forces in 1975 exacerbated unemployment problems. In general, the economic problems faced by the newly united Vietnam were daunting. The country suffered a serious drought in 1977, followed by floods that intensified the land cultivation problems created by the residue of war bombing and herbicides. As a result, food was scarce. Ly, a woman in her thirties, conveys a sense of the panic and economic desperation that gripped many South Vietnamese at this time:

1975 was terrible. I cried a lot because I didn't know what the Communists were like and I heard rumors that they would kill everyone. Then people started selling their own things because they needed money . . . TVs, refrigerators, electric fans, anything you could sell, even clothes. Life was so hard in those years that people just wanted to keep enough clothes to wear for one day; if they had extra clothes they would sell them. So I would buy those things and then sell them in the market.

While the years after 1975 were economically difficult for urban South Vietnamese in general, the Communist victory was economically particularly devastating for certain segments of the population. After 1978, the government moved toward the nationalization of private businesses. Small businesses, however, were allowed to remain open so along as they did not deal in government-controlled goods. The government also enacted currency reforms in an effort to bring the economy under state control and to deter black marketeering. Particularly affected were the Chinese-Vietnamese, the traditional business group in the south. The economic losses suffered by the group, along with the outbreak of hostilities between Vietnam and China, led to the massive exodus of Chinese from Vietnam at this time (Duiker 1980).

Government economic policies generated losses for other segments of the business class as well. Those Vietnamese who had owned stores, for example, lost control over their business and found their profit margins to be reduced: "After 1975, the local government came to take control of some of my family's stores. We had several different stores by 1975. But after 1975 we had only one store left, and we had to pay a lot of taxes. And the store wasn't our own anymore. We had to report to the government, and the police came to check the store sometimes. So life became much harder after 1975."

A number of my informants asserted that the nationalization campaign engendered corruption rather than economic growth. This is suggested by the account of a man whose bus transportation business was affected by government nationalization policies:

> In 1975, after the Communists took over, half of me wanted to leave for the United States, but I didn't want to go because I was afraid I would lose my property. I had two buses at that time. And another reason I didn't go was that although I knew what the Communists were like, I also thought that they had something good because they always won and there were a lot of people following them. So I wanted to stay to find out what was good about them.

65

In 1978, my buses became collectivized. Actually, the bus was still my bus, but the government took all the money. The bus had fifty-four seats, so we sold tickets for all those seats, and the government took all the money. My assistants and I took care of the bus, so if sometimes there was a flat tire we had to fix it ourselves, using money from my own pocket. When the tires were worn out I asked the government for new ones; sometimes they gave them to us and sometimes not. Each month they paid me ninety-six *đồng* for driving. Each month they sold me nine kilos of rice and a few packets of cigarettes. But you see, ninety-six *đồng* at that time was only good enough to cook the rice soup. So even honest people had to cheat. We cooperated with the ticket seller; we told him to sell just forty tickets and give the rest to us. The official price of a ticket to Vung Tau was two and a half *đồng*, but we sold the tickets for thirty or forty *đồng*. If a person had cargo we sold him a ticket for less, but then we charged him a lot for the cargo. That way we could live, repair the bus, and spend on other maintenance expenses. No matter how honest a person was, he had to cheat. All the people who worked for the government were like that. Everyone became a thief.

Together, the political retributions and economic losses experienced by the urban middle class after 1975 created a drastic shift in their lifestyle and outlook. Among the younger generation, the optimism of the pre-1975 years was replaced by a deep pessimism. The security and privileges that they had come to expect were now gone. The children of former army officers in particular found themselves at a disadvantage—their families underwent close surveilance and they experienced discrimination at school. Dinh, one of my male informants, described some of the changes in his life:

> Life got worse and worse. Anything we wanted to say, we couldn't say; my parents would tell me to keep quiet. We couldn't express ourselves. We lived then in a group of ten families. Every group of ten families had a leader, so if a relative wanted to come he had to be reported to the leader. The leader reported all the information about what was going on to the Communist police. We were controlled by them. The ten families had to do some work together, like grow vegetables in the garden.
>
> I went to school at that time and there, too, we were controlled. We were divided into many classes and each class was treated very differently. In the bottom class, the worst class, there were children of the former officers, people like me. In the top class there were the children of the people in the Communist government. Those children got special benefits, like good

food supplied by the government, and they got better teachers, better grades.

Their disadvantaged place in the educational system was one of the most troubling aspects of the 1975 takeover for most of my younger informants. It highlighted for them their loss of status and their potential inability to attain in the future the prosperity of their lives before 1975. In the following passage, a young informant described how the events of 1975 eventually led him to become a fugitive from the government:

Before 1975 I was the best student in the school, in fact, in the province. But after 1975 everything changed; only the students from the right background passed. I failed the test [to enter college] two times. So I forged my background. I passed the test and entered into a technical school, away from Saigon. Eventually I started teaching there, but I just taught for three months; I was considered antirevolutionary because of my opinions. I was drafted into the army on January 17, 1981; they sent me to Cambodia, sixty-three kilometers over the border. I escaped after twenty-three days. After that I had no name; I moved around and stayed with friends for a few days. I had a temporary life at that time; I spent all my time trying to escape. I learned how to forge an ID. I had all different kinds of paper, and I forged all kinds of IDs so I had a different name and occupation, depending on the place and situation.

As in the past, kinship ties continued, for many, to provide the support that was necessary to survive and cope with the changes occurring after 1975:

After 1975, we went to the countryside near Hue to do farming, in my paternal grandparents' village. But I didn't like living in the countryside, so after a few months my mother and the children, we went to Vung Tau, and my father stayed behind in the village with his sister. In Vung Tau we lived in a small house near my mother's relatives. My mother's relatives were very rich before 1975, and they managed to hold on to some businesses, so they could easily support us at that time.

But the years after 1975 also had some disruptive effects on family life. First of all, men's economic dominance in the family was threatened. As the South Vietnamese army and government bureaucracy was dismantled, and large businesses lost their profitability, the position of men as the primary breadwinners of the family was shaken. When men endured years of confinement in reeducation camps, their authority was further affected by their absence from their families. In men's absence, women often assumed a more dominant position in the household. For one thing, the income of women became more crucial to the household. After 1975, many women turned to small-scale trading to support their households (cf. Dorais, Pilon-Le, and Nguyen Huy 1987, 83). Huong, a woman informant, described this activity: "After 1975 we had to close the store because the taxes were too high. My father was in the reeducation camp for one year. My mother and I sold things in the market, like food and clothes. She also sewed, and I helped her. That was how we survived that time."

In a few cases, the return of men from reeducation camps was accompanied by their efforts to restore their economic dominance in the household. In one of these cases, when the husband returned from the reeducation camp after two years, his wife immediately quit her clerical job at the insistence of her husband, who then began working two jobs to make money for the family. More commonly, however, men were unable to find jobs after their return. For example, Khanh, a male teenager, described the continued economic losses suffered by his father after his return and the tension between his parents that ensued:

> My father went to jail for about three years when the Communists came. He came back, and the Communists didn't let him work. During the time he was away my mother opened a restaurant, and she was doing really good with it; she made a lot of money. Before 1975 my mother was a housewife. When my father came back he was very depressed, and he and my mother had a lot of fights. [What kinds of things did they fight about?] Oh, everything. I think the one who earns the living is more powerful. Before 1975, my Dad made the money, but after 1975 my Mom was the one who was like the head of the house. I think that's why they fought so much.

The changes of 1975 upset not only gender relations but also relations between the generations, specifically between parents and children. The authority of parents weakened as they lost their former status and were treated as pariahs by the new regime. The Communist government's policies and programs at school also sought to create a wedge in the political and cultural outlook of parents and children (Dorais, Pilon-Le, and Nguyen Huy 1987, 81). Their efforts seemed to have met with the most success with younger children whose recollections of life before 1975 were dimmer than those of older children. In the following passage, a young man who had left Vietnam in his late teens described the divisive effects that the Communist government policies had on families:

One thing we did after school was join in the activities of the Ho Chi Minh Youth Group. It was supposed to be voluntary, but it wasn't really. What we did was study about Ho Chi Minh, sing patriotic songs, and do work like cleaning the school, because there were no people who cleaned the schools. Sometimes we also cleaned the roads, and we went outside the city on trips to do some farming, like planting rice and vegetables. They wanted to give us the experience of being workers and farmers, because for them, the farmers were the best people in the country, but only after the Communist party people. I was actually happy then; I thought I was doing a good thing. I felt patriotic; I thought the Communists would help all the poor people in Vietnam. When I started to believe the government my parents were angry. We had problems then because my parents didn't like the Communists and I did. My parents tried to tell me something different, but they couldn't say much about it; they had no control over me. If they said anything too loud then the Communists would come and blame them. I grew up and slowly I learned the truth about the Communists. In school I tried once to express myself, give a different opinion, and I got into trouble. The teachers said, "Your generation is too corrupt; we will concentrate on the younger ones who will be pure Communists." I think what the Communists tried to do was move us apart, separate us from each other so that we have no power. No one trusted each other. Neighbors couldn't talk to each other because they were afraid. It was even like that in many families; the children would report the parents to the police or the wife would report the husband to the police. So everyone just kept their ideas to themselves.

Some of my older informants also suggested that in the years after 1975, there was a rise in premarital sexual activity among the urban young due to the after-school programs set up by the government. Ly, a woman informant in her early thirties, suggested that these programs created more opportunities for boys and girls to have unsupervised contact with each other:

In the groups after school, the boys and girls spent a lot of time together, and it was alone some of the time. They weren't with their families. Sometimes they would even stay overnight outside the city; there was some chance for boys and girls to be alone together. That's why there were a lot of abortions after 1975 with the young people. But I think a few years later the Communists became stricter when they saw what was happening.

More generally, there was a sense among my older informants that the post-1975 era was a time of moral decay, a period of disintegration of traditional sexual mores. Suong, a woman in her midfifties, talked to me

69

about the sexually corrupt environment that she felt had been created by the Communist regime: "After 1975, there were many abortions because the Communists encouraged children to not listen to their parents. The Communists were themselves corrupt; they had many wives and girl-friends and many children they abandoned. I heard that now in Vietnam it's worse; the whole society has become like that."

ESCAPE FROM VIETNAM

Within the urban middle class, two groups were especially motivated to flee Vietnam after the Communist victory: men and the young—a fact that is reflected in the age and sex profile of Vietnamese refugees in the United States (see Gardner, Bryant, and Smith 1985, 13–16). As I have described, many of the men suffered a serious loss of status. The younger generation faced disadvantages at school and were pessimistic about future opportunities. Also, young men faced the military draft that was imposed by the government in the late 1970s because of conflicts with China and Cambodia. In addition to these factors, by the early 1980s, some Vietnamese were also motivated to join relatives who had left and been resettled in other countries. Two of my informants had also left unintentionally, because of unforeseen circumstances: "I went with my younger cousins to the boat where they were to escape. They were very young, about thirteen, and my aunt asked me to take them there. I went with them and then the police were coming, so the man in the boat told me to jump in, so I did that. The boat left and I was still on it."

Leaving Vietnam meant separation from kin, both close and distant. For one thing, the expenses associated with the escape process meant that families were compelled to be selective about which members would leave. Because of this, men sometimes left alone, with the hope that their wives and children could join them later. Young men and children were also sent by their parents, sometimes with relatives, in the hopes that they could find more opportunities elsewhere. The elderly often declined to leave, preferring to remain in Vietnam. Those who were successful in leaving Vietnam then faced the trauma of the boat journey (see Freeman 1989; Grant 1979; Wain 1981). One of my informants lost her husband when he was pushed off the boat during a scuffle between passengers. In another case, a male informant's sister was kidnapped by Thai pirates and was never recovered.

The next step in the escape process involved a period of waiting for resettlement in refugee camps in various countries in Southeast Asian and

East Asian regions. As Freeman has noted (1989, 292), the refugee camps differed in their conditions and treatment of inhabitants. However, informants' accounts of camp life invariably touched on boredom and a lack of privacy. Many felt frustrated with the camp bureaucracy, especially the long periods of waiting in lines that were required in order to obtain food and other provisions. But most informants spoke positively of the English language classes and the orientation programs that they were required to attend before resettlement in the United States. Materially, camp life was easier for those who received money from relatives who had already been resettled abroad.

A few informants spoke of increased tensions within the family, especially between spouses, and between parents and children, during the refugee camp period. These were caused, they felt, by the uncertainty and tension of waiting to hear from foreign delegations as well as by the somewhat anarchic social milieu of the camp. But the period in the camp also cemented and generated many kin or kinlike relationships. Cousins grew closer to one another, single men and women formed intimate relationships, and lifelong friendships were forged. These relationships helped to ease the frustration of waiting and wondering about the future.

CONCLUSIONS

Migration was a prominent theme in the personal and family histories of my informants, in ways that reflect the turbulent events and changes that have rocked much of South Vietnamese society in recent times. These events and changes shaped family life and gender relations in important ways. I have suggested that traditional patterns of family life in Vietnam were informed by two basic models of kinship: a patriarchal Confucian one and one that was more diffuse and flexible, and less hierarchical in character. In the latter tradition, the family group was a broad and inclusive entity that was a source of mutual aid and support. The traditional Vietnamese family system brought together and integrated both these traditions. However, war and urbanization raised the more flexible model of kinship into prominence, as in the face of a shifting social fabric in which other community institutions were weak, Vietnamese turned to available kin to help them survive and cope with the turmoil of the era. In short, the circumstances of the time were such that Vietnamese emphasized the cooperative and inclusive aspects of kinship tradition in constructing their family lives.

The emphasis on the more flexible model of kinship did not, however,

71

mean that Confucian ideology did not continue to shape the family lives of urban middle-class South Vietnamese. Although tempered in certain respects, the hierarchical vision of family prescribed by Confucianism continued to have significance in a social context that preserved gender and generational hierarchies. Men continued to retain power in the social and economic institutions of South Vietnam, and so women remained subservient to men who held the key to middle-class status and respectability. For children, too, the economic and social resources of their parents remained critical to their success in the fairly closed class structure of urban South Vietnam. These social conditions helped to sustain the force and meaning of Confucian family ideology. For the urban middle class, Confucianist ideals of family life were also important in their symbolic value, serving as standards toward which to aspire or as markers of elite status.

But familial gender and generational hierarchies were threatened by the post-1975 social and economic environment. The Communist victory of 1975 threatened the established lives of the urban middle class in several ways. The urban middle class lost much of its former status and privilege. Men were sometimes no longer the primary breadwinners in the household, and the authority of parents over their children was reduced by their loss of economic resources and their pariah political status. In short, the post-1975 years undermined the social class status of the former urban middle class as well as the established hierarchies of family life.

In the chapters that follow, I explore how the kinship traditions and experiences that I have described here entered into the family life constructed by Vietnamese in the United States. I will show how, in the United States, it was the flexible, cooperative model of kinship that once again rose to prominence as the Vietnamese turned to kinship, as they had in the past, to help them deal with the vicissitudes of migration and settlement in the United States. But whereas in the past this flexible and cooperative model of kinship had coexisted in relative harmony with Confucianist family traditions, in the United States this was no longer the case. The hierarchical vision of family life prescribed by Confucianism, one in which women were subordinate to men, as were the young to the old, was being threatened in serious ways by the conditions of life in the United States.

Patchworking

HOUSEHOLDS IN THE ECONOMY

> A hundred years—in this life span on earth
> talent and destiny are apt to feud
> You must go through a play of ebb and flow
> and watch such things as make you sick at heart
> Is it so strange that losses balance gains?
> *(Nguyen Du, "The Tale of Kieu")*

THE VIETNAMESE IMMIGRANTS recounted feelings of euphoria in the days immediately following arrival in the United States. There was excitement at being in a country that carried images of great material wealth and personal freedom. The material prosperity of the United States was confirmed by the abundance of food and other goods at stores, a finding that initially delighted my informants. But this initial elation soon dwindled. It was replaced by often overwhelming anxieties about the task of building a new life[1] and of regaining the middle-class status that had been lost in the years following 1975. Eventually, Vietnamese Americans came to understand the experience of immigration as an ongoing struggle, one in which they labored to achieve gains that could balance the losses that had been incurred in the migration process.

When asked about their economic experiences following resettlement in the United States, Vietnamese Americans inevitably praised the greater economic freedom of the United States, in particular the freedom to engage in business activities—a freedom that was not present in Communist Vietnam. At the same time, many felt pessimistic and troubled about their economic prospects in the new homeland. Indeed, some felt that the difficulties of living in Communist Vietnam had simply been replaced by another set of problems, in which financial worries were paramount. As one woman put it: "There I worried about the Communists; here I worry

---

[1] The results of other studies suggest that this movement from elation to depression, one that is typically followed by recovery or psychological rebounding, may be a consistent pattern in the psychological experience of displaced minorities (Portes and Rumbaut 1990, 161–63).

about money and the children." And another informant said: "We have a lot of freedom here, but we're not free because of money." As these comments suggest, there was dissatisfaction about the manner in which financial anxieties had come to overshadow or dominate life, more so than in the past. Some informants related these anxieties to the larger and seemingly infinite need for consumer items of various sorts in the United States: "In Vietnam the man can earn enough for everyone, it's cheaper to live there. Here, people need more; everyone needs to get a TV, a car, a house. Here I work very hard and very long, and still I'm not sure, do I have enough money? Because there's always something more I have to buy."

In general, Vietnamese Americans assessed economic life in the United States in ways that were ambivalent and somewhat contradictory. On more than a few occasions, praise for the freedom and justness of economic life in the United States was immediately followed by a lengthy discussion of the obstacles faced by Vietnamese Americans in their efforts to succeed. Ba, a man in his late twenties, spoke of the problems he faced in the labor market due to his minority status:

> Life is more fair here than in Vietnam. Here [in the United States] it's good because you have freedom; if you want to buy something or have a business, you can do that. But for me, it was much easier to do well in Vietnam because there was no discrimination. Here, everywhere I go, I'm a foreigner. The white Americans, the black Americans, even the Asians from Hong Kong and Korea, they don't like us; if it's a good job, then they don't want to hire us. Once when I worked at a Chinese restaurant for a few weeks, the waiters from Hong Kong, they came to me and said: "All Vietnamese are dogs."

Like Ba, other Vietnamese Americans also spoke of their racial-ethnic marginality in multiple terms. They felt themselves to be outsiders not only among whites but also in relation to other minority groups—African Americans as well as many, if not most, segments of the Asian American population. In the face of such obstacles, many Vietnamese Americans channeled efforts to attain middle-class status in directions other than achievement in the labor market. One of these was the education of the young. As I will discuss more fully in chapter 6, educational attainment was viewed as a route by which the young could effectively achieve the acceptance and prosperity that was out of reach for older Vietnamese Americans. Families thus invested in the education of the young, expecting to share in the rewards that it would bring in the future.

In addition to this long-range strategy, another way in which Vietnam-ese Americans reached for middle-class status was by acquiring consumer items such as cars, televisions, videocassette recorders, and stereo systems. In certain ways, these items symbolized middle-class status, reflecting the significance they had carried in Vietnam, where such consumer electronic goods had been scarce—certainly far more so than they were in the United States. Thus, much like they did for the Dominican immigrants described by Grasmuck and Pessar (1991, 195), these goods served as symbolic markers of middle-class status for Vietnamese Americans. Their acquisition was also a watershed of sorts, signifying a transition from newcomer to veteran, to established immigrant. An excerpt from my fieldnotes recording a visit to the household of a woman named Nguyet gives a sense of the significance imparted to the acquisition of such goods. Nguyet lived in a crowded two-room apartment that housed about six people:

> At Nguyet's the TV is on with the volume turned way up, perhaps to compete with the noisy play of the children in the room. There is a game show on TV—"The Price Is Right"—in which the contestants compete to guess the prices of items. Nguyet's sister-in-law, who has been ill for some time and is lounging on the bed, tells me she loves these shows: "I want to go there, how can you do that? Do they let Vietnamese people go there? Look at all the things they give you." Nguyet laughs. A large stereo system with huge speakers appears on TV, and Nguyet says they're going to buy a stereo like that. I ask her about the stereo they already have. She replies that the old one was too small and the sound quality wasn't good. They would try to sell it and then buy a new one, putting together her own money as well as her nephew's money.

The value placed on expensive cars and other consumer goods was noted and disparaged by a few of my informants. One man in his early forties viewed it as representing a rise in materialistic values among Viet-namese refugees. He was especially bothered about the social status that he felt was attached to the ownership of certain types of cars:

> The Vietnamese people here are different from those in Vietnam. If I don't make as much money as other people, they look down on me. There are people who were very poor in the camp, but when they get here they buy a new, no, an almost-new car. When they're driving it, they don't even want to look at those people who drive older cars. Many Vietnamese people, they arrive here and soon after, they buy a Toyota Camry for $17,000,

so each month they have four checks and they spend three checks paying for it.

It is worth pointing out that contrary to the image of reckless spending suggested by the man above, most Vietnamese Americans I observed were selective and careful in their decisions about the purchase of large-ticket items, particularly when the purchase involved the use of credit loans. In addition, although cars, televisions, and videocassette recorders were status symbols, these items also fulfilled important practical functions for the new immigrants. Television, for example, aided in efforts to learn English (cf. Gold 1992, 103). Videocassette recorders allowed the immigrants to view Vietnamese language movies, an activity that helped to ease feelings of cultural alienation. This point was noted by a Vietnamese American clergyman, who also talked about the stark contrast posed by the expensive electronic items to the otherwise bleak surroundings of the homes he visited:

I'm sure you've noticed, every single Vietnamese family here has a nice big color television, a VCR, and a good stereo. Even I don't own a VCR or a big TV at home! They may have nothing, absolutely nothing else. No good furniture, nothing like that. But they have these few things. And after they come here, they'll work extra hard for the money to buy these things. I think it's because they're sad here, they feel lonely. These things help them feel good. With the VCR they can watch Vietnamese movies, you know, the Chinese movies that are dubbed in Vietnamese.

In magnified ways, the significance with which the acquisition of televisions and videocassette recorders were imbued were also attached to home ownership. Owning a home represented prosperity, stability, and integration into the economic mainstream of U.S. society. For informants such as Dao, a woman in her midthirties with three children, it was also a way to combat economic insecurity and residential instability:

All I want is to buy a house. When I buy one I won't be scared anymore. If we don't have money for the rent, then where will we go? Sometimes I have dreams that we have to live on the streets. In Vietnam, life was hard, but I didn't feel scared. If you didn't have money or a job, you could go to the countryside and do farming. Here you can also save money if you buy a house; that's what everyone says. And if we buy a house, there's no problem with landlords. Since I came to Philadelphia we moved three times because of problems with landlords.

Of the twelve households that formed the core sample of my study, three had bought homes by the end of 1986, five to seven years after arriving in the United States. Four other households were making plans to buy houses in the near future. How Vietnamese Americans strove to achieve such aspirations as home ownership, and why some were more successful at fulfilling these aspirations than others, are questions that I turn to next.

PATCHWORKING

Studies of economically disadvantaged communities have found the pooling of resources within domestic groups and networks to be a common response to conditions of economic scarcity and uncertainty (Bolles 1983; Glenn 1991; Stack 1974). Vietnamese Americans were not an exception to this pattern. The pooling or sharing of resources, concentrated within the household or co-residential unit, was in fact one of the central economic practices[2] by which Vietnamese Americans worked to survive and realize economic aspirations. I found, however, that *pooling*, a term that has had currency among social scientists, was an inadequate conveyer of the dynamics of economic cooperation that I observed in Vietnamese American households. These dynamics were more fully and powerfully suggested by *patchworking*, a term that presents an image of jagged pieces of assorted material stitched together in a sometimes haphazard and uncalculated fashion. Whereas pooling connotes the sharing of income or finances, to the neglect of such salient assets as information, services, and education, patchworking conveys the merging of many different kinds of resources.[3] Patchworking also better conveys the often uneven and unplanned quality of members' contributions to the household economy, both in substance and in tempo.

Although patchworking—the bringing together and sharing of disparate resources—was a common practice in Vietnamese American house-

[2] The term *household practices* has been suggested by Diane Wolf as a replacement for *household strategies*, a phrase that assumes the presence of planning and rationality in household economic activities (1992, 262–63).

[3] The practice of bringing disparate resources into the household that I describe here is similar to the income diversification that has been observed by scholars of developing societies to be a common strategy for dealing with risky economic contexts (Agarwal 1992, 91; Perez-Aleman 1992, 244).

holds, it was not one that always produced the same results. There were variations among households so far as the economic outcomes of patch-working were concerned; the extents to which household economic needs and aspirations were fulfilled by patchworking differed. In part, these interhousehold differences grew out of variations in the composition of the households. One aspect of household composition that has attracted the attention of social scientists is the size of the household, or the number of people it contains. Scholars have considered large households, as represented by the extended family household form, to be valuable for economically disadvantaged groups (Angel and Tienda 1982; Wallerstein and Smith 1991). Quite simply, this is because a larger household is likely to have a greater number of labor force participants and thus a higher wage-earning capacity. Although additional members do also raise household expenses, the fixed costs and subsequent economies of scale that are associated with setting up a household mean that on the whole, additional members tend to augment rather than subtract from collective household resources (Brown 1982).

I was often told by informants during my fieldwork that the presence of a large family in the United States was critical to understanding why some Vietnamese Americans fared better economically than others. Clearly, size was a feature of household composition that had important economic repercussions. But the effects of size were mediated by another aspect of household structure: the age and gender composition of the household. I found that Vietnamese American households that were not only large but also more internally varied and complex, composed of members who were different in age and gender status, were more successful at patchworking. This was because a high degree of status differentiation expanded the reach of the household, enabling it to connect successfully to a variety of social arenas and institutions and to take advantage of the resources contained within them.

The ethnic community was a social arena that provided important resources for my informants. In the absence of strong formal organizations, the local ethnic community was one that was structured around informal social networks. While these social networks revolved around kinship and neighborhood ties, they were also based on such factors as age, gender, and social class background. In other words, the personal social networks of individuals reflected not only their kinship ties and neighborhood of residence but also age, gender, and social class background. Because of this, Vietnamese American households that were more varied in their status composition were also more likely to be hooked into a set of social networks that was more wide-ranging. But although connection to a wide range of networks potentially expanded the ability of a household to access more resources in the ethnic community, in reality, being hooked into an extensive set of social networks was not always a boon for a household. As Carol Stack's (1974) study of a low-income community suggests, social networks have the capacity not only to enhance but also to drain a household's assets. In assessing the economic consequences of social networks for Vietnamese American households, I found that what was relevant was not simply the fact of wide-ranging integration but also the quality of the networks. For example, those Vietnamese American households that were connected to social networks that were prosperous in their resources were more likely to derive benefit from these connections.

In general, the dynamics of patchworking, including the economic benefits of a household membership differentiated in age and gender, cannot be understood independently from the particular economic context of Vietnamese American life. So I turn next to a discussion of two central axes in the structure of opportunities that surrounded my informants: the labor market, and government programs and institutions. As my discussion will show, the structure of opportunities for Vietnamese Americans was such that it offered an array of resources that were scarce and unstable in quality. The availability of certain resources was also restricted to certain segments of the Vietnamese American population. Under such conditions, it was economically advantageous for households to gain access to as many different resources as possible, thereby enhancing the scope of their assets, and also guarding against fluctuations in supply.

THE STRUCTURE OF OPPORTUNITIES

Labor market opportunities were limited for the Vietnamese Americans, a reflection of both the conditions of the local economy and the job skills of the group. During the 1980s, the Philadelphia city economy was highly polarized, with a professional high-income sector and a service sector that in contrast provided mainly low-paying semiskilled or unskilled work.[4]

[4] Reflecting these polarization trends, the Census Bureau reports a decline during the 1970–80 period in the number of persons in traditional blue-collar occupations in the city of Philadelphia, especially for operators and laborers (−37.7 percent) and craft and repair occupations (−30.2 percent). In contrast, there was a rise in white-collar occupations from 47.5 percent in 1970 to 54.5 percent in 1980, with a 5.2 percent increase in managerial and

This polarization reflected ongoing shifts in the city's economic base, similar to those taking place in other northern urban centers in the United States (Wilson 1987). There was a decline in manufacturing industries and a rise in business and consumer services, along with a gravitation of manufacturing industries from the inner city toward outlying suburban areas (Adams et al. 1991, 30). The increasingly limited range of employment opportunities for city residents was reflected in high unemployment and poverty rates, which were further aggravated by the nationwide economic recession of the early 1980s.[5]

Besides these general economic conditions, the labor market options of Vietnamese Americans were negatively affected by their minority ethnic status as well as their lack of job experience and skills that were appropriate to the U.S. labor market. In Vietnam, most had been in the military or small business and trading—all work experiences and credentials that could not be easily marketed with success in the United States. It is not surprising, then, that unemployment rates tended to be high. For example, in mid-1984, roughly 35 percent of the adult men in the twelve households of my core sample were unemployed. But what is not addressed by this figure is the shifting character of the Vietnamese immigrants' employment experiences. Because of the seasonal or unstable character of the jobs they occupied as well as their constant search for more lucrative work, there was continuous movement into and out of jobs. Shifts in employment were a particularly strong feature of women's work histories.

Under these conditions, the jobs that were the most easily available to my informants were low-level service sector positions. These jobs, such as cleaning and waitressing, had the characteristics of secondary sector employment, as it has been described by the dual economy model (Doeringer and Piore 1971). That is, the available jobs tended to be poorly paid, part-time, unstable positions, devoid of fringe benefits and opportunities for advancement. Given these unattractive features, many Vietnamese Americans preferred work in the informal economy or the sector of the

---

professional jobs. These figures refer to jobs held by Philadelphia city residents only and not total employment within the city (Philadelphia City Planning Commission 1984).

[5] In 1980, unemployment rates in Philadelphia were double (11.4 percent) that of the national figures (6.6 percent). The percentage of persons in poverty in the city of Philadelphia had risen from 15.1 percent in 1970 to 20.6 percent in 1980. In comparison, nationally the number of persons in poverty in 1980 was estimated at 12.4 percent (Philadelphia City Planning Commission 1984).

economy with no official government sanction or monitoring.[6] In the informal economy, income and payments are not subjected to taxes, and minimum wage laws are not acknowledged. The conditions of work are often below government health and safety standards, and workers receive no benefits. My women informants were especially likely to be involved in informal sector work, most commonly in garment or small-scale food preparation industries. In both cases, the industries were mostly owned by Chinese Americans and Korean Americans who actively recruited Vietnamese and other Southeast Asian refugees for these jobs.

Those who worked in the informal economy usually saw it as an attractive income-generating option, given the alternatives. Foremost among its attractions was the fact that the wages from such work were protected from the scrutiny of welfare and social service agencies as well as from government tax regulations. Work hours were flexible and, in some cases, the work could be performed at home. Thus on several occasions, I was told that jobs in the formal or "legal" sector made little sense, because after subtracting taxes and the cost of transportation, one was left with virtually no pay. In addition, women, especially, talked of how informal sector work had the advantage that it could be discontinued and resumed at one's own convenience. Many women also felt that the terms of payment—usually per completed unit—were better, because one was paid according to how much work was actually done, in comparison to fixed-wage jobs, in which hard work went unrewarded. Among the disadvantages of informal sector work that were mentioned was the absence of health insurance benefits and the vulnerability of workers to abuse by employers. I was told of cases in which workers were misled about the wages they were to receive for jobs, and also of situations in which women were sexually harassed by managers and owners. One of my informants, Huong, began working at a garment shop after being told that she would receive $3 an hour for part-time work and $3.50 an hour for full-time work. But after working five hours a day for three weeks, she received only $30 for all her work. Despite her vigorous protests to the manager, she was unable to recover the money owed her.

These types of employer abuses were supposedly less common in Vietnamese American businesses because of the closer social and economic ties of these businesses to the local Vietnamese American community. Ethnic economic enclaves or concentrated "pockets" of ethnic businesses

[6] The movement of Vietnamese Americans toward the informal sector economy has also been noted by Baker and North (1984, 100–13) and Gold (1992, 113–14).

have been identified by social scientists to be important to the economic adaptation of many immigrant groups (Portes and Bach 1985). The distinctive features of ethnic enclave businesses include their reliance on personalistic relationships within the ethnic community for capital and labor as well as for clientele. In certain ways, the conditions of work in ethnic enclave enterprises resemble those that I have described for jobs in the informal sector. For example, wages are usually low, and there are often no health insurance or other work benefits. Despite these disadvantages, my informants viewed jobs in Vietnamese ethnic businesses with favor. For one thing, the social environment of these jobs was more comfortable and enjoyable because they involved contact with other Vietnamese Americans. Ties of a more personal nature between employer and employee also meant that there was some flexibility in work schedules and conditions. Finally, income was often unreported to the government. But whereas all these considerations made working in a business owned by co-ethnics attractive, it was not an option that was widely available to my informants. At the time of the study, the number of Vietnamese ethnic businesses in Philadelphia were relatively few in number.

The range of employment opportunities that I have described was one that was dominated by unstable jobs that offered low pay and limited benefits and opportunities for advancement. What significantly widened the scope of available resources for Vietnamese Americans was their relationship to the governmental arena. The political refugee status of Vietnamese Americans gave legal legitimacy to their presence in the United States and also provided access to a federal aid and resettlement system, or what Rubén Rumbaut has described as "the structure of refuge" (1989a). According to this system, VOLAGS, or voluntary social service agencies, play a leading role in finding housing for new refugee arrivals and in providing information on services available to refugees such as English language classes, job counseling, and income support.[7] So far as

[7] The system is described in detail in the 1980 Refugee Act, which formalized and supplemented the ad hoc, nationality-specific refugee resettlement system that existed prior to this time. As specified by the act, the initial step of the resettlement process rests (as it has since 1975) in the hands of VOLAGS, which are contracted by the United States Department of State. The VOLAGS receive "Reception and Placement" grants from the federal government in accordance with the number of refugees they sponsor. During the first ninety days, these agencies are responsible for ensuring that the refugees receive needed services. These are roughly defined to include English language lessons, job counseling, health assessments and income support. Most agencies have worked through a variety of sponsorship models, using a different combination of relatives, U.S. families, congregations, and professional staff to assist the refugees for at least this initial period (Office of Refugee Resettlement 1983).

income support is concerned, all Vietnamese Americans and other refugees are eligible for cash assistance and medical benefits through RCA (Refugee Cash Assistance) and RMA (Refugee Medical Assistance) programs after their arrival. When eligibility (based on length of residence in the United States) for refugee cash assistance expires, those meeting family composition and income level eligibility requirements can continue to receive assistance through programs available to U.S. citizens, such as AFDC (Aid to Families with Dependent Children), SSI (Supplemental Security Income), Medicaid, food stamps, and GA (General Assistance).[8]

The cash and medical assistance available to Vietnamese immigrants by virtue of their refugee status has often been identified as an important economic boost for the group. What has been less frequently noted, perhaps because it is less visible, is the access provided by the system to valued social relationships. In other words, the "structure of refuge" generated "social capital"[9] for the group. For example, out of their initial contacts with VOLAGS and sponsors, some of the refugees developed close relationships with individual social service agency workers or sponsors, relying on them as a source of information about jobs, bank loans, and educational opportunities. In one particular case, members of a church congregation that had collectively sponsored a refugee household helped the household to obtain a bank loan that they needed to open a business. For some of the Vietnamese refugees, the social relationships that were generated via contact with the structure of refuge were the only relationships outside the ethnic community and thus especially valued as a source of help for dealing with institutions outside the ethnic community.

Although the basic features of the federal aid and resettlement system

[8] AFDC targets low-income families with young children under the age of eighteen. In two-parent families with neither parent incapacitated, certain conditions were to be met in order to qualify for eligibility. In brief, these conditions were a work history requirement whereby either parent had to establish a substantial connection to the work force. SSI is reserved for low-income persons who are aged, disabled, or blind. GA has been described as an income transfer program of last resort for those unable to qualify for other programs. GA programs tend to vary greatly by state. In Pennsylvania, two subcategories of GA recipients were specified: the chronically needy and the transitionally needy. The chronically needy were those with prolonged sickness, those over forty-five years of age, or those attending school before the age of eighteen. The transitionally needy included those who were unemployed or had inadequate income, a group that was eligible to receive assistance for a period of ninety days out of twelve months.

[9] I use the term *social capital* to mean a resource that is embedded in the structure of social relations (Coleman 1988).

for refugees remained consistent during the 1980s, some noteworthy changes also took place during this time. In 1982, federal reimbursement to the states for Refugee Cash Assistance declined from a period of thirty-six months to eighteen months following arrival in the United States.[10] The Refugee Assistance Amendments of 1982 required refugees to register for employment services within the first sixty days of arrival and to participate in job and language training as a condition for receiving assistance. In effect, these changes removed some refugees from cash public assistance soon after arrival (Office of Refugee Resettlement 1983). Another important consequence of funding restrictions was that social services designed to ease the adjustment of refugees such as ESL (English as a Second Language) classes and job training programs were curtailed.[11]

These various policy changes, along with differences in assistance programs across the country by state,[12] produced a fair amount of confusion among potential recipients about the exact eligibility requirements for cash and medical assistance programs. Vietnamese Americans often pointed to differences in how eligibility had been judged across individual cases. For example, a woman named Ha, who was married and had three children, felt that she had been unfairly deprived of welfare benefits. She and her family had received assistance for a year, after which they were informed that they were no longer eligible for support. Ha began to work as a housekeeper at a downtown hotel, but she was unhappy with the job because it did not provide health coverage for her children. She compared her situation to that of a close friend whose financial and family circumstances were similar to her own. Her friend, however, had been receiving cash assistance for over three years.

Such incongruities were believed by informants to be partly a result of differences in the manner in which applicants presented and documented their economic status to welfare officials. For example, the receipt of General Assistance required evidence of an active job search through enrollment in an employment search program. According to a number of

[10] In 1988 the period was further reduced to twelve months (Office of Refugee Resettlement 1989, 36).

[11] VOLAG officials informed me that because of funding cuts of about 60 percent in 1982, Pennsylvania reduced the number of refugee services from twenty-four to five. The services that remained, although reduced in scope, were case management service, employment services, ESL classes, translation and interpretation, and vocational training. The eliminated services included day care, family planning, outreach, information, and referral.

[12] See Rumbaut (1989a, 103) for a description of differences in levels of AFDC benefits and eligibility requirements across states.

informants, this requirement could be interpreted quite broadly and was sometimes not subject to close scrutiny. In addition, the receipt of AFDC required that household income and resources not exceed certain minimal amounts. But the common Vietnamese American practice of patchworking resources within households that were often composed of people who were distant relatives and friends, was one that was largely invisible to the welfare bureaucracy. What also contributed to the perception of inconsistency in the allotment of cash public assistance were differences in how social service agency officials interpreted eligibility requirements. Agency officials were believed to have considerable discretion in the determination of eligibility. Thus some informants felt that the amount and length of time over which one was able to receive welfare depended on the VOLAG through which one was sponsored and the particular caseworker to whom one was assigned.[13]

All these conditions contributed to an understanding of cash public assistance as a highly ephemeral and unstable resource, short-lived in its availability and subject to abrupt termination at any time. It was also considered to be a resource that was restricted in availability to certain social groups. Given the eligibility requirements, it is not surprising that those who were elderly, disabled, under the age of eighteen, or single parents were most likely to have a long-term relationship with the cash and medical assistance programs.

Another institutional arena that carried important resources but was restricted in access was public education. Schooling was a resource to which households with children under the age of eighteen had greater access in comparison to others. The public schools provided the opportunity to gain educational credentials, to learn English, and to acquire other cultural skills important for life in the United States. Because of this, households with schoolgoing children were often at an advantage in dealing with institutions and persons outside the ethnic community, since the children could serve as reliable interpreters. In addition, much like the refugee assistance system, the schools were also an arena through which the immigrants could develop relationships with teachers and other school officials who could serve as important sources of information and assistance. One high school teacher in the community often assisted the

---

[13] The power of caseworkers to determine eligibility is suggested by Jeremy Hein's (1988, 468) research on refugee social service agencies. He describes the conflicts often experienced by agency officials who are members of the refugee group about whether to guide the refugee toward cash public assistance or toward immediate employment.

families of his students in filling out forms for home loan mortgages, while another teacher provided much-needed information about the complex regulations of the public assistance bureaucracy.

As this discussion suggests, the structure of opportunities for the Vietnamese Americans was such that it gave them access to a whole range of resources. However, for the most part, the assets potentially available from any one source were limited and unstable in quality. These qualities clearly characterized labor market opportunities. They also characterized the structure of refuge, which, in addition to being an unreliable source of assets, was also one that, when taken alone, provided subsistence at only minimum levels.[14] Given these conditions, the patchworking of resources within households was an effective response in several respects. For the individuals, it created an economic buffer or safety net that helped them to survive and to overcome vacillations in their means of livelihood. Patchworking also enlarged the scope of resources available to individuals. Thus, for example, a person who was cut off from the refugee assistance system could nonetheless enjoy some of its benefits through another household member. In addition, because access to such resources as "welfare" was restricted to certain social groups, the composition of the household—and in particular the age and gender composition of its members—was of importance. In effect, having many different kinds of people expanded the arms of the household, allowing it to forge more effective channels of access that could allow it to take advantage of opportunities situated in a variety of arenas and institutions.

Patchworking Processes: Case Studies of Households in the Economy

I turn next to a description of three Vietnamese American households, focusing on the history of their economic experiences following arrival in the United States. By looking at household economic experiences over a period rather than a particular point in time, I attempt to convey the shifting quality of Vietnamese American economic experiences. In gen-

[14] According to a 1984 information sheet of the Community Services Department of the Philadelphia County Assistance Office, a family of four persons was eligible to receive a monthly allowance of $429. In the 1984–85 period, low-cost, one-bedroom rentals in the city ranged from $200 to $300. A family of four solely dependent on public assistance would thus have anywhere from $100 to $200 for expenses other than rent, in addition to food stamps and medical benefits.

eral, through these three detailed portraits, I hope to capture the intricate and contingent character of Vietnamese American economic experiences—traits that tend to remain submerged in statistical economic descriptions of the group.

The three households, selected because of their diversity in size, age, and gender composition as well as because of the quality of their social networks, illustrate some of the complex ways in which household structure entered into household economic dynamics. The experiences of the households also suggest that conflict was an important feature of household economic relations. In other words, patchworking was rarely a smooth process. It was, rather, one that was marked by contention and clashes over economic activities and decisions among household members.

Household One: Nga and Vinh

I became acquainted with Nga and Vinh through a Vietnamese American teacher, who introduced me to the couple as a university student who was studying Vietnamese refugees in the United States. The household consisted of five people: Nga; her husband, Vinh; and three children—one daughter and two sons. Another daughter, who was now living with Nga's mother, had been left behind in Vietnam because of some unforeseen complications during the escape journey. The family lived in a one-bedroom, third-floor apartment in an old brick building situated on a busy street. Across the street, in an identical building, other family members lived in two separate apartments. One of the apartments housed three of Vinh's younger brothers as well as the wife and child of one of the brothers. Nga's brother and three of his friends lived in another apartment across the street. The kin group (including all but one of the brothers) had left Vietnam together in 1977, although they had been resettled in the United States at slightly different times. Nga, Vinh, and their three children had arrived in 1979 and had been resettled in Philadelphia by a social service agency. Initially they had lived in another apartment in the area, which they had eventually vacated because of a rat infestation in the building.

Before 1975, in Vietnam, Vinh had been a warrant officer[15] (*thượng sĩ*) in the South Vietnamese army. He had about twelve years of education. After 1975, he had spent about a month in a reeducation camp, after

---

[15] A warrant officer ranked between a sergeant and a lieutenant.

which he had driven trucks for the new government. Nga originally came from a small town in Ben Tre, where her parents had owned and run several small variety stores. She had attended school for eight years, after which she had worked in the family stores. After she and Vinh married, she continued to live with her parents for a few years. Eventually, she moved to Saigon, where Vinh was posted. During this time, she sometimes sold homemade goods (usually food) for some extra money. But Nga never worried about money because her parents were prosperous and regularly gave her generous cash gifts. She told me that she had been the youngest child in her family, spoiled and accustomed to spending a lot of money. Because of her close attachment to her parents, she had been reluctant to leave Vietnam when Vinh had suggested it. But after his release from the reeducation camp, Vinh had been determined to leave the country. He was sure that, along with his brothers and children, he would always suffer discrimination in Communist Vietnam because of their association with the previous regime.

For about a year after their arrival in the United States, Nga, Vinh, and the children lived solely on the public assistance available to newly arrived refugees. Vinh attended some job counseling and ESL classes for refugees. Nga also attended some ESL classes but did so less regularly, because she was busy looking after the children and the household. At this time, Vinh's younger brothers arrived in the United States and lived in the household for about six months, before renting their own apartment.

About a year later, Nga began working as a cook at a Vietnamese-Chinese restaurant located a block away from the apartment. The restaurant belonged to a friend whom Nga had known from her days in Saigon. Vinh did not want Nga to work, but, according to Nga, he could not argue much about it because they needed the money. The money available through RCA was barely enough to live on and certainly did not allow them to send money to their daughter and other family members in Vietnam. Working at the restaurant, Nga made about $120 a week. Besides, the restaurant job had certain fringe benefits, despite its long hours and low (below minimum wage–level) pay. Nga could take leftover food home from the restaurant, and the informal quality of the work environment allowed for her children to spend time with her during the day at the restaurant. Also, her relationships at work were a source of companionship and kept her mind distracted, away from the daughter and mother she had left in Vietnam.

While Nga worked at the restaurant, Vinh continued with his English language classes, but this time at the local community college. At other times, he stayed at home or visited friends. Vinh complained of severe headaches and exhaustion. He also drank heavily. Once, about four years after the family's arrival in the United States, he had tried unsuccessfully to commit suicide by hanging himself in the kitchen. When I interviewed him, Vinh, a normally quiet and reserved man, talked at some length about the disappointments he had experienced in the migration process:

> I don't want to talk about higher or lower, but living in America I'm disappointed. Here, money is above everything; if you don't have money, you're not good. I came to America because there's no freedom in Vietnam now, and my children can't get an education. I heard that life in America was hard but fair. I still think that's true, except for old people. When I first came I thought I could be a truck driver, because I drove American trucks in Vietnam. But I found that you have to know good English or no one will give you a job. So I try to learn English but it's very difficult.

Vinh's words expressed the high costs of the move to the United States for many Vietnamese Americans. He suffered from a deep sense of loss. He had hoped to carry his work experiences and skills from Vietnam over into the United States. Unable to do so, he had lapsed into chronic unemployment. He was unwilling to accept unskilled service sector jobs (such as those of janitor or cook) that represented a drop in occupational status in comparison to his situation in Vietnam.

In 1983, the household no longer received cash public assistance, but they did receive food stamps and medical benefits. The household met its expenses from Nga's wages and money from Nga's brother who lived across the street. Vinh's brothers also contributed money to the household, but far less regularly, as they themselves had limited income. One of Vinh's brothers was attending high school, and the other was chronically unemployed.

Notwithstanding its financial difficulties, in 1986 the household moved into a home they had bought. According to Nga, she and her brother had jointly decided quite early on (in 1982) that Vinh's employment prospects were slim. Given this, the only way for Nga to gain some measure of economic security in the United States was to own a home. They felt that it would be financially easier, and in the long run more profitable, to own rather than rent a home. Nga's brother contributed his savings, and, with loans from neighborhood friends as well as from an uncle in New York, they were able to gather together about eight thousand dollars, enough to make a down payment on a small house in a growing Vietnamese American enclave in another part of the city. Nga, Vinh, and the children moved into the house in 1986.

In the task of building a life in the United States, it was Nga rather than Vinh who had assumed a position of leadership in the family. With the assistance of her brother, Nga appeared to play the dominant role in organizing and managing household resources and making decisions about the direction of household goals. Nga talked of how it had been different in Vietnam, where Vinh had dominated the relationship and she had gone along with his decisions. It was clear that settlement in the United States had seriously upset the balance of power in the family. Vinh was no longer the primary breadwinner in the family, and so his position of dominance—as husband, father, and older brother—had been eroded. It is not surprising, then, that this particular family was a hotbed of conflicts and disputes.

The household's limited access to the labor market and government assistance programs meant that they were heavily dependent on help from kin. The purchase of the house was accomplished only with the aid of kin. It is notable, though, that it was Nga's brother and uncle in particular, rather than the entire kin group, who were a financial resource for the household. Nga's brother and uncle, although undoubtedly not without personal sacrifice, were both in a financial position whereby they could contribute to the down payment of Nga's and Vinh's house. This was particularly true of the uncle, who had been in the United States since the early 1970s and was the owner of several restaurants in New York. His situation contrasted sharply with that of Vinh's brothers, who themselves were barely getting by. Nga's relationship with her uncle was also such that she could expect to receive help from him. Nga told me that her uncle had a very close relationship with her mother (his older sister) in Vietnam. Out of respect and affection for his sister, he felt a deep sense of obligation to come to the aid of his niece.

Household Two: Tuan and Thanh

Seven people lived in this household, which included a woman named Thanh in her late fifties, her three adult sons, two daughters, and one son-in-law. I originally came to know the household through Tuan, the eldest of the three brothers. Tuan was charismatic, talkative, and energetic. He was proud of his English language skills, which he had managed to acquire in just six months of intensive ESL classes. The household had arrived in Philadelphia in 1981. Their escape out of Vietnam had been facilitated by the fact that Thanh was half Chinese (her mother had been of Chinese origin).[16] With the help of some relatives, they had managed to forge some Chinese identification papers, which eased their passage out of Vietnam at a time when the Vietnamese government was unofficially allowing the Chinese minority to leave the country (see Duiker 1980).

Thanh's husband had died in Vietnam shortly after 1975 from a stomach ailment. In his younger days, he had worked as a tax collection officer for the government, but in the years prior to 1975 he and his brothers had opened a restaurant outside of Saigon. Before getting married, Thanh had worked in her brother's jewelry store. Later, she worked in the family's restaurant, supervising others and doing the bookkeeping. Tuan was twenty-eight years old when the family arrived in Philadelphia. In Vietnam he had attended school for nine years. According to him, he had been a "lazy and bad student," more interested in riding his motorcycle around town and going out with girlfriends than in studying. After leaving school, he traveled around the country and worked at a variety of odd jobs and eventually settled down to working the family restaurant. It was Tuan who had initiated and organized the family's escape in 1979. The family had suffered serious financial losses in the 1975 political transition, and, perhaps more importantly, Tuan and his brothers faced the military draft.

About seven months after arriving in Philadelphia, Tuan and his brothers found work at a meat-processing plant in New Jersey, for three and a half days per week. A friend who had been working at the plant helped them to apply for the jobs. Tuan had been quite happy with the situation because in his assessment, the work paid well relative to other available unskilled jobs. He and his brothers were paid $7.10 an hour, which was at least $1.50 more than the wages paid by other competing meat processing plants in the area. In addition, he and his brothers were able to drive to and from work together, thus minimizing transportation costs. The job was not unionized, however, and did not offer them work benefits. It was also unstable and seasonal, as Tuan found out when, two months later, cuts in production resulted in the family's dismissal from the plant.

Tuan and all the adult members of the family, with the exception of Thanh and Pat (the youngest daughter), then began working in a garment

---

[16] The family's Chinese identity was nominal at best. Both Thanh's father and her husband had been ethnic Vietnamese. Family members identified themselves as ethnic Vietnamese and spoke Vietnamese at home.

shop in Chinatown for long hours, at piecework rates. During this time, Thanh and her two daughters received food stamps and income support from AFDC and SSI programs. For about three months, Tuan and his brothers also received some money from the RCA program. Pat, who was attending junior high school, offered to find a part-time job to help with household expenses. But her mother and brothers insisted that she spend her time studying in preparation for college admission. A member of the church congregation that had been the family's U.S. sponsor regularly tutored Pat in English and helped her with homework.

All of the family turned over most of their earnings to Thanh, who kept some cash for food expenses and then gave the remainder to Tuan to manage. Tuan had decided that the entire family should work in the garment shops because the work was easily available and it also generated undeclared income that would not affect public assistance benefits. He was, nonetheless, unhappy about working in the garment shop himself because he felt that sewing was not appropriate work for men. What made the situation tolerable was that it was a temporary phase. Soon after arriving in the United States, Tuan had decided to focus his energies on opening a family business, preferably a restaurant—a goal fully endorsed by his mother, Thanh. In Tuan's assessment, the goal of a family business made sense, because of both the family's previous entrepreneurial experience and the absence of good alternative employment opportunities. During an interview, Tuan also talked of cultural differences between Americans and Vietnamese and of how a lack of loyalty to employers was an unattractive feature of U.S. businesses:

> For us, a business is best. Because we don't have much education and we're foreigners, so we can only get bad jobs. But if we have a business, we can work hard and make some money. Better to fish where there's water. Also, we had a business in Vietnam and we know something about it. I don't like working in a job for American people; I prefer my own business. [Why is that?] Because Americans and Vietnamese are very different. With Americans, sentiment (*tình cảm*) is weak and dry, like ice and cold. If I like you, I like you forever, unlike Americans. With Americans, you work for a company and you're a good worker for ten years, but they'll fire you immediately if you make a small mistake.

After working in Chinatown for about a year, Tuan and his family bought a food vending truck with which to sell Chinese-Vietnamese food in the downtown business district area. They were able to lease a truck and purchase the necessary license from a Chinese-Vietnamese man who regularly sold such services to the ethnic community. They drew together the necessary money from family savings and small personal loans from friends. The truck did well for about a month, but business declined rapidly in the summer. After consulting with some friends, Tuan sold the truck and placed the money he received in a savings account in the bank.

Two years later, after another period of working in a series of temporary, low-paying jobs, Tuan decided once more to try the family's luck in the food business. They bought an old, declining Italian restaurant, located in another section of the city, which they hoped to renovate and convert into a Vietnamese-Chinese restaurant. This time, the household relied not only on family savings and loans from friends but also on a bank loan that had been co-signed by a friend of Tuan's named Jack. Tuan had met Jack, a white American, when he was working in New Jersey. The two had become close friends after a few long evenings of drinking beer at a pub in New Jersey. Jack often came over to eat at the house, where he was welcomed warmly by Thanh and the others.

Following the purchase, the family decided (under the leadership of Tuan and Thanh) that in order for the restaurant to be financially solvent, family labor would have to be divided between the family business and other jobs that could generate immediate income. Tuan proposed that he, Thanh, and his older sister work in the family enterprise, while his brothers and brother-in-law continue to make as much money as they could through other employment. Tuan argued that the work in the restaurant was such that it would easily enable his mother and sister also to meet their housekeeping and childcare responsibilities. Since he was the oldest in the family and the most proficient in English, it was only natural that he take charge of the restaurant.

However, one of his brothers was unhappy with this arrangement and suggested that he, rather than Tuan, run the restaurant. The brother generally resented the dominant role played by Tuan in the family. He had not agreed with Tuan's decision to sell the food vending truck, and he also blamed Tuan for the failure of that particular venture. But other members of the family, and especially Thanh, supported Tuan's decisions and his authority. Thanh often spoke proudly of her eldest son. In Vietnam, he had been irresponsible and uncaring about the family, whereas here he thought only of the family's interests. Faced with a lack of family support for his position, the rebellious brother defected from the household after his dispute with Tuan. He moved in with a woman he had been dating for some time. This further incensed his mother, Thanh, because the woman involved was not of Vietnamese or even Asian origin.

A striking aspect of this household was the diversity of the social and economic resources that it was able to draw upon. At various times and via various members, the household drew on RCA, AFDC, and SSI programs, relationships with sponsors, English language classes held by social service agencies, and jobs in the informal and formal economies. Through Pat, the household was also able to take advantage of public education opportunities. The household's ability to access these various resources was enhanced by its relatively large size (seven persons) as well as by the complexity of its age and gender composition. Although the household did not have kin in the United States, its members were connected to social networks that provided small financial loans and information about jobs. Access to these various resources enabled the household to gather together the capital necessary to open a small business.

Household Three: Long, Dinh, and Thach

The third household consisted of five men, all single, in their twenties, and unrelated to one another. When I first became acquainted with the household, three of the men—Long, Dinh, and Thach—had been sharing an apartment for over a year. Shortly after I met them, they moved into a larger apartment and acquired two new roommates. The new apartment was located next to an Irish neighborhood bar. The apartment consisted essentially of a large room and two smaller adjoining rooms.

Long, Dinh, and Thach came from similar social class backgrounds in South Vietnam. Both Dinh and Thach had fathers who were college educated and high-ranking military officers (i.e., captain and major, respectively) before 1975. Long's father had been a fairly wealthy businessman who had owned several stores. All three recalled the days before 1975 with nostalgia. They had lived in prosperous homes with servants and access to such items as cars and televisions. For all three, a primary motivation for leaving Vietnam had been avoidance of the military draft.

Of the three men, Thach had been in the United States the longest, since 1979. He had no relatives in the country. After arriving, he had lived in a suburban area with his sponsor, a man who owned a tailoring shop. After a few months, he had moved into the city, and with the resources available under government assistance regulations, he spent a year learning English and attending high school. It was at this time that he met Long, and the two had instantly hit it off. They decided to rent an apartment together, and after about a year, they were joined by Dinh.

Unlike Thach, who had no relatives in the United States, Long had an older married sister who lived in the neighborhood. Long maintained a close relationship with his sister and her children, but he did not live with them because her apartment was very crowded. Dinh's only family member in the United States was an older brother who was living in Oklahoma. Dinh had thought about moving there to join him but decided against it because he did not want to live in Oklahoma. He also admitted that he had never gotten along with his brother.

The three men told me that they were "like brothers," and, as evidence of the closeness this implied, they pointed to how they shared whatever they had with each other. Long, due to both his age and his aptitude, was in charge of managing the household finances. He collected money from each household member to pay for rent and utilities. Ideally, all members paid an equal amount, but in reality, as they all conceded, this was often not possible. For example, as Long described, at one time he had been between jobs for a couple of months and had had no source of income. Dinh and Thach had chipped in to cover his share of the expenses, agreeing that he would pay them back at some later point. Food was shared in the household, although there was no system in place to ensure that the contributions of household members were equivalent. Both Dinh and Thach felt that Long rarely paid for groceries. But this was not a problem, because Long had been the one to purchase the large color television and stereo system for the houshold. Also, they frequently ate over at Long's sister's place. At other times, when they did not eat out, Thach was the one to cook meals for the household because he was the only one who could cook Vietnamese food. The young men understood these household exchanges to be an expression of their kinship, which made giving and receiving a natural and expected part of their relations: "We trust each other absolutely, otherwise it's not possible to live like we do. We're like brothers; there's no difference. For instance, I have a car and we all use it, we share it. In that way, we're very different from Americans. The American way is that you pay for what you get. I have two American friends and when we go out somewhere, everyone pays separately; that's not like us."

The brotherlike trust that defined the relationship of Long, Dinh, and Tang did not preclude squabbles in the household about how resources should be shared. For example, although the quarrels were short-lived and relatively insignificant, Long, Dinh, and Thach often argued about the use of the household car. The fragility of the exchange system was highlighted for the members of the household in a more serious manner when one of the two men who had joined the household later behaved in what the others saw as a reckless and irresponsible manner. He borrowed and damaged Long's car, and, in addition to showing no remorse, he made no effort to pay for the repairs. What further irked Long, Dinh, and Thach was that although he was working at a fairly well paid job, he failed to pay the rent for two months. In general, he showed no concern for the collective welfare of the household. Eventually, after an argument which ended in a physical fight, he left the household.

Besides this particular incident, exchanges within the household, particularly among Long, Dinh, and Thach, worked smoothly. For the three men, household cooperation provided an important method by which to cope with the uncertainties of the economic environment. Of the three men, Thach's financial situation seemed to be the most stable. After attending high school for over a year, he had been forced to drop out because he was over eighteen years of age, which made him ineligible to receive government assistance while attending school. Thereafter, his sponsor began to pay for him to attend a tailoring school. In return, Thach was obligated to work for his sponsor at set wage levels for a few years after finishing the tailoring course. The living expenses that Thach received from his sponsor were enough to cover food and rent but not other occasional expenses. So, Thach sometimes worked at odd jobs to supplement his income, and he also relied on his housemates for incidental expenses. Thach was also studying on his own at home in preparation for the high school equivalency test. He hoped eventually to take the test and go on to study computer programming.

Long's economic prospects were more uncertain. In his first year in the United States, he had received public assistance and taken English language classes. He had also done home work for a Chinatown company. In one of these jobs he had wrapped colored thread around pieces of wood to make napkin holders, receiving two dollars for every dozen completed napkin holders. With the income from these jobs, he managed to save some money to send to his sister who was in a refugee camp in Indonesia. After his first year, through the contacts of a friend, he found a recycling plant job that paid minimum wages. After working at the plant for four months, with the help of loans from relatives and friends, he began a course on machine repair at a technical institute. He completed a six-month course but was unable to find a job. Discouraged, he began to investigate the possibility of opening a small store or other business in the area, although he was pessimistic about his ability to obtain the money necessary. He had recently taken the city exam to become a firefighter, which he felt was a highly desirable job because it was part-time and yet provided benefits. But since there were a thousand applicants and only a handful of positions, he did not feel optimistic about getting the job.

Dinh's early employment history was also characterized by instability. Recently, however, he had been fortunate enough to find a well-paid position in a trucking company. But, as he discussed during an interview, he was unhappy in the job because of harassment from fellow truck drivers:

The first job was at a factory making plastics; it paid $3.75 an hour and nothing else. Our sponsor found that for us, but it wasn't a good job. I found a job at another factory making army machines. That paid better, but they didn't keep us for more than six months; they didn't have many jobs. And it was very far; I had to drive to New Jersey. Now I work as a truck driver for a company, but I don't know how long I'll stay there. It's a good job; I make almost $10.00 an hour. But the Americans don't like the Vietnamese or the other Asians who work there; they make trouble for us. They say: "Hey ching chong, go back to your country." They try to get you in an accident, or sometimes they beat people up. Once they followed me, five American truck drivers, all the way from New York; they wanted to beat me up. I called my friend and he came and called the police. But the police didn't come for a long time. I'm scared after that; I don't know how long I'll stay in this job. I want to buy my own tractor and then I'm not an employee. Maybe I'll still have trouble on the road, but I won't work for anyone. But I have to get money for that, and it's difficult for me to save because I send money to my mother in Vietnam and also I'm not good at saving.

For Long, Dinh, and Thach, the household that they had created was an important economic buffer, helping them to survive, particularly when their own resources were low. Household sharing also made it possible for members to stretch their resources and gain access to such goods as cars. However, what is also evident in this particular case is the paucity of the household's collective resources. This was striking to me as an observer because in terms of their social class background in Vietnam, the members of this household tended to outrank other informants. But in contrast to the more diverse household that I described earlier, this household was composed of young men of similar age, all facing a fairly similar structure of opportunities. All three men had arrived in the United States at an age that had prevented them from taking full advantage of public education opportunities in the United States. As young, able-bodied, single men, they were also rarely eligible for government assistance programs.

The household was also deficient in its resources because of the quality of the social networks to which they were connected. Although two of the men had siblings who lived in the United States, in neither case were these siblings a significant resource for the men. In fact, Long's sister, although she did often provide meals for Long and his friends, was a significant drain on Long's resources. She had five young children and often turned to Long for help with rent or other necessities. In fact, all of the men were periodically called upon to provide financial assistance to family members, not just in the United States but also in Vietnam. As young men who were single and thus bereft of any competing familial obligations, they were expected to assist parents, married siblings, and children. The friendship-based social networks of Long, Dinh, and Thach, although they were less of a drain on their resources, were nonetheless not prosperous enough to benefit them in significant ways. For the most part, the three men were hooked into social networks composed of other young Vietnamese American men in predicaments similar to their own.

.   .   .   .   .

As the three case studies suggest, household patchworking, or the bringing together and sharing of resources within the household, was a common practice by which Vietnamese Americans responded to the uncertainties and limitations of the economic environment. However, the quality of patchworking differed a great deal among households. In sharp contrast to the third household (Long, Dinh, and Tang), the second household (Tuan and Thanh) patchworked in a very effective manner, drawing together a large variety of resources. Whereas the larger size of the second household was clearly relevant to this difference, the greater age and gender homogeneity of the third household exacerbated the economic disparities between the two households. I encountered other Vietnamese American households that were as large as or even larger in size than the second household but yet unable to patchwork as effectively because of the homogeneity in age and gender of their membership.

The case studies also suggest the importance of another feature of household structure: the quality of the social relations and networks to which a household was connected. On the whole, the first household seemed to benefit the most from its relations with kin located outside the household. Nga's brother and uncle not only had resources to offer to her but also felt a deep sense of obligation to help her out. In contrast, the third household was unable to benefit from its kinship networks in the United States. Besides being relatively sparse, these networks were more of a drain on than a contribution to household assets.

PATCHWORKING AND THE IDEOLOGY OF
FAMILY COLLECTIVISM

As suggested by the three case studies, in the households that I studied, the economic activities of members were cooperative in many respects. Yet household economic life was also marked by dissension and discord. Besides calling attention to the essential fragility of the patchworking process, these conflicts also called into question the view of the household that has been embedded in much of the research on pooling and other cooperative household economic practices—a view in which the household is a reciprocal, consensual, and altruistic "moral economy" (see Grasmuck and Pessar 1991, 134; Wolf 1990). According to this perspective on the household, the sharing of resources is a natural response, given the essential unity of household interests. Rejecting this uncritical view of the household, I suggest that it is more useful to see such cooperative household economic practices as patchworking not as natural outcomes but as negotiated processes that are generated and supported by specific structural and ideological contexts.

Among Vietnamese Americans, household economic cooperation was supported by an ideology of family collectivism, an emergent set of beliefs about the nature and significance of family life. The ideology of family collectivism, which drew on Vietnamese kinship traditions, undergirded the economic patchworking of Vietnamese American households in several ways. It advanced the view that economic reliance on family ties was an appropriate and judicious response to the economic demands and opportunities of the migration process. It also helped to promote a collective, cooperative approach toward economic resources and activities among household members by stressing and indeed idealizing the unity of family interests.

Central to this ideology of family collectivism was the notion that the kin group (*gia đình* or *họ*) was an entity of far more significance than the individual. This dimension of the ideology of family collectivism drew strength from Confucian family ideology and tradition, including the practice of ancestor worship. Family altars consisting of a small shelf or table with incense and photographs of deceased relatives were a common sight in the Vietnamese American households that I visited.[17] Although some households were more attentive to these altars on an everyday basis than others, occasions such as the death anniversary of an important departed ancestor and *Tết*—the Vietnamese New Year—were almost always observed with the performance of rites to honor ancestors. Ancestor worship affirmed the sacredness and essential unity of the kin group as well as its permanence in comparison to the transience of the individual. It also highlighted obligation as a key feature of a member's relationship to the kin group. One was, for example, obligated to produce male descendants who could maintain the continuity of the kin group and continue to honor the spirits of ancestors. More generally, familial obligation was defined by the idea that the needs and desires of the kin group took precedence over personal ones.

But if the ideology of family collectivism defined the individual's relationship to the kin group as one in which the individual was obliged to submerge him- or herself into the family collective, it also reassured members that the kin group would be there to help that individual out in times of need. Among my informants there was a strong belief that kinship ties were an economic safety net, a belief that had been cultivated by the long years of social turmoil in contemporary South Vietnam during which time kinship ties had been a source of security for many Vietnamese. Thus repeatedly, and in a variety of contexts, Vietnamese Americans talked to me about how kinship was the most reliable source of support for the individual—the only institution that could be counted on for assistance under all circumstances. To emphasize this point, one elderly man related a proverb that he had heard as a child: "Give the surplus to kin and rely on kin when in need."

The economic practices of my informants in the United States, centered around economic interdependence and cooperation with kin, were informed by these beliefs about kinship. But the realization of kin-centered economic practices also required Vietnamese Americans to engage in a process of rebuilding kin groups in the United States. In other words, because the process of migration to the United States had been so disruptive to kin relations, a process of kin group reconstruction was an essential precursor to kin-centered economic practices among Vietnamese Americans. The rebuilding of kin groups was made easier by the presence

---

[17] I observed such altars in eight of the twelve households. When I asked about their absence in the other households, I was told by members that they did not believe in ancestor worship or, more commonly, that someone else in the family (such as the older brother) had assumed responsibility for the family rites.

of Vietnamese kinship traditions that defined the boundaries of the kin group in an inclusive manner. An example of kin rebuilding was provided to me by Xinh, a woman who had arrived in the United States with two children. Xinh's husband had died during the boat journey from Vietnam. Shortly after she arrived in the United States, she met Toan. During an interview, she recalled her decision to marry him. Her recollection suggests the tremendous importance that she placed on the kinship ties that would be forged by the marriage:

> When I first came here I was so lost and lonely. There was no family here, no one to help me, to look after the children. I felt that I was still on the boat at sea, with nothing around me. Toan was my neighbor's friend, and he wanted to marry me. At first I thought no; he didn't have a good job and couldn't speak much English. Why should I marry someone like that after all the trouble I took to come to America? And I didn't love him; I still loved my husband who died. But then my friend's mother, she talked to me like my mother. She said, "I see that in that family the mother and daughter-in-law are happy, snorting like young pigs together. Because of this, you should marry him. If he has another woman, the grandparents will take care of the children. If your father leaves you, you still have your uncle; if your mother leaves you, you can nurse on your aunt's milk." I listened to her, I saw that he had a big family in Philadelphia. I saw that he would be a good father to my children, he was strong inside, he never angered easily. So I said okay, I wouldn't be so lonely, and I would have people to help us if I had some trouble.

Another, more common way in which Vietnamese Americans worked to ensure the presence of kin in the United States was by sponsoring relatives who were waiting for resettlement in refugee camps in Thailand. When I met Nguyet, a woman informant, she was thinking of sponsoring her nephew and his family of four, who had written to her a month ago from a refugee camp in Thailand. Considerable tension had developed between Nguyet and her boyfriend, Phong, over the sponsorship decision. Nguyet and Phong had been together with their three children (two from Nguyet's previous marriage) for about seven years, since they had met in a refugee camp in Thailand. Phong remained married to a woman who was still living in Vietnam—a fact that, not surprisingly, was a constant source of tension for Nguyet and Phong. Phong told me that he was opposed to the sponsorship of the nephew because of the heavy financial obligations that it entailed. He also mentioned that he was worried that Nguyet would leave him after the nephew's arrival—a threat that Nguyet often made during their many quarrels. Phong also talked of how Nguyet's relationship with the nephew was too distant to justify the sponsorship. Nguyet had never actually met the nephew, who was the son of a first cousin whom she had seen perhaps once or twice as a child.

Confirming some of Phong's fears, Nguyet viewed the presence of the nephew and his family in the United States as a potentially important source of support for herself. She spoke of how she had no relatives in the country, in comparison to Phong, whose sister lived in Philadelphia. Although it was true that she did not know much about her nephew, she nonetheless felt that his presence would ease her sense of isolation in the United States. Notwithstanding all these arguments in favor of the sponsorship, she was extremely worried about the financial burdens that it would create for her: "You know the woman next door, she sponsored her sister's family, four people, and now it's terrible. Ten people living in two rooms. She doesn't work, she gets welfare money for her four children, and her husband doesn't work. Her sister has to wait 'til the end of March to apply for welfare. It's terrible; they don't have money for food. If I sponsor my nephew, we'll be like that."

Despite these misgivings, as well as the opposition of Phong, Nguyet eventually proceeded with the sponsorship. It was clear that in the absence of other kin in the United States, she placed great significance on having her nephew near her. The sponsorship of her nephew and his family was part of her attempt to rebuild a kinship group in the United States: "I don't know my nephew, but I want his family to come here. And you know I have no family here. All my brothers and sisters, my mother and father, they're dead or in Vietnam. Phong has a sister here, that's all, and you know she's not nice. So I think that if my nephew and his family were here I would feel better. A bitter relative is still a relative; a sweet stranger is still a stranger."

As this particular case suggests, in many ways migration to the United States had reinforced the dimension or component of Vietnamese kinship tradition that defined the kin group in an inclusive and flexible manner. Just as the absence of kin in the United States had elevated the significance of a relative that Nguyet would have considered distant in Vietnam, for many other Vietnamese Americans some of the other distinctions that had previously been used to distinguish between close and distant kin had receded in importance. For some informants, for example, in-laws had assumed greater significance in the context of life in the United States. A twenty-eight-year-old man, who had been resettled in Chicago but had moved to join his sister and her family in Philadelphia, talked of how he perceived his brother-in-law as a substitute for his brothers who were in Vietnam: "Here in America it's different because I have no brother here; they're all in Vietnam. So my brother-in-law and me, we have to help each other, like brothers. I think there's no choice."

The inclusive manner in which Vietnamese Americans defined kinship also allowed for household members who were unrelated to one another by traditional criteria to redefine one another in familial terms and to engage in the economic exchange and cooperation that was expected of kin. Thus, for example, Long, Dinh, and Thach of the third household defined one another as "brothers" and also shared resources with one another. Even more common was the adoption by extended family households of individuals, especially single men, into the kinship group. One of my woman informants, named Ha, described a young man named Kim who was living in her home as her "brother." Once I even saw Kim taking care of the family's ancestral altar, an act that emphasized the extent of his integration as a kin member into the household. Kim had, however, joined the household just two years ago when Ha's younger brother (who also lived in the household) brought his friend Kim home to live with them. Ha described Kim's status in the household as follows: "Kim is just like another young brother, my children's uncle. You see on Tết how he gave money to the children just like my brother. He lives with us for three years now. He has no family here. He wants to bring his brother from Vietnam, so he sends him money to escape. Sometimes if I have some money I don't need, I give it to him to send to his family in Vietnam."

For Vietnamese Americans, the rebuilding of kin groups was driven in part by the notion, embedded in the ideology of family collectivism, that kinship ties constituted an effective way of coping with economic scarcity and uncertainty, as they had in the past. But although this idea that kinship ties were a reliable economic safety net reflected kinship traditions and experiences of the past, it was a belief that was also being strengthened by the economic conditions surrounding settlement in the United States, which, in their poverty and uncertainty, fostered reliance on kinship as a means of survival and mobility. In other words, economic conditions and kinship beliefs worked together, in interactive ways, to generate and support such cooperative household economic practices as patchworking.

But if migration to the United States had reinforced beliefs about the economic significance of kinship ties, it had concurrently weakened other components of the ideology of family collectivism. As I have mentioned, the ideology of family collectivism idealized the unity of the kin group and its interests, promoting a conception of the family in which its natural and moral order was one of unity and consensus. One of the ways in which this perspective fostered economic cooperation and interdependence among household members was by helping to hide the reality of multiple and differing interests within the household. The belief in the essential unity of the family functioned as a means of social control whereby those who refused to go along with the decisions made by dominant household members were widely condemned (by kin and friends) for a lack of commitment to family solidarity. Thus intrahousehold conflicts were often interpreted by my informants as evidence of moral shortcoming, or a failure to adhere to traditional values among those involved, rather than as a genuine conflict of interest. For example, in the case of the second household (Tuan and Than) that I described earlier, the united image of the household was marred by Tuan's dispute with his younger brother. The younger brother perceived the dispute to be a result of Tuan's efforts to promote his own interests and power in the family. Tuan and Thanh, on the other hand, felt that the younger brother's actions reflected his lack of commitment to collective family interests—a view that seemed to enjoy support among neighbors who were acquainted with the household. It is notable, however, that despite Tuan's and Thanh's admonishments and the disapproval of neighbors, the younger brother eventually left the household. Thus despite its potency, the invoking of the ideal of family unity was clearly not enough always to ensure the compliance of members to household authority.

In fact, in certain ways, migration to the United States had weakened the power and meaning of the ideal of family unity for Vietnamese Americans. As I will discuss in the chapters to follow, migration to the United States had created conditions of greater equality among household members, particularly between the young and the old and between men and women. Whereas prior to migration, especially in pre-1975 South Vietnam, the ideal of family solidarity had been invoked in a structural context that supported the authority of certain household members (men and the elderly) over others, in the United States the lines of authority were in a state of tremendous flux. The diminished power of men and the elderly had opened up opportunities for traditionally less powerful groups in families to challenge the authority of men and the elderly. The resulting conflicts weakened the ideal of family unity by exposing or bringing to the surface underlying differences of interest within families. In short, migration had scratched the ideological veneer or facade of family unity and consensus.

CONCLUSIONS

Vietnamese Americans responded to conditions of material scarcity and uncertainty by engaging in cooperative household-based economic practices.[18] What I have described as patchworking helped Vietnamese Americans to survive economically as well as to reach toward the goal of regaining their middle-class status. By stretching the scope of individual resources, patchworking helped my informants to acquire consumer items and homes as well as to make investments that were expected to yield profits and, eventually, aid movement into the middle class. Among these investments was the formal education or vocational training of selected household members, usually children or adult males. For some households, particularly those that had entrepreneurial experience from Vietnam (such as the second household), patchworking was oriented toward investment in a small business.

Although patchworking was a response that was common to the households that I studied, it was one whose effectiveness varied according to differences in the kinds of social networks to which households were connected as well as to the size and age and gender composition of households. The households that were particularly successful at patchworking were able to draw on multiple and disparate sources of income and other assets. It is, however, important to emphasize that the economic advantages conferred by diversity in household composition were very much tied to the particular qualities of the structural environment faced by my informants. In other structural contexts—for example, one in which women did not have access to valued resources—a household that was diverse in its gender composition would perhaps not have an advantage over others. The specific economic consequences of variations in household structure vary across different economic contexts.

My findings on the effects of variations in household structure on the household economies of Vietnamese Americans suggest the need for an expansion in our conception of the resources and the social institutions and arenas that are relevant to the dynamics of the household economy. For immigrant households, it is not just income from the labor market but also resources from state institutions and the ethnic community, including job training, education, information, and services, that are rele-

---

[18] The particular practice among Vietnamese refugee households of relying on a combination of income sources has also been noted by Caplan et al. (1989, 58).

vant to their economic situation (cf. Pedraza-Bailey 1985; Portes and Rumbaut 1990).

For Vietnamese Americans, the federal refugee aid and resettlement system provided important resources. The availability of resources through this system, including not only cash assistance but also medical benefits, education, training opportunities, and valuable social relations, is one aspect of the economic experience of Vietnamese Americans that clearly distinguishes them from historical and contemporary immigrant groups in the United States who do not hold political refugee status. Although eligibility for RCA and AFDC programs was highly valued by my informants, the use of these programs was considered very much a temporary phase, one that was part of their initial adjustment to U.S. society. Vietnamese Americans also saw these programs as just one resource among many that could be "patchworked" into the household economy. These programs were used as a collective rather than an individual resource, an approach that perhaps enhanced their economic effectiveness. There was no evidence to suggest that the refugee assistance programs were used as a permanent crutch or that they acted to discourage Vietnamese Americans from striving to achieve socioeconomic mobility. Studies based on longitudinal survey data also show that dependence on government cash assistance programs drops for Southeast Asian refugees in the United States over time (Caplan et al. 1989, 57; Rumbaut 1989b).

Social scientists have suggested that the expansion of household boundaries to include more members as well as such cooperative kin-based economic practices as pooling, are both responses to conditions of economic deprivation (Bolles 1983; Stack 1974; Wallerstein and Smith 1991). My materials on Vietnamese American experiences do not contradict these insights. However, they do also suggest that these practices are informed in critical ways by ideologies of family life. Studies of the cooperative household economy usually fail to explore the ideological factors that underlie such practices as the pooling of resources and the expansion of household boundaries. They thus offer a one-dimensional and ultimately unsatifying understanding of the forces that motivate people to exchange and share resources in their domestic groups and to expand the membership of their households. I found that for Vietnamese Americans, an ideology of family collectivism informed and supported the process of economic patchworking. And in rebuilding their kin groups, Vietnamese Americans drew on Vietnamese kinship traditions that defined kinship in a fluid and inclusive manner. These ideologies and traditions of family life were, however, not static or "given" but themselves being reworked by the conditions of life in the United States. For example, while the rebuilding of kin groups drew on Vietnamese kinship traditions, it was also clear that these kinship traditions were themselves being reshaped to cope with the loss of kin that migration to the United States had entailed.

Too often, studies of the economic behavior of households have reified the household, simply assuming that it acts unitedly, in ways that are unmarred by conflict, resistance, and noncompliance among household members (e.g., Harevan 1982; Massey et al. 1987). This view, one that has been thoroughly critiqued by feminist scholars (Benería and Roldán 1987; Wolf 1990), was belied by the abundance of conflicts over economic (as well as other) matters that I observed in Vietnamese American households. Patchworking was far from a smooth process. In fact, while household economic behavior may be inherently discordant because of the conflicting interests of household members, there were certain conditions operating to make these conflicts exceptionally prominent in the Vietnamese American households. Migration had thrown the established lines of household authority into disarray, by creating conditions of greater equality between men and women and between the young and old.

107

The Family Tightrope

GENDER RELATIONS

Tomorrow I will be home and someone will ask
What have you learned in the States?
If you want to give me a broom
I'll tell you, I am a first class janitor.
I wash dishes much faster than the best housewife
And do a vacuum job better than any child
Everyday I run like a madman in my brand new car
Every night I bury my head in my pillow and cry
In the States I learn the meaning of vastness
But love here seems the size of a toothpick
Such naturalness they appear like kids
But my soul is aged by a thousand years.
The speech art becomes a physical exertion
The more you talk, the more muscle you get
And your mother tongue is used only for cussing
Or at best to pen verses on nights of despair
The big lesson I learn since coming to the States
Is this boundless craving for my land
(Cao Tan, "Tomorrow I Will Be Home")

THE IMMIGRANT EXPERIENCE, particularly in its early years, is typically one that is imbued with a sense of uncertainty and liminality—of being in a dynamic state of transition. For Vietnamese Americans, especially men, changes in the relations of men and women were central to the experience of disorder that accompanied settlement in the United States. There was a widespread feeling that a breach in the world had transpired. This feeling found expression in a tongue-in-cheek description, recounted to me by several men, of the transformation in gender relations that had been brought about by the move: "In Vietnam the man of the house is king. Below him the children, then the pets of the home, and then the women. Here, the woman is the king and the man holds a position below the pets."

A profound sense of loss is conveyed by this statement, with its suggestion of a dramatic reversal of the traditional Confucian sexual hierarchy. Underlying this perception of loss were the largely unanticipated challenges to male power that had occurred with migration to the United States. There had been a shift in the gender balance of resources, one that had shrunk the differential gap between the level of men's and women's access to and control of key resources.

This shift in the balance of resources between men and women was a source of tension and change in the relations of Vietnamese American men and women. However, contrary to what one might expect, the shift did not result in a radical transformation or restructuring of gender relations. While Vietnamese American women exercised greater influence in their families as a result of their relatively greater control over resources in comparison to the past, they did not use their enhanced power to challenge traditional conceptions of gender relations and family life. Instead, Vietnamese American women worked hard to incorporate the new realities of their lives into the ideological confines of the traditional family system. They walked an ideological tightrope—struggling to take advantage of their new resources but also to protect the structure and sanctity of the traditional family system.

MIGRATION AND THE GENDER BALANCE OF POWER

In certain ways, the move to the United States had resulted in greater losses for Vietnamese American men than for women. There was a sharper difference, for men, between their social and economic status in pre-1975 Vietnam compared to the United States. In pre-1975 South Vietnam, men had been in middle-class occupations, in sharp contrast to their position in the lower tiers of the occupational structure in the United States. Besides providing them with an income that supported a middle-class lifestyle, their occupational positions in Vietnam had meant that they had been relatively privileged in their dealings with government institutions and bureaucracies. In the United States, in contrast, men found themselves to be "foreigners"—disadvantaged in their dealings with institutions located outside the ethnic community. In general, I found among men a profound sense of alienation from the social institutions of their new homeland. Many spoke to me of experiences of powerlessness and loss of face in their contacts with U.S. bureaucracies and officials:

Americans look down on us, the Vietnamese, because we don't know about their culture, their language. For example, I went with my son-in-law to the bank to borrow money to buy a house. A man was there, he was a young man, I could be his father. He was very rude. My son-in-law didn't understand what he said so he asked him to repeat and the boy said, "Come back here after you learn some English," and he just got up and walked away. I just said let's go. But things like that happen all the time to us, it's difficult because we're not used to it. In Vietnam I could go any-where and do anything. Here, nothing.

The loss of middle-class status and privilege that had accompanied mi-gration of course affected not just men but women as well, since in Viet-nam women had derived status and benefit from the occupational status of men. However, while both women and men had lost these former priv-ileges, the losses had nonetheless effected a change in the position of women vis-à-vis men. Whereas previously men had through their occupa-tional position held the key to middle-class status for women, in the United States this was no longer the case. Migration had worked to create greater equality between Vietnamese American men and women in their relative control of societal resources. In other words, relative to that of men, the level of women's control of societal resources had improved. As figure 1 shows, the extent of women's inequality, as measured by men's and women's relative control of resources, had shrunk with the move to the United States.[1]

In a variety of ways, this greater equality permeated the relations of Vietnamese American men and women. Among both men and women, there was an acute awareness of the negative consequences of this greater equality for the self-esteem of Vietnamese immigrant men. This was sug-gested by a male informant in his midtwenties, who also identified several economic and social advantages enjoyed by Vietnamese refugee women over their male counterparts in the United States. His claim that women had fewer financial obligations to kin in Vietnam was, however, contra-dicted by women, both married and unmarried, who often talked to me about their struggle to send remittances to relatives in Vietnam.

The Vietnamese women, when they come here they have more opportu-nity, they become more active. The difference between Vietnamese men and women is that the women don't have the responsibility to support the

---

[1] It is important to emphasize that I refer here to the status of Vietnamese American women within the group rather than in comparison to women in other groups or socie-

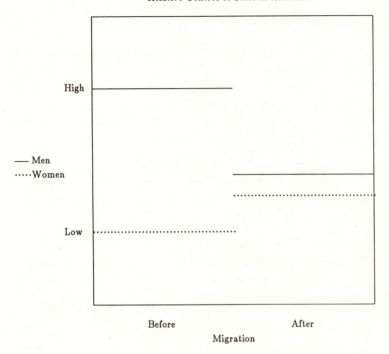

FIGURE 1. Shift in the status of Vietnamese American women

family back home. The women, they can get AFDC for a while if they have children, get some skills, take some classes. The men have to get a job immediately, because unlike the women, they have to send money to Vietnam.

Things also change because here women have more chance to go out and women get less discrimination from the local people than the men do. [Why do women get less discrimination?] I think the women are friendlier than the men, and the friendlier you are, the more opportunity you get. The men are also defensive, upset. They have the feeling that their dignity has been damaged, and sometimes they react very stupidly.

Both women and men were particularly cognizant of and concerned about the inability of men to fulfill adequately, as they had in pre-1975 Vietnam, the role of the primary economic provider for their families.

---

ties. As Janet Chafetz has suggested, "the concept 'sex stratification' refers to a comparison of access levels by the two sexes within a given society at a given time" (1984, 5).

111

During interviews, the negative repercussions of this inability for the status and authority of men in their families was often mentioned. As one man in his late thirties put it:

> In Vietnam, the man earns and everyone depends on him. In most families, one or two men could provide for the whole family. Here the man finds he can never make enough money to take care of the family. His wife has to work, his children have to work, and so they look at him in a different way. The man isn't strong anymore, like he was in Vietnam. In Vietnam I felt I could always take care of my family, but here I know I can't.

Another male informant, who was in his early fifties, offered a similar analysis. But he also spoke pragmatically of the adjustments that were necessary for men to make in their relations with women as a result of the decline in men's earning power:

> There have been a lot of changes. In fact, to anyone, whether you're in Vietnam or here, whether you're a man or a woman, it's the same. The women who depend on their husbands for money, those women respect their husbands. Now when they come to America and they can work, they have money, they can support themselves, they don't have to depend on the husband. So the husbands here should change the way they treat their wives and not keep the customs.

The decline in men's earning power and, more generally, in their social status, was central to the shift in the gender balance of power that had been generated by migration. There were, however, a number of other conditions that also contributed to the shift in the gender balance of power. In the following pages, I discuss three of these conditions: a high sex ratio, challenges posed by dominant U.S. culture, and an expansion in the scope and significance of women's homemaking responsibilities.

The High Sex Ratio

One condition that affected gender relations among Vietnamese Americans was a high sex ratio—a surplus of men over women, particularly in the prime marrying ages.[2] As Guttentag's and Secord's (1983) analysis of

---

[2] A high sex ratio (120 males to 100 females) among Vietnamese refugees is reported by Rumbaut (1989b, 158), based on his research in San Diego. There is also evidence that the sex ratio has been particularly skewed for Vietnamese Americans aged twelve to twenty-four. For example, the Office of Refugee Resettlement reports (1984, 10) that among 1984

the impact of sex ratios on women's status suggests, the surplus of men in the Vietnamese American community often appeared to be a source of dyadic power for women.[3] In other words, women used their comparative scarcity to exercise greater power in their relationships with men. However, not all Vietnamese American women clearly benefited from the high sex ratio, the impact of which was highly uneven, differing markedly for married and unmarried women.

Young, single men in the community tended to be quite bitter about the shortage of young, available Vietnamese American women. For males who were unattached, the scarcity of Vietnamese American females meant that women had greater choice than men in marriage partners and could "look around" in a more leisurely fashion for the most desirable match. Men often spoke of how single women used the high sex ratio to search for the most financially lucrative match: "Here, because there are not so many girls, the men have to chase after the girls. And the girls choose the man with the most money. In Vietnam the girls were more honest and simple. They stayed with you because they loved you. But here, money and job are more important to girls than love."

Men's references to the preference of Vietnamese American women for "money over love" were in fact incessant (cf. Gold 1992, 123), reflecting the economic insecurities that the migration process had generated for men. One man in his forties, who had a wife and children remaining in Vietnam, spoke angrily of this: "If I say I love a woman, she will ask me if I have a lot of money in the bank and if I have a new car. So how do I have enough means to satisfy her? I came here to make money and help my relatives in Vietnam, and not to get together with her."

The young women that I talked to disagreed with such analyses, denying that women used the high sex ratio to their advantage. Nonetheless, some women informants did mention specific incidents in which women had taken advantage of the increased vulnerability of Vietnamese men in the United States: "The men say that the girls just want their money; that's not true. But it's true, some girls are like that. When I lived at ——— there was a man who was very ugly but had a lot of money. Twice, Viet-

---

Vietnamese refugee arrivals, men outnumbered women by more than two to one in the twelve- to twenty-four-year age group.

[3] Guttentag and Secord (1983) also predict that the dyadic power accruing to the sex in short supply will be counterbalanced by the ability of the group with greater structural power (i.e., control over important societal resources) to limit and restrict the activities of the other.

namese women came and lived with him and then ran off with his money. He was so angry, the second time it happened he just came out and told everyone in the neighborhood how bad that girl was."

Because of the high sex ratio, the consequences of ending a relationship were, in a certain sense, more damaging for men than women, for whom there was no shortage of future partners. According to my informants, the situation was almost a reversal of that in South Vietnam, where because of the war, eligible men had been in short supply in the decade or so before 1975. The scarcity of Vietnamese women in the United States meant that women were able to use the threat of leaving a relationship to push partners to meet their demands. In one specific case, a woman demanded that her boyfriend spend less time hanging out and drinking with buddies. In another case, a young man's fiancée threatened to break off the engagement if he did not start taking courses at the local community college or make some other moves toward acquiring a better-paid job. In a situation that involved a couple, Duyen and Ba, Duyen demanded that Ba reform himself if he wanted her to remain in the relationship:

> Before we were married, Ba had many girlfriends, not just Vietnamese but American, Spanish. After we started going out, he liked to keep on seeing them sometimes. I heard from lots of people, "Oh, I saw Ba with that girl." I was embarrassed. I said to Ba, this isn't Vietnam, you can't have so many girlfriends, there are no Vietnamese girls here who will go out with you if you act like that. So I said to him, this is your choice; if you don't stop seeing other girls, then I won't go out with you.

Although Ba was not pleased with these demands, he agreed to them. Like many other men, he was acutely conscious of the greater bargaining power that women had because of their shortage: "Vietnamese men have to chase after the women, do whatever the women want, at least until they get married. In Vietnam, I would never listen to a girl who told me what to do, I would just say goodbye and find someone else. It was easy to do that in Vietnam, because there were so many nice, beautiful girls."

The high sex ratio had other, somewhat less explicit effects on the relations of unattached men and women. It deeply affected the social texture or ambiance of the social life of young, single men and women in the community. For example, in social gatherings, much of the public attention was focused on the women, highlighting their scarcity and "value." My fieldnotes recording a party thrown by a group of young Vietnamese American males conveys some sense of the quality of public interaction between young men and women that I observed. Parties such as that described below took place frequently in the community. Sometimes they were part of weddings, birthdays, or celebrations to mark the one-month birthday of a newborn child. But more often than not, they were organized with no specific occasion in mind. Although the guests of such parties tended to be young and single, they also included children as well as older and married persons.

The party was at one of the apartment buildings on Orchard Street, in the home of Lien and Hung and the four young men (friends of Hung) who were sharing the apartment with them. When I arrived at 9 P.M., about fifteen people were crowded in the small kitchen eating fried rolls, noodles, and potato chips. Hung's older brother and sisters, their spouses, and their children were all there. Eight-year-old Lan excitedly showed me the black lace gloves ("just like Madonna's") that she had brought specially for the party. A steady stream of guests, mainly young men, poured into the kitchen. Men helped themselves to the cans of Budweiser while the women drank Coke or Seven-Up. One guest, dressed elegantly in a suit and tie, took instant Polaroid snaps and handed them around.

I went outside to the balcony overlooking the main street. The five or six older men at the party sat there drinking beer and talked about the possibility of starting a poker game. Later, a group of young men moved out to the balcony to smoke cigarettes and talk outside the din of the blaring music in the living room. Hung came out and urged everyone to start dancing. Dinh replied that there was no one to dance with, and he said, "Do you think we're gay, huh?" For a while, the conversation on the balcony turned to the cost and merits of the cars going down the street. At one point, a car driven by a young, attractive, blonde woman came down the wrong way on the one-way street. Two of the young men stood up, started whistling, and yelled, "Wrong way, wrong way, baby. Over here!" Everyone laughed except two of the older men, one of whom shook his head in disgust.

In the inside room adjoining the balcony, a large area had been cleared of furniture, for dancing. When Lien put on some Vietnamese music, three couples danced the cha-cha-cha, a dance that had been popular in Vietnam. On one side of the room there was a group of about twelve men drinking beer. Man and I talked about the small number of women in the room; he counted five unmarried women in the room. Man then called over his sixteen-year-old niece and asked her to invite some of her Laotian girlfriends from school so that there would be "more girls." She said she would try, but their parents didn't usually let them go out at night. When Man put on a Michael Jackson record the dance floor became crowded. A group of about ten children under the age of ten moved around wildly on one side of the room.

By about 11 P.M., the five unmarried women were dancing constantly. I talked to Patricia, who was in her late teens and had dropped out of high school recently and begun a beautician's course. Patricia, who was dressed in a silver-colored miniskirt with black sequins, told me that she never danced with anyone more than once or twice because if she did they would "get some ideas." She said that if you danced with only one Vietnamese guy, he and everyone else would think they were girlfriend and boyfriend. Our conversation was interrupted by Sang, who asked her if she wanted to dance. When she refused, he offered to bring her a fresh drink. While he left to get the drink, Patricia got up to dance with someone else.

I went into the kitchen where Dinh and some other males were drinking shots of Johnnie Walker whiskey. Dinh showed me the bottle, which he said had been full an hour ago and was now about empty. He said that it was the "Vietnamese custom," that when a man asked another man to drink, he couldn't refuse. So it was impossible to stop. A couple of the men turned to me and complained about the lack of women at the party, and suggested that I call up any women that I knew and ask them to come over. I told them I couldn't think of anyone. They talked about leaving and going to a bar in Chinatown. Man suggested they drive over to the Atlantic City casinos.

At about 11:30 P.M., a heated argument broke out between two of the young men about their relationship with Tia, a senior in high school. Khanh said that Tia was his girlfriend and that Duc had no business dancing with Tia all night. Duc claimed that Tia had told him she was not going out with anyone so Khanh shouldn't interfere. In the midst of the argument Tia left the party with her older sister. Both Khanh and Duc left at about the same time.

At about midnight, Suzy, an Amerasian (of Vietnamese and American parents) woman in her midtwenties, came to the party. I had heard stories before from the men (Dinh and Man) about her exceptional beauty. Suzy sat in the only armchair in the living room and talked to a couple of the men. After a while, Man and a few others came over to me and talked about how they didn't like Suzy. Man talked about how Suzy was like some of the Vietnamese girls here who acted "royal." The girls thought they were special because they knew that they were beautiful and that many Vietnamese guys wanted to go out with them. He also said that "girls like that are no good" and that nobody would want to marry them after a few years. He talked about how Suzy went out with the guy who had the most money and the nicest car and then eventually left him for a wealthier suitor. Lien, who was standing with us, laughed and said it was true that Suzy had too many boyfriends but Man was just jealous of her because he didn't have a girlfriend. Another man there shrugged and said that no one wanted to marry girls like that anyway. I asked what he meant and Lien said that a lot of people wouldn't marry Amerasians because their mothers had been prostitutes in Vietnam.

Because an important underlying goal of these parties was to provide an occasion for young women and men to meet and to develop amorous relationships, the parties dramatically highlighted the fact of the high sex ratio among Vietnamese Americans. In parties such as that described in the preceding, men vied for the attention of the few available women. As a result, a striking dynamic of these gatherings was an emerging sense of rivalry and competition among the men, along with the ensuing tensions. The interactions between men and women were marked by acts of deference by men toward women. Women found themselves at the center of attention as men brought them food and drinks, asked them to dance, changed the music to suit their taste, and offered to drive them home.

This attention, however, was not entirely beneficial for the young women in that it tended to circumscribe their social activities. The focus of the "public eye" on women, combined with sexual rivalries among men, strengthened community monitoring of the sexual reputations of women. In general, a high value was placed by Vietnamese Americans on the virginity and fidelity of young women. Curiously enough, the importance of these values was often emphasized to me by those young, unattached women who had come to the United States without family members. These women often went to some lengths to make sure that in the absence of close family members, they had other guardians who could protect their sexual reputations. As one woman in her late teens, recently married, put it:

Dating for the Vietnamese here is similar to Americans but more conservative. Usually the girl doesn't go out with the guy the first few times he calls. If her family is here, then he has to meet them, but then it's serious. I didn't go out with my husband 'til I talked to him a few times. Before we got married, we wrote to our parents in Vietnam and they met each other. My parents wanted to find out if he was good or not. Some girls here, usually without parents, they just go crazy and get into a lot of trouble. I didn't have my parents here, but I listened to my friend's parents, took their advice, and tried to learn from them.

For another young teenage woman, her older male cousin had stepped into the role of surrogate guardian:

> I don't think sex before marriage is good, because if the woman gets pregnant, she's in trouble. I know there are some Vietnamese girls here who do it, but I don't think it's common. The girls who do it are very Americanized. After coming here, I've changed a little bit, but not much. In Vietnam, girls and boys can't hold hands. Here I think, forget it, it's just a hand. But when I go out I always ask my cousin, "Can I go out with this person? And I'll come back at this time." Before I went out with my boyfriend, I asked him to come over to meet my cousin. I don't have to do that, but I don't want to change.

For those unmarried women whose parents were present in the United States, the supervision of their parents ensured that they did not develop a reputation for sexual promiscuity. At the same time, parents also sometimes encouraged their unmarried daughters to take advantage of their numerical scarcity by looking around and waiting for a partner who had good economic prospects. In part, such attempts by families to ensure that younger members made a "good" marriage choice grew out of a recognition that kin groups had a stake in the marriage decisions of the young, which could translate into either a drain upon or an extension of collective familial economic and social resources. An unmarried twenty-six-year-old woman talked about her family's "wait and see" attitude regarding her boyfriend: "My family liked Trac, my first boyfriend. He was quiet and polite. He worked at our store and my family knew that we liked each other. My parents told me, Trac is okay, if you really like him you can marry him. But we advise you to wait because there are a lot of Vietnamese men here, and some of them are smarter and make more money than Trac."

The high sex ratio entered into the lives of my married informants somewhat differently, although for this group too, it undoubtedly complicated the relations of men and women. Almost all of my married informants (both men and women) felt that migration had been an unsettling factor in their marital relationships. Dissatisfactions and conflicts in marriages were far more common than in Vietnam. According to men, these tensions grew out of the greater freedom and power of women in the United States. In women's accounts, marital conflicts were provoked by what the women saw as men's irrational jealousies. As one woman put it:

> We have many, many fights; it's not good. I'm an old woman now, but when I go out somewhere, to the store, he says, "Oh, you went to see your

boyfriend, I know; you want to make love with the American men who have big cocks." He says that in front of the children; I feel ashamed. Many Vietnamese men here are like that, when they get angry they say, "just go with the American men who have more money."

Other women, too, talked of the jealousy and the propensity of their partners to compare themselves unfavorably with men of higher social and economic status, especially "American men." It was clear that the high sex ratio was viewed by Vietnamese American men as an additional aggravation to the other losses that they had suffered in the migration process. Much like their unmarried counterparts, some married men spoke of the high sex ratio as a source of power for women, because men had more to lose than women from the termination of a relationship: "Many Vietnamese men are afraid that their wives will leave them because it's easy here in America to get divorced. The man who gets divorced, maybe he will live alone for the rest of his life. I think it's hard for an old Vietnamese man to find a Vietnamese wife. But for the woman it's different; I think it's easier for her to marry again."

However, the impact of the high sex ratio seemed more symbolic than real for those who were married, in the sense that married Vietnamese American women faced a variety of social and economic pressures to remain in their marriages. In other words, although the prospect was greatly feared by men, women rarely initiated the ending of a marriage. Some of the social pressures that encouraged Vietnamese Americans to remain in unsatisfactory marriages were revealed by Nga during an interview. Nga and Vinh were having conflicts in their marriage. Although Nga had seriously considered leaving Vinh, she did not do so, in part because of pressure from kin. Like many other women, Nga feared the disruptive effects of divorce on her familial relationships:

The Americans, they get divorced so easy; they change their husbands like changing clothes. That's not our custom. But the Vietnamese, we don't think well of the man and woman. If a husband and wife don't like each other, they should still stay together because of their children. But sometimes Vinh says, do you want to divorce? Vinh doesn't care so much about the children. He can't find a job, but he gets angry when I go to work. He says I talk to other men at the restaurant and that makes him jealous. One night he called me at the restaurant and said I had to come home. I said I couldn't do that because I had to clean everything and close the restaurant before I came home. He came to the restaurant and started pulling me out, pushing me onto the street. I told him I wanted to divorce, and he started crying and said no, he doesn't want that. I took a bowl of water and threw it on the floor and said, if you can put back the water in the bowl then I'll stay with you. But after that, I decided not to divorce. Vinh's younger brother lived with us at that time and he was upset. My children were very sad. Then my uncle and his wife in New York; they called me and talked to me. They wanted us to stay together; they said America is a new place and we have to stay together. They told Vinh to find a job and stop being jealous. But everything is the same. Vinh asks me for money all the time, and he gets angry when I don't give it to him.

Similarly, in another situation, a marriage on the verge of collapse was saved by kin who persuaded the woman to remain in the marriage. This particular case also illustrates the economic pressures that often underlie women's decisions to remain in unsatisfactory marital relationships. Lan had come to the United States with her children in order to join her husband Hai, who had left Vietnam a few years earlier. Upon her arrival, she found out that Hai had been living with a Cambodian refugee woman for some time. Hai refused to end his relationship with the woman and continued to visit her. Despite Lan's tremendous anger about the situation, she remained in the marriage. As the interview transcript suggests, her decision to do so was guided by the idea that it was important for her son to have his father around. But what is also revealed are the economic considerations that shaped her decision. A divorce from Hai would cut her off not only from Hai but also from his kin, who were an important source of economic assistance for her:

> My destiny is bad; I have a difficult fate. I think Cambodian women have a lot of charms. After I came here, my husband said a man has several hearts; one stays with his wife, others wander to other women. I was always waiting for him at home; I cooked a meal and waited, like the woman waiting forever for her husband to return (*Hòn Vọng phu*).[4] I wanted to leave him. But it's different for us, for the Vietnamese people, it's not like the Americans. I told my friends and my sister and they said no, I should stay with him because he's the father of my son. A son without a father is like a house without a roof. But still, I said, I'm going to leave him. I told Hai's brothers and they were upset. They said, how could I do that? All except one brother, he never liked me. Then I started thinking, if I leave Hai and his family, how can I live with my children? I know I'll get welfare but that's not enough. Hai's family, they give us food and money all the time. All I have is my sister, and she doesn't want me to leave Hai.

[4] *Hòn Vọng phu* refers to a Vietnamese folk legend of a woman with her child, waiting for her husband to return; she waits so long that she eventually turns into stone.

As these two situations suggest, social and economic pressures from kin often compelled Vietnamese Americans to remain in unsatisfactory marriages. Although these pressures operated for both men and women, for women they served to mute the options potentially generated by the high sex ratio. Thus for my married informants, the effect of the high sex ratio was ultimately somewhat ambiguous in that it did not clearly empower women in their relations with men. What was clear was that references to this demographic condition sometimes served as a symbolic vehicle for the expression of men's frustrations. It also accentuated the greater fragility of male dominance and, more generally, the traditional family order in the context of the United States. But for unmarried women, the high sex ratio enhanced their value in the "marriage market,"[5] thus giving them an immediate kind of power in their relationships with men. At the same time, the high sex ratio worked to strengthen the community's preoccupation with young women's sexual purity.

Cultural Challenges

Many of my informants felt that the most decisive challenge to the integrity of Vietnamese culture and identity in the United States stemmed from cultural forces. Among other things, "American culture" was viewed as extremely corrosive to traditional Vietnamese patterns of gender relations. United States culture affirmed the equality of men and women and also challenged appropriate norms of feminine behavior. There was much variation in feelings about these cultural challenges, depending on the age and social background of the informant. Reactions ranged from complete disapproval to some degree of endorsement of the perceived state of gender relations in U.S. culture. One of the most conservative reactions was voiced by Binh, a man in his early fifties, a former middle-ranking military officer:

> In Vietnam, we accepted that men and women were different—both equally important, but different. Women and men dressed differently; talked and walked differently; women were different. Only the women who had no families smoked cigarettes, drank beer, wore clothes that showed their bodies. Women were devoted to taking care of their families, their children. American women are different, and the Vietnamese women

[5] The marketplace metaphor has been used in theories of mate selection to explain patterns of homogamy or in-group marriage (Goode 1982). In the most explicit use of the metaphor, exchange theorists have hypothesized that people "trade off" their traits in the marriage market to get the most desirable partner or to "bargain" in the marriage market.

121

want to be like them when they come here. Sometimes I see the young Vietnamese girls here, they walk and talk in ways the girls would never do in Vietnam.

A younger male informant who had grown up in Can Tho (a city in South Vietnam) also expressed concern about changes in the behavior of Vietnamese women with the move to the United States. Once again, Vietnamese American women were chastised for imitating their U.S. counterparts: "Some of the Vietnamese women here are like Americans. They talk and laugh so loudly, you can hear them far away. I don't like that. The Vietnamese women in Vietnam are more honest. They have less contact with society, they're more isolated, so they don't try to imitate."

Such negative reactions to alleged changes in the conduct of Vietnamese American women came not only from men but from women as well. Dao, a woman in her early thirties, who had grown up in a coastal village in the south and had moved to the city in her teenage years, made the following comment; within the spectrum of opinions that I encountered, her reactions were more conservative than most others:

> Even the clothes women wear here are different from in Vietnam. There they wear the baggy trousers, the *aó dài*; only the rich wear jeans and things like that. But here they wear anything. Some Vietnamese women, they want to be like the American women. I don't like the freedom of American women; it's too much. The way some American women dress is so bad, only girls who work in bars dress like that in Vietnam. And some women here, they act just like a man, smoking. American women are too loud, not shy, and they do things like kiss on the street.

Another woman, from Saigon and in her late thirties, also spoke with some disdain about the alleged changes in Vietnamese American women. But for her, as for many others, the most disturbing aspect of these changes was not so much their substance as the rapidity with which they took place. The speed of the changes was taken as a sign of an absence of integrity in the individual involved:

> Women come here [from Vietnam to the United States], and they are mothers of the men. Many women change a lot, those women don't know anything, but they heard that it's "ladies first" here. I've even seen some young couples where the wife hits the husband. I think those women are looking up, and they don't want to look at their past.
>
> Life here is ten thousand or a hundred thousand kilometers different from in Vietnam. I, myself, am exactly who I was in Vietnam, and I tell you

the truth. My friend who came here, in Vietnam she had to wear black pants and one leg was shorter than the other. She wore slippers, and she had to get a string to keep them together. But after she came here she started acting like the wife of the mayor.

Not everyone, however, agreed with the idea that women had changed or that these changes should not be welcomed. A vastly different response to the issue of changes in women's behavior came from Huong, a single woman in her late twenties. She angrily suggested that it was men rather than women who had changed; it was men who no longer fulfilled the norms of masculine behavior:

> Here the women can do whatever the men do; they can go to school, work in the same kind of job, drive a car. The men who complain about it, they're the ones who don't act like a man any more. They come here, they get depressed because they can't stop thinking about Vietnam. And what do they do? They sit around the house and drink beer. They don't want to learn English, to go out and talk to people. Yes, I think it's the men who don't act like men any more; it's not the women who have changed.

United States culture not only challenged appropriate norms of male and female behavior but also cast doubt on the legitimacy of male authority. While my informants perceived a variety of social agents, including the popular media, to be implicated in this challenge, U.S. legal principles concerning family relations were seen to be at the forefront of this challenge to male dominance. The significance of these principles was dramatically highlighted to my informants by cases of police intervention into domestic quarrels among Vietnamese Americans. These cases embodied the absence of support for male authority in U.S. culture.

In three of the twelve households that formed my core sample, members told me that physical assaults by men on women occurred quite frequently in their homes. However, informants (both male and female) also felt that wife beating was less common among Vietnamese immigrants in the United States than it was in Vietnam. This was, in part, because such behavior was no longer "legal." Indeed, Vietnamese Americans were highly conscious of the illegal nature of wife beating, frequently mentioning it as one of the most important differences in the position of women in Vietnam compared to the United States. While I was conducting fieldwork, I heard of two instances in which women telephoned the city police for protection during physical confrontations with their partners. One involved Nguyet, a woman in her early thirties, who had been living with

Phong for six years, since her days in the refugee camp. She described the incident to me a few days after it occurred:

> That time when Phong started hitting me I was so mad I called the police. He's crazy sometimes, if I just go out for an hour, he says to me, "Did you go to meet your boyfriend?" When he gets angry I'm scared that he might kill me with a knife; the Vietnamese men are like that. When Phong saw the police he was scared; he doesn't speak as much English as I do. The police came and asked him if he lived here, and to stop hitting me. The police told me they couldn't do anything because we lived in the same house.

The effect of the intervention of the police in situations such as this was to underscore for Vietnamese Americans the illegitimacy of traditional Vietnamese conceptions of male authority in the context of the United States. In the weeks that followed the visit of the police to Nguyet's home, the incident was widely discussed and recounted around the neighborhood where she lived. Both men and women expressed surprise at Nguyet's audacity in initiating contact with the "American police." On the whole, reactions to Nguyet's actions were ambivalent, among both men and women. In part, this ambivalence stemmed from the refugees' deep and historically rooted distrust of government and police officials. But it also reflected the fact that there was support, although certainly to varying degrees, for the right of husbands to chastise their wives physically under certain conditions. Not uncommon were the attitudes of a woman in her late thirties who spoke of how men were naturally prone to physical violence and of how such violence was justified in the case of the wife's sexual infidelity:

> I said to my husband, if I really do sleep with other men like you say I do, then you can hit me. But there's no reason, so I get angry. Sometimes I say to him, what time do I have to see other men like you say that I do? I work all the time, at the company [shampoo factory], or I cook and clean. I don't have time to see other men. Men are different from women. If they get angry, they want to hit someone. That's the way men are. That's okay, if the wife does something wrong.

The ambivalence regarding police intervention also stemmed from concern about the potentially destructive consequences of such interventions for parental authority as well. There were men and women who pointed out to me that the intervention of the police into domestic quarrels could undermine not only the position of men in relation to women but also that of parents in relation to their children. Male authority and parental authority in the family were viewed in symbiotic terms, as suggested by a woman in her late twenties, who commented disapprovingly on Nguyet's decision to call the police:

> I don't like that she called the police, because we're Vietnamese and we should take care of our own problems, not ask the American police. [What do you think Nguyet should have done?] Phong has a sister here; Nguyet must talk to her first. Maybe the sister can help her. Nguyet did something bad when she called the police. I think the children learn from her that if their mother or father hits them, they can call the police. But if you don't hit the children, how will they learn?

The Expansion of Women's Homemaking Activities

In the Vietnamese American households I studied, it was women rather than men who were seen as the household caretakers—the people who held primary responsibility for making sure that the basic material needs of household members were met. As part of this responsibility, women performed the bulk of housework and childcare tasks. Although men sometimes babysat children, they rarely seemed to participate in such work as housecleaning and cooking. The one notable exception to this was in the case of households that contained no women, a situation that forced the male members of these households to perform household caretaking tasks.

But if for the most part Vietnamese American men's involvement with homemaking activities had not changed dramatically in comparison to the past, migration had affected Vietnamese American women's homemaking experiences in crucial respects. In the context of market economies, household caretaking involves not just the provision of services such as housework and childcare to household members but also the work of acting as intermediary or liaison between the household and social institutions that are located outside the household and contain resources that are critical to the well-being of household members (Gordon 1990, 12–13). For Vietnamese immigrant women it was this intermediary aspect of homemaking that had changed; it had expanded in scope and significance. Whereas in Vietnam, too, women had negotiated with social institutions such as government bureaucracies and schools on behalf of the household, in the United States this mediating work had taken on new dimensions. For one thing, in the United States, this work involved dealing with a wider range of complex, large-scale bureaucracies. These bridging activities had also become more difficult to perform because of language barriers and a lack of familiarity with U.S. bureaucratic

125

procedures. Indeed, it was perhaps because of the difficulty of such bridging work, and the feelings of marginality and powerlessness often accompanying it, that men were often willing and even eager to leave these tasks up to women.

For some households, dealings with utility companies were particularly irksome. Problems arose when utility bills were not paid on time because of money shortages or were misinterpreted because of language difficulties. Also, two households did not contain any members with bank accounts, so they sometimes postponed the time-consuming process of going to the post office and getting a money order. Problems with telephone bills were frequent because of the constant and open flow of neighbors and others into the households who did not hesitate to make long-distance calls. Partly because of this, the recipients of bills were often puzzled about the long-distance charges on their bills and wanted more information about them.

Women were compelled to deal with utility companies, as they tended to be the ones to manage the portion of the household budget that was allocated for basic living expenses. On a few occasions, I accompanied women to shops or to utility companies where they attempted to return purchases or get information about bills. At one time I accompanied Nguyet to the local office of a utility company. Nguyet and other family members had recently bought a house. But since the previous morning, they had had no electricity or gas in the house. As suggested by my field-notes, for Nguyet, playing the part of intermediary between the household and such bureaucratic organizations as utility companies was time-consuming and difficult work.

> As we drove over to the office, Nguyet talked about how before they moved into the house she had spent all her time taking the bus all over town and arranging to have the utilities turned on. Luckily, her friend's teenage daughter had been able to help her, particularly in filling out application forms. She had called the electric company at the beginning of the summer, so she didn't know why they had turned it off. The same thing had happened to their Vietnamese next-door neighbor.
>
> At the office, there were two long lines. We talked about which line to stand in; one was in front of a sign saying "bill payment," and the other, "information." I suggested the "information" line and Nguyet agreed. We waited for about twenty minutes. When it was our turn, the service representative said, "What can I do for you ladies?" Nguyet replied there was no electricity or gas in her house and the man said he would look into it. He asked for the address of the house but didn't understand Nguyet's answer.

After Nguyet's second try I gave the man the address. After about five minutes he returned and said that their records indicated that we had not made any payments over the past three months, and we should have responded to the several bills and notices that had been sent to the house. Nguyet took out a thick sheaf of papers from her handbag and started searching for the bill, and after a few minutes I searched with her. The service representative looked on exasperatedly. There appeared to be no bill in Nguyet's papers. I asked the man about what needed to be done to get the service resumed. He replied that we could pay now or fill out a form requesting deferred payment. I explained this to Nguyet, after which we went to another line to fill out the necessary form.

I also found that it was women rather than men who most often dealt with the health-care system on behalf of the household. Indeed, women were widely acknowledged to be the health-care "experts" so far as both U.S. doctors and the more traditional Sino-Vietnamese medical practitioners (*đông y sĩ*) in the community were concerned. Thus on a few occasions, I saw men turning to women for information when they needed to consult a doctor. Once, when everyone in a household of five single men was quite ill, one of the men called his sister to help them consult a doctor. The men waited for several days for her to return from an out-of-town trip because, as they told me, they had no idea how to get medical attention. The sister, however, knew all about hospitals and doctors because her children had been sick so many times.

The prominence of women in negotiating with the health-care system was viewed as a natural extension of women's homemaking activities. It was in the process of taking care of children and others in the household that women were compelled to deal with medical practitioners. The structure of the public cash assistance system also reinforced the tendency of women rather than men to become the health-care experts. Many Vietnamese American women with young children received medical care, both for themselves and for their children, through AFDC or other public assistance packages. Social service agency workers sometimes helped women to become familiar with the bureaucratic procedures of the public assistance and health-care system. Women's greater intimacy with the health-care system was fostered in other ways as well. For some families, childbirth marked their first sustained contact with U.S. doctors. The process of giving birth, including pre- and postnatal care visits, forced women rather than men to have direct contact with doctors and hospitals and thus acquire some fluency in dealing with the medical establishment.

Although it was far less exclusively the responsibility of women, Vietnamese American women also participated actively in the task of finding housing and dealing with negligent landlords. Once again, women dealt with landlords in an effort to fulfill their domestic caretaking responsibilities. On several occasions, I saw women attempting to contact landlords to demand home repairs. In a building that housed several Vietnamese American households, the problems of peeling paint, uncollected trash, and inadequate heat grew exceptionally severe one winter. Some of the Vietnamese immigrant women in the building took on the job of calling and badgering the landlord to fix the problems. After the landlord failed to respond, one of the women spoke about the situation to a social worker with whom she was acquainted. The social worker, through complaints to the mayor's housing office, was able to pressure the landlord to provide more heat throughout the winter, although the other complaints of the residents remained unanswered.

In the effort to fulfill the demands of their domestic caretaking responsibilities, Vietnamese American women relied heavily on the support of female friends and kin. Most women were part of female exchange networks that were centered around kin and neighborhood ties. While hanging out at informal social gatherings, I observed women exchanging food and material goods of various sorts as well as money to help one another with emergencies or unusual expenses. Women viewed the lending of money as an important source of economic security, as it obligated the borrower to the lender in ways that could prove useful in the future. For Dao, a woman in her early thirties with three children, the monthly struggle to pay household bills intensified when, after a family quarrel, her brother left for New York. Dao turned to women friends to make up for the financial gap created by the loss of her brother's income. She spoke of how she knew she could rely on one friend in particular, to whom she had lent about $200 when the friend had a baby and had needed money badly. Dao spoke to me of how it was wise to give money and other goods to people because they would then be obliged to help you out later.

Women exchanged not only money and material goods but also such tasks as childcare and cooking. They traded information on where to find good buys on food and other items for the household and on how to cope with and maximize gains in dealings with welfare and social service agencies, hospitals, and schools. The women also shared knowledge of available jobs and other income-generating opportunities, as suggested by my fieldnotes recording a visit to the neighborhood Vietnamese American hairdressing establishment. The store was run by a Chinese-Vietnamese woman who had been a hairdresser in Vietnam. She had yet to obtain the necessary license, and so she ran her business in the basement of her house, which was located on a busy street. Trang, one of the assistant hairdressers, had invited me to visit her there in the midafternoon, a slow time for customers. Her sister and a number of friends were also visiting her at the time:

> One of the women talked about how she badly needed money to send to her sister and mother in Vietnam; her welfare payments were not enough to do this. She needed to find some work, but she didn't know where to look. Trang's sister said that her cleaning job at a downtown hotel was a good one, she could take her over there and introduce her to the supervisor. Another woman said that she sewed clothes at home and that might be better because then she would still get welfare. The woman who was look-ing for a job questioned the two closely about the wages she would receive by working at the hotel and sewing clothes. Trang then broke in to say that she might also consider working at a Vietnamese restaurant—there was a new one in another part of the city, and Trang knew the owners well.

As suggested by the preceding, in a variety of ways, ranging from the exchange of money loans to information about jobs, women's networks helped them to meet the demands of their household caretaking responsi-bilities. I have suggested that migration had expanded the scope and sig-nificance of these responsibilities in that women were more heavily in-volved than before in the work of mediating between the household and large-scale, complex bureaucratic institutions containing resources valu-able to the household. But a caveat must be attached to this assessment: it would be extremely misleading to suggest that in Vietnam, women were completely confined to the domestic sphere or that they had not had di-rect contact with large-scale bureaucracies or institutions prior to settle-ment in the United States. Nor do I wish to suggest that Vietnamese American men never engaged in dealings with bureaucratic institutions outside the ethnic community or even that women occupied a position of substantial dominance over men in the extent of such dealings. My point is, rather, that there had been a relative shift in the involvement of men and women with such institutions. Women's contacts had grown, whereas those of men had shrunk.

The expansion in both the scope and significance of women's home-making activities both reflected and contributed to the overall decline in the resources of men, relative to that of women. Despite the fact that negotiating with bureaucratic organizations on behalf of the household was onerous work, it was also a process that ultimately equipped women with valuable skills, which were a resource for women in their efforts to exert control over household affairs. But the disruptive impact of these enhanced skills on traditional gender relations was curbed by the manner in which the expanded homemaking activities of women were viewed and defined by my informants. In Vietnam, women's domestic caretaking responsibilities had carried them into a wide spectrum of activities, ranging from managing household budgets to running businesses. The variety of tasks that had traditionally been associated with women's homemaking made it relatively easy for Vietnamese Americans to see the new activities of women as simply another dimension of women's homemaking tasks. It was, after all, the responsibility borne by women for meeting essential household needs that led them to negotiations with stores, hospitals, social service agencies, and so on. Women's homemaking responsibilities had simply stretched to include the complex tasks of negotiating with bureaucratic organizations that held resources and services that were necessary to the functioning of the household and the well-being of its members. These tasks were easily defined as part of the job of looking after the household. They had become part of the larger body of women's "invisible" work, the work that had been traditionally referred to in Vietnam as "the work with no name" (*việc không có tên*).

On the whole, migration to the United States had impoverished the social and economic resources of Vietnamese American men relative to those of women. In comparison to Vietnam, particularly in the pre-1975 era, there was greater equality in men and women's control of social and economic resources. The high sex ratio, cultural challenges, and a shift in the scope and significance of women's homemaking activities all reflected and deepened men's losses. The shifts in the gender balance of power had set the stage for deep-seated changes in gender relations. But women's responses to their improved control of resources were ambivalent in certain respects, in ways that reflected the complexity of their relationship to the traditional family system.

WOMEN AND THE TRADITIONAL FAMILY ORDER

Vietnamese American women often spoke to me about the importance of preserving Vietnamese family traditions in the United States and of not assimilating into the familial behavior of people in the United States. When I questioned women about exactly what it was that they valued about Vietnamese family traditions, they invariably compared the close family ties of Vietnamese men and children to the looser and more distant ties they observed among families in the United States. The close familial ties of Vietnamese men and children were fostered by the prescriptions of the traditional Vietnamese family system, according to which men and children were obligated to orient themselves and their activities toward the kin group. Women feared the disruptive effects of settlement in the United States on men's and children's obligations to their families. These fears, while especially pronounced among those who were wives and mothers, were also present among other women, who anticipated the familial ties of men and children to be significant to their lives in the future.

Women feared the weakened familial ties of men and children for several reasons. For one thing, the potential defection of men and children threatened the cooperative household economy and such practices as patchworking. Thus women often expressed support for those elements of traditional Vietnamese family ideologies that articulated and buttressed the economic obligations of men and children to their families. For example, Vietnamese American women spoke approvingly of how according to the dictates of Vietnamese culture, in contrast to those of U.S. culture, men were expected to devote themselves, at whatever personal cost, to provide economically for their families. A young unmarried women made the following comment: "I respect my father a lot because he worked hard to support the family. After 1975, he worked at three jobs to make money for the family. I think that's one difference between American and Vietnamese men. Some American men, they don't take responsibility for the family."

It is worth noting that women, both married and unmarried, continued to value men's breadwinning obligations despite the decline in men's ability actually to fulfill this obligation. Frequently however, women viewed the inability of Vietnamese refugee men to provide economically for their families as a temporary aberration, a transitory phase in the process of adjustment to the United States. It was expected that in the future, men would regain their ability to generate income—an expectation that was strengthened by the inclination of some households to invest in the vocational training of adult male (rather than female) members. In short, women valued the economic contributions, both actual and potential, of men, and they identified the familial economic obligations of men as an aspect of the traditional family order that they wished to preserve.

Traditional Vietnamese family ideologies upheld not only the economic obligations of men to their families but also those of children. As part of their filial obligations, children were expected eventually to provide economic resources to parents and other family elders. It was in fact partly this strong expectation of future payoff that led households to make considerable financial investments in the education of the young. For many households, it was the achievements of the young that were the key to moving up in the socioeconomic ladder of the United States. Thus Vietnamese American mothers, along with other kin elders, feared the prospect of vitiated ties between children and their families because it jeopardized familial socioeconomic aspirations.

But the trepidation of women about the weakening of children's familial bonds was driven not just by economic considerations. Underlying it were also deep-seated concerns about the erosion of their authority, as mothers, over children. The attenuation of parental authority meant a loss in the ability of mothers to exercise control over children's lives, in matters ranging from modes of dress to such important life decisions as marriage. In fact, when asked about the greatest drawback of living in the United States, Vietnamese American mothers invariably expressed fears about the loss of control over their children:

> The biggest problem of living here is that it's difficult to teach your children how to be good and to have good behavior. The children learn how to be American from the schools, and then we don't understand them and they don't obey us. The customs here are so different from our culture. The children learn about sex from TV. Maybe American parents think that's okay, but for me that's not okay because I know the children will learn bad behavior from watching TV. Also, I worry that when my children grow older they won't ask me my opinion about when they have girlfriends and they get married.

The deep-seated anxieties of Vietnamese American women, particularly those who were mothers, about the erosion of parental authority also found expression in their ambivalence about the protection offered to them from domestic violence by the U.S. legal system. As I have mentioned, although many women felt positively about the illegitimate quality of wife beating in U.S. society, there was also widespread concern that the intervention of the law into family life detracted from the authority and rights of parents to discipline their children as they chose. In a historical study of domestic violence in the United States, Elizabeth Pleck (1984) describes similar attitudes among European immigrant women in the early part of the century. These immigrant women welcomed the greater rights and authority accorded to them by U.S. legal institutions, but they also resented the intrusion of the state into their authority to discipline their children as they chose. Their ambivalent attitudes regarding police intervention into episodes of domestic violence, like those of Vietnamese immigrant women, highlight the complexity of women's position within the patriarchal family order (Gordon 1990). This was an order that assigned women to a position of subordination to men but also gave authority and power to women in their relations with children. The latter was one aspect of the traditional family system that Vietnamese American women were reluctant to relinquish and that was threatened by egalitarian modes of family life.

All these considerations led Vietnamese refugee women to express considerable general support for the maintenance of traditional Vietnamese family relations in the context of the United States. However, Vietnamese American women were not simply staunch supporters of the traditional Vietnamese family system. That is, women's support of the system did not preclude them from working to improve their situation within it or to soften the force of male authority. This became apparent to me as I observed women attempting to protect and support the struggles of individual women against men in their household using traditional family ideologies, interpreting them in ways that were to their advantage. Women's ideological manipulations emphasized the fluid and multifaceted quality of traditional Vietnamese family ideologies as well as the duality of women's relationship to the traditional Vietnamese family system. Women strove both to preserve this system and to moderate their position of subordination to men within it.

Vietnamese American women who were having conflicts with men in their households sometimes brought these conflicts to the attention of women kin and friends. While hanging out at various places where women informally gathered, I observed women talking of such conflicts. One case I heard of involved a woman named Thuy and her husband Chau. Chau had been severely beating Thuy for some time. Following a particularly violent incident, Thuy's sister, Dao, appealed to her close women friends for help with the situation. Together, the women condemned Chau, not only for his acts of violence but also for his lack of commitment to providing for the family. A former military officer, Chau had been largely unsuccessful in finding work in the United States. Among other things, the women described Chau as "a bad father."

Several women were gathered at Dao's house. Dao brought up the situation of her older sister, Thuy. She said she hadn't wanted to talk about it before, but now it was so bad she had to talk about it. Thuy's husband, Chau, was hitting her often. The other day, Dao had to take Thuy to the hospital, when Chau had hit Thuy on the face. One of the women said, "What about Chau's brother? Does he say anything?"

Dao replied that the brother had told Chau to stop it. But nobody really cared about what the brother said; certainly Chau didn't. The brother was very old. He did nothing but eat and sleep. And he hardly talked to anyone any more, he was so sad to leave Vietnam. Dao started crying, saying that if her parents were here, they could help Thuy.

Dao's neighbor said that maybe Thuy should leave the husband. That wasn't a bad thing to do; when the husband was so bad, the woman should leave the husband. Chau didn't even take care of the children; he wasn't a good father. He also hit the children, even the smallest one, who was only three years old. No good father would do that. Dao said that yes, that was true, Chau wasn't a good father. He also didn't like to work and have a job. Thuy had talked about leaving Chau, but she was scared because she thought maybe Chau would come after her and the children. One of the women said that she would appeal to her brother, who was Chau's friend, to talk to Chau and tell him "not to make trouble" for Thuy. Several other women mentioned people they knew who were in some way associated with Chau. They all said they would talk to these people about Chau. Someone remarked that Thuy was "a good woman" who took care of her children and family, in contrast to Chau, who was "no good."

Dao and her friends were an important source of support for Thuy. Largely through gossip, the women were able to bring pressures to bear on Thuy's husband. The women's exchange networks that I described earlier also functioned as gossip networks. Chau found his reputation among kin and friends to have been affected by the rapidly disseminated judgments of the women. In conversations with a number of men and women about the situation, I found that Chau had been ostracized, not only by the women but also by male friends and relatives. Chau left the city to join a cousin in California. There were no legal divorce proceedings, but the marriage had been dissolved in the eyes of Vietnamese Americans in the neighborhood. Thuy and her children continued to live in the city, receiving help and support from family and friends. Chau, in contrast, severed almost all relationships in the area.

The process by which women collectively worked to sanction Chau was one in which they engaged in a selective interpretation of traditional Vietnamese family ideologies in order to garner support for Thuy. In other words, to legitimate their support of Thuy, women interpreted these ideologies in ways that they chose, emphasizing certain elements and ignoring others. The women supported Thuy in breaking ties with her husband, a course of action that conflicted with beliefs about women's familial obligations as well as ideals of family unity and solidarity—central dimensions of the ideology of family collectivism that I have described earlier. But in Thuy's case, women worked to create an interpretation of the situation in which her husband Chau was responsible for the breakup because of his lack of commitment to the collective welfare of his family. He had not fulfilled his obligation to provide economically for the family; he had abused his paternal authority. Thuy, in contrast, as suggested by the women, was faithfully upholding her familial obligations. Through their selective mobilization of traditional family ideologies, the women were able to support Thuy but also to present themselves as the moral guardians rather than challengers of the traditional Vietnamese family system.

There were other instances in which women stepped in to protect the interests of female kin and friends who were in conflict with men, most often husbands, in their families. These situations involved not only domestic violence but also disputes between women and men over various sorts of household decisions. In one situation that I encountered, Lien was supported by female kin and friends in her decision to seek employment despite the objections of her husband. After completing six months of training in haircutting, Lien had her second child. She planned to leave the baby in the care of her aunt while she worked as a hairdresser in Chinatown. Lien's husband objected to her plans, feeling that it was important for her to stay at home with the baby. While Lien agreed that it was preferable for her to remain at home, she argued that her husband's frequents bouts of unemploment made it necessary for her to go out and work. With the support of other women, Lien's aunt intervened in the couple's dispute in a powerful fashion. At a gathering of friends, Lien's aunt discussed how she had talked with Lien's husband and emphasized to him that Lien was not deviating from traditional women's roles but merely adapting out of necessity to economic circumstances. Because of the gossip that ensued, Lien's husband found himself under social pressure to accept Lien's decision to work.

In another case women mobilized neighborhood opinion against a man who forbade his wife to see her brother, whom he disliked. Ha, a woman in her early thirties, had been living in the city with her husband and their children. Some time ago, Ha's brother and his four children had arrived in the city from the refugee camp to join Ha. Ha described the household atmosphere as tense and uncomfortable during this time. Her husband,

Nhat, was in "a bad mood," because he was not able to find a suitable job. Nhat and her brother had been fighting constantly over small matters. Because of these problems, after a stay of two months, the brother and his children moved to another apartment in the area. Ha went over to see her brother frequently, usually every other day. She often cooked for her brother's children, and sometimes she lent her brother small amounts of money. Nhat resented Ha's involvement in her brother's life and eventually told her to stop visiting them. Ha became incensed and told women kin and friends that she would divorce Nhat if he did not allow her to take care of her brother. Although women kin and friends discouraged Ha from leaving the marriage, they also attempted to change Nhat's behavior and attitude toward Ha's relationship with her brother. The women were able to muster considerable support for their position. Because of their efforts, Nhat felt social pressures from kin and friends to allow Ha to maintain a close relationship with her brother. The women suggested that Nhat was violating the foremost value of family solidarity; they used the ideal of family unity to condemn Nhat's behavior.

It is important to note that although they were extremely powerful, women's groups were not always successful in their interventions in family disputes, particularly when they encountered opposition from their male counterparts. In one such case, a group of women supported the efforts of a member named Tuyet to dissuade her husband from purchasing an expensve car with household savings. Tuyet told women friends that the purchase of the car would significantly postpone their plans to buy a house. Despite the gossip that followed and the women's disapproval of his actions, Tuyet's husband went ahead with the car purchase, supported in his decision by male friends.

In all the cases I encountered of a group of women intervening on a woman's behalf, the process by which the groups attempted to influence the outcome of disputes was similar. Women collectively derived influence from their ability to interpret situations, define who was right or wrong, and impose these interpretations through gossip and the threat of ostracism. In the process of collectively constructing responses to disputes between individual men and women, women drew on elements of traditional Vietnamese family ideologies, such as family unity and the economic obligations of men to their families. What was revealed by this process was the active relationship of women to these ideologies as well as the malleable quality of these ideologies.

But although Vietnamese American women often used traditional Vietnamese family ideologies to support the struggles of individual women, they were careful to do so in ways that did not seriously challenge or undermine the traditional family system. Above all, women remained committed to upholding the normative obligations of men and children to the kin group. As part of this commitment, women also affirmed the obligations of women to their families. In fact, the women's gossip networks that I have described sanctioned not only men but also those women who were thought to have seriously violated their familial obligations—by, for example, neglecting their domestic caretaking responsibilities. Women seemed especially harsh in their judgments of those among them who displayed signs of sexual promiscuity and infidelity. In such cases, women did not hesitate to condemn the woman involved and sanction her through gossip or ostracism.

In summary, the traditional Vietnamese family system—an intricate, crisscross configuration of ideals and beliefs about family life—was one that was generally supported by women. Women's support of this system reflected the power that it accorded them as mothers as well as its centrality to the collectivist household economy. The collectivist household economy, which women (and men) saw as central to their ability to survive and to achieve potential socioeconomic mobility, was organized around and legitimated by the traditional family system. The traditional family system, for example, obligated men and children to contribute economically to their families. Particularly in the context of a precarious economic environment, Vietnamese immigrant women valued the ability of the traditional family system to support and legitimate men's and children's familial obligations. In short, the continued material salience of family ties in the United States helped to preserve the meaning and attraction of the traditional family order for women.

Besides reinforcing women's dependence on the collectivist household economy, there were other ways in which the economic environment that surrounded my informants worked to circumscribe the extent of change in the relations of men and women in families. In the section that follows I explore Vietnamese immigrant women's wagework experiences. In a variety of ways, the structure and quality of Vietnamese American women's employment experiences reinforced rather than challenged gender inequality in the household.

WOMEN AND WAGEWORK

The characteristics of the paid work that Vietnamese American women performed were such as to create continuity and minimize the separation between women's paid and unpaid work experiences. The absence of

137

clear boundaries between women's paid and unpaid work had important consequences for gender relations. By minimizing the disruptive effects of women's wage employment on their domestic caretaking activities, it stifled the impetus for renegotiation between men and women concerning the gender division of household labor. The absence of a separating line between wagework and homemaking also gave women's paid work an invisible quality, one that allowed it to be defined by Vietnamese American women and men as work that was secondary in importance compared to that of men.

The paid jobs that Vietnamese American women performed, located in the lower tiers of the service sector or the informal sector, were often seasonal or unstable in their duration. Somewhat ironically, this quality gave these jobs a certain flexibility for women. That is, the instability of these jobs allowed Vietnamese American women to engage in wagework and also to meet their domestic caretaking obligations by alternating between periods of employment and periods of unemployment during which they could turn their attention to meeting pressing household needs. Given the insecurity that was inherent in their jobs, women felt few compunctions about quitting their jobs when family demands were pressing. It was also a relatively easy matter to find similar work later, given the fairly limited competition for such low-paying and low-status jobs. As a result, it was common for Vietnamese American women to move in and out of the labor market and specific jobs, often in response to various needs and emergencies at home. Lien, for example, alternated her wagework with periods during which she withdrew from paid employment in order to take care of her child. Lien had quit her cleaning job in a downtown restaurant a few months before giving birth. She remained at home for about eight months, but when financial difficulties at home became severe (her husband Hung was unemployed), she began working at a Chinatown grocery store. Although the wages were below the minimum, the job was convenient because she could take the baby with her to the store. During this time, she also worked on weekends as a waitress at a Vietnamese restaurant owned by friends. Six months later, when the baby began requiring more active attention, Lien quit working outside the home for a four-month period. Following this period, she began working at a shampoo factory located just outside the city. She was able to leave the baby in the care of her sister-in-law during this time.

As this brief description suggests, Lien was involved in a cycle of paid work that took her into a variety of paid jobs that were nonetheless fairly similar in their low paying "dead-end" qualities. She continuously moved around, alternating between unemployment and low-paying jobs in the service and manufacturing sectors and in the informal and ethnic enclave economies. Her movements in and out of paid employment were triggered by immediate financial or childcare needs. This strategy of fluctuating employment minimized the disturbance caused by Lien's wagework to the fulfillment of her domestic caretaking responsibilities. For example, it lessened the need for a renegotiation, between herself and her husband, of childcare responsibilities. The structure of employment was such as to allow for a bypassing of any such renegotiation of the household division of labor.

Besides instability, much of the wagework in which Vietnamese American women were involved was also characterized by proximity, both spatial and social, to their unpaid domestic labor. Spatial proximity was particularly pronounced in the case of home work—informal sector work that was performed at home. Because this kind of work was done at home, it was highly interwoven, in women's experiences, with their unpaid domestic work. Women who sewed garments at home, for example, often simultaneously took care of young children, in addition to doing cooking, cleaning, and other housework. Like many other immigrant women, they used home work "to reconcile the responsibilities of domestic care with the need to earn a wage" (Fernandez Kelly 1990, 184). During a visit to her home, an informant named Xinh talked to me of the advantages of home work. Among them was the opportunity that this kind of work gave her both to meet her domestic caretaking responsibilities and to generate income:

> In the corner of Xinh's kitchen there was a large, black sewing machine, surrounded by neat piles of materials. Her brother-in-law and sister-in-law pulled up with a van outside the building. They had been downtown to pick up the week's batch of orders and materials from the garment shop. Xinh and her sister-in-law divided up the materials. The work consisted of sewing collars and sleeve hems on shirts.

> Xinh told me that the manager of the garment factory was a man from the Philippines who was well known in the neighborhood because he employed many Vietnamese refugee women to sew at home. When she had arrived in the United States, her sponsor had helped her to find a cleaning job at a downtown restaurant. But she had quit after four months because she was spending so much money on bus transportation, and she had heard from friends that her welfare benefits might get cut off if she continued working. She also quit because by working at home instead she could cook and take care of her children at the same time. She usually made about $80 a week from sewing at home, often with the help of her sister-in-law.

When Vietnamese American women worked in family businesses—businesses collectively owned by households or kin groups—the line separating employment and household life was even harder to discern. In fact, some women who worked in family businesses told me that they did not "work," despite their long hours of labor in the family business. They saw such work as part of their domestic caretaking obligations—a perspective that was reinforced by the fact that they were generally not paid a wage. In family businesses, the continuity of women's work experiences was also fostered by the informal and familial conditions of the workplace. Thus for Suong, a fifty-eight-year-old woman, a mother of seven and a grandmother to six children, her work in the small ethnic grocery store owned by the family was considered, both by herself and by other family members, an integral aspect of her domestic responsibilities rather than something separate from them. Suong worked at the store most of the day, assisting customers, cleaning, and doing inventories of goods. She usually had a number of grandchildren with her, because her daughters-in-law, while at their own jobs, left their children in her care. The informal conditions of the workplace allowed her to combine such "family work" with taking care of the store. Indeed, in many ways, with Suong working at the store, the locational center of many household activities had moved from the house to the store. The school-aged children of the household would always stop at the store for a few hours after school. Here they would chat, get snacks, and help their grandmother. In the evenings, household members would often sit at the back of the store and watch Vietnamese-language movies on the VCR while waiting for customers.

Also contributing to the continuity of women's paid and unpaid work experiences was the fact that the content of their work in both spheres was similar in certain respects. In her study of Japanese immigrant women, Evelyn Nakano Glenn observes (1990, 368) how *issei* (Japanese immigrant) women's roles in both employment and family life were "defined as service to another." Similarly, for Vietnamese immigrant women, the paid jobs in which they worked, especially those in the service industries, drew on such domestic skills as cooking, cleaning, and sewing. These similarities in substance created continuity between women's experiences of employment and domestic caretaking.

By minimizing the disjuncture between women's paid work and domestic caretaking, the structure and quality of Vietnamese American women's employment helped to maintain established gender relations in the household in important ways. The attributes of women's employment were such that they did not compel a renegotiation of the established division of household labor. By allowing women's paid work to be seen as secondary in importance to that of men, these qualities also had a preserving rather than challenging effect on the relations of men and women. In short, women's employment did not challenge the structure of household life, especially the established division of labor between men and women. Instead, the gendered structures of employment and the household reinforced each other (Glenn 1990, 368).

There were other reasons why the wagework of Vietnamese American women had minimal disruptive effects on established patterns of gender relations. For those groups of immigrant women for whom paid work is a new experience, the experience of employment, by creating a sharp disjuncture between the past and the present, may provide a powerful impetus for renegotiating gender relations. For Vietnamese American women this was not the case—the vast majority of my adult female informants had engaged in wagework at some point in their lives in Vietnam. Moreover, the structure or quality of women's employment in Vietnam had been fairly similar to that of their experience in the United States. In Vietnam, women's employment had been sporadic, with women turning to wagework during those times when household financial needs were urgent or exceptional. Much of women's employment had been part of a family enterprise or in the informal sector, involving small-scale trading activities. Finally, women's wagework had usually been viewed as transient and of secondary importance, in comparison to that of men. In all these respects, there was much continuity in the structure of women's employment in Vietnam and the United States. What this continuity did was lessen the disruptive effect of women's employment in the United States on the established structures of family life.

CONCLUSIONS

Vietnamese Americans had experienced a shift in the gender balance of power due to changes in men's and women's relative degree of control over social and economic resources. This shift in power was viewed and experienced by men and women differently, depending on their age, marital status, and socioeconomic background prior to migration. However, a general consequence of this shift was the presence of a deep and widespread sense of malaise among Vietnamese American men about the state of gender relations in the United States. Related to this uneasiness was an

141

increase in conflicts and tensions in the relations of men and women in households, which reflected the enhanced ability of women to challenge the authority of men in the context of the United States. More than ever before, idealized notions of the household as a consensual and unified entity were being shaken by widespread and visible conflicts among household members.

However, changes in the relations of men and women had a conservative quality to them, in part because Vietnamese immigrant women themselves were deeply concerned about preserving the basic structural and ideological parameters of the traditional Vietnamese family system. Like many other groups of economically vulnerable women in the United States, Vietnamese American women worked to limit changes in family life because they valued the economic protection and support that was an integral aspect of the traditional family system (Ehrenreich 1983; Klatch 1987; Stacey 1990). Like their Cuban and Dominican counterparts, Vietnamese immigrant women also aspired toward a middle-class life-style, one in which the men were the primary breadwinners and women the homemakers (Fernandez Kelly and Garcia 1990; Grasmuck and Pessar 1991, 155). These middle-class aspirations encouraged Vietnamese Americans to view the shift in the gender balance of power as a temporary phase, one that would be followed by the social and economic prominence of men over women once middle-class status was restored. Such expectations helped to curb women's impetus for engaging in a radical restructuring of family life. However, as Grasmuck and Pessar (1991) note in their work on Dominican immigrants, for Vietnamese American women these expectations may be difficult to sustain in the long run, particularly if the attainment of middle-class status is elusive and men continue to be unable to fulfill their primary breadwinner responsibilities effectively. Furthermore, even in the event that women's expectations are fulfilled and male power is restored, the period that I have described—one in which men and women have relatively equal control over resources—is likely to leave a permanent mark on the relations of men and women. In other words, any changes in gender relations generated by this period are unlikely simply to be discarded in the future. As Pierrette Hondagneu-Sotelo observes (1992), behavioral changes generated by phases in the migration process that call for a departure from traditional gender arrangements are unlikely simply to disappear when conditions of normalcy return.

Vietnamese American women also supported the traditional family system because of the power it gave them, as mothers, over children. Although the patriarchal family order is often viewed simply as one in which women are oppressed by men, my materials suggest the need to see this order in more complex terms, as one that is composed of multiple relations. As Linda Gordon eloquently puts it (1990, 182), this order is one in which "mothers . . . are simultaneously victims and victimizers, dependent and depended on, weak and powerful." As I have described, Vietnamese American women saw maternal authority and power to be threatened by U.S. society. U.S. society impinged on their rights as parents over children, in particular their rights to discipline their children as they chose. But what was in many ways a far bigger threat was the potential cultural defection of the young, fostered by the powerful forces of cultural assimilation in U.S. society.

Generation Gaps

Today you started school
Carrying your lunchbag
You looked so sad and ready to cry
Helpless, my child, so sweet!
At day's end I came back
Happy to take you home
You grabbed me and did not let go
Tears overflowing your eyes:
"I won't go back to school
I have no one to play with
I spoke Vietnamese
And the whole class burst out laughing."
Tonight before going to sleep
You turned and tossed
Caressing you, I said: "You'll get used to it
You are different from the class
Because you are Vietnamese
That's what we have been
For thousands of years
Your ancestors are Nguyen Trai
Le Loi and Quang Trung . . .
Remember the story of Hoa Lu and Thanh Giong?
The shining examples of Trieu and Trung?"
Suddenly you shook my arm:
"Yes! I remember now
The story of the Rush Battle
And Phu Dong who went to the sky
I will tell them all
So they won't dare . . . laugh."
(Truong Anh Thuy, "The First Day of School")

ON THE MORNING of April 4, 1991, three brothers—Loi, Pham, and Long—told their parents they were going fishing. After leaving the house, they were joined by another young Vietnamese American male, Cuong Tran, aged seventeen. But instead of making their way to the Sacramento

River, the four proceeded to a nearby Good Guys electronics store, armed with two nine-millimeter pistols. What followed was a eight-and-a-half-hour siege in which they held forty people hostage at the store. Although the exact motives of the young men were unclear to observers, it was later reported that the gunmen had talked to their hostages about the difficulty of finding jobs in the United States and about their desire to go back to Southeast Asia to fight the Viet Cong. The siege ended with a shootout in which six persons were killed—three of the hostages and three of the gunmen.[1]

According to news reports, the four gunmen were members of a gang called the "Oriental Boys." Despite their gang affiliation, many of those who had known the young men were shocked and puzzled by the incident. Although none of the youths had been successful in school, their teachers recalled them as obedient and pleasant, as did the priest of the Vietnamese Catholic Church they attended. Particularly stunned were the parents of the three brothers, who could offer no explanation for their sons' actions. A Vietnamese American acquaintance of the parents, however, suggested the following: "In this country, there is too much freedom. We cannot tell the kids what to do. They were nice guys, but they grew up in this country. They watched the TV. They learned a lot of bad things" (Paddock and Ingram 1991).

The incident, which received wide coverage in the mainstream media, countervailed the image of young Vietnamese refugees as highly studious and obedient to their family elders—an image that has been perpetuated by many media reports of Vietnamese Americans. The incident in Sacramento instead suggested a picture of deeply troubled youth, unsuccessful at school and distant from their families. It is clear that both these extreme images seriously distort the experiences of Vietnamese American youth, most of whom would certainly not conform to either of them. Nonetheless, I suggest that when meshed together these images do contain, albeit in simplified fashion, elements central to the familial experiences of Vietnamese American youth. The process of migration to the United States had generated distance and conflicts between the young and their families. At the same time, young Vietnamese Americans upheld and affirmed the importance of family ties in their lives and expressed support for preserving the traditional Vietnamese family system in the United States.

[1] This account is drawn from the following news reports: Richard C. Paddock and Carl Ingram, "Priest Calls Youths in Store Siege Obedient," in the *Los Angeles Times* (Sunday, April 7 1991); and Richard C. Paddock and Lily Dizon, "Three Vietnamese Brothers in Shoot-Out Led Troubled Lives," in the *Los Angeles Times* (Monday, April 15, 1991).

INTERGENERATIONAL BATTLES

Vietnamese Americans, both young and old, felt that migration had enhanced intergenerational tensions among them. At the root of these tensions were growing cultural schisms between the generations as well as a decline in the power and authority of family elders. As both young and old conceded, younger Vietnamese Americans were becoming more "American" in many ways, ranging from dating practices and modes of dress and speech to their increasingly individualistic orientation toward life. Further exacerbating the depth and significance of these cultural changes was the growing inability of family elders to control the young—to halt or slow down the pace of cultural assimilation.

In a study of European immigrant women at the turn of the century, Elizabeth Ewen writes (1985, 91) of how immigrant mothers felt that "American institutions—the public school, the factory and the urban street—conspired to steal their children." Echoing these concerns, Vietnamese American kin elders viewed the central culprit in the battle between the generations to be the social environment of the United States—in particular, such powerful cultural agents as U.S. television, popular music, and schools. The tendency to pinpoint blame for generational conflicts on the cultural environment of the United States was perhaps facilitated by traditional Vietnamese beliefs about the importance of social environment, rather than inherent personality characteristics, in molding personal character. These beliefs are expressed by such traditional proverbs as "If you live in a round thing you become round; if you live in a long thing you become long" and "If the straw is set near the fire, sooner or later it will catch fire." Given the ubiquity of U.S. social and cultural institutions, many elders felt that they were involved in an uphill battle in their efforts to socialize the young properly. This was suggested by Toan, a father of three children, who was in his early forties: "I have children and I can't educate them. The films and TV show bad things, things which are not suited for an Asian culture. On TV, they show love couples doing things, and I think that way it directly teaches the children bad behavior. Books and magazines show naked pictures of women, and the children who don't know, they see it and try to find out about it. If one plays with the ink, one will get black."

Besides the popular media, schools were another important cultural culprit. The school environment led to the adoption of popular cultural fads by Vietnamese American children who sought to emulate their school peers: "A lot of Vietnamese kids behave like American children; they compare themselves to the American children. The question the children here usually ask their parents is, why can those children do things and why can't I? They want to do things like go out late at night and spend their parents' money."

One problem often discussed by parents was the increasing demands made by children for toys, clothes, and other items that were in vogue among their peers at school. Some elders also spoke disapprovingly of the lax discipline in the schools, which failed to inculcate respect for elders and teachers into their students. After looking over the report card of her son and finding a complaint from his teacher that he was too disruptive and talkative in class, one woman made the following comment: "I don't understand the schools here. If he talks too much, they should punish him. One day I went to the school and I saw a class in which the children were laughing and talking. And the teacher didn't do anything. In Vietnam they would hit you if you did that."

Nga went so far as to forbid her teenage daughter to attend a prestigious public high school to which she had gained admission because she believed that despite the school's reputation for academic excellence, its environment was too loose. Although the family was not Catholic, she preferred that her daughter attend a Catholic school for girls that was closer to home and had a more regulated environment. For Nga, these considerations overrode many others, such as the facts that the parochial school was academically less prestigious and that attending it cost money—$800 a year, a tuition that was reduced to $450 for work-study students.

For family elders, U.S. society not only offered a cultural environment that countered their efforts to educate and socialize the young in ways that they chose; migration to the United States had also, in a variety of ways, weakened the strength of their efforts to enforce appropriate values and norms on the young. For one thing, as so many family elders told me, U.S. society did not support the right of parents to discipline their children as they chose. This absence of support for parental rights was dramatically highlighted for my informants by situations in which school or police officials directly intervened in conflicts between children and their family elders, often in response to complaints of physical abuse made by children. A Vietnamese American educator talked of the tremendous symbolic significance of these cases for Vietnamese Americans. He also identified messages from the media as an important influence on the children's actions: "I often hear of fathers hitting their children and the children calling the police. Because the children have seen the ads on TV, that's how they learn about it. Unimaginable, in Vietnam. In one situation I saw, the parents were in complete shock about it; they didn't understand it at all."

I heard of several cases of Vietnamese American children turning to school authorities or to the police for protection from physical assaults by older family members. For older informants, these cases symbolized the impotence of the old in relation to the young in the context of U.S. society. One such case involved a sixteen-year-old named Tin, who had been in the United States since the age of eleven. Tin's father had held an administrative position in a military hospital in South Vietnam before 1975, but since his arrival in the United States in 1979, he had been chronically unemployed. Conflicts between Tin and his father had become increasingly frequent since Tin's alleged involvement with a Vietnamese American youth gang in the city during the past year. Tin frequently skipped school and sometimes stayed out all night. During one confrontation with his father, Tin called the police. About two weeks after this occurred, his mother described the incident:

> When Tin came home that night, his father was angry. I don't know about him [Tin] anymore; I just hope he finds a job and doesn't steal money from other people. His father was so mad he hit him with a stick. And Tin hit him back. We were surprised because in Vietnam the son can never hit his father. Tin went into that room [an adjoining room], he locked the door, and called the police. Then he came out and his father hit him again. The police then came to the apartment. Everyone from the building came to see what happened. The police told my husband to stop it or they would arrest him. Then they told Tin not to be so bad. My husband was sad that Tin called the police, and he didn't understand why the police thought he was doing a bad thing, hitting his son.

The intervention of the police not only helped to undermine the legitimacy of the father's authority but also represented a profound loss of face for the father. Shortly after this incident, Tin dropped out of school and moved into an apartment with friends. Embittered by the situation, Tin's father grew increasingly despondent and was eventually hospitalized for acute depression.

Much as when the legal authorities were called upon in incidents of wife beating, episodes such as this were widely recounted in the neighborhoods of study, serving as a focal point for discussions about the conflicting nature of family life in Vietnamese and U.S. cultures, particularly with regard to parental rights and authority. The importance of parental guidance and discipline of children was frequently mentioned to me by adult men and women in the community. Several proverbs were reiterated to lend support to the idea that parental discipline was crucial to molding the character of children. One of the most popular of these was "The fish that is not preserved in salt will be rotten; the children who disobey their parents will be corrupted." Others included "Bamboo trees, when they are still young, are easy to bend" and "If one has children and does not educate them, it's better to spend one's time rearing pigs for their tripes."

The following comments from two men provide a sense of the anger often felt by parents about the lack of support for their authority from legal and educational institutions. Also revealed is how, for many men, the decline in parental authority exacerbated the more general sense of loss that had been part of the migration process for them:

> In Vietnam the whole society followed the same rules and standards so when the children did something wrong, the parents and people around them would look down on them and scold them. They [the children] understood then themselves about their wrongdoings. I have children and I can't educate them, and sometimes I get mad and beat them, but society is on their side; not much I can do. When you enter a house, follow the rules of that house.

> The way people teach their children here is different. With my children, too, if I can't educate them, they will be like Americans. It bothers me if you come to visit me and my children don't greet you properly. I would beat up my children if they don't obey me, even if I have to go to jail for it. I feel sad here, even though I'm comfortable about money, but I feel sad.

Not only had the authority of parents and other kin elders diminished because of the legal and cultural context of life in the United States; the social and economic resources that had previously supported the authority of elders had also waned. In the previous chapter, I described how the decline in social and economic status that had been part of the process of migration had transformed gender relations in certain respects, weakening the power of men over women. These same changes had affected intergenerational relations, damaging the power of parents over children. Some parents, especially those with teenage or adult children, spoke pointedly of how the greater economic opportunities available to the young in the United States had weakened the control of parents over their children. Binh, in his early fifties and the father of two sons in the United States, spoke of this at some length:

> In Vietnam, parents raised children and paid for their schooling. When they come to America it's different, they can get help from the government, the government will pay for their schooling. For instance, my older son is supported by the government in college and even in high school. So he can study, and if the government doesn't give him enough he can work in the summer for money. Slowly, he lives like Americans. The children don't listen to the parents because they are not supported by them.

In the extremely competitive and closed educational system of pre-1975 South Vietnam, children had depended on financial support from their families to make it through the system. Family elders, for example, had paid for the young to attend private schools, a necessity for the large numbers of students who were unable to qualify for entrance to the public schools (Dorais, Pilon-Le, and Nguyen Huy 1987, 61). As Binh's words suggest, with migration to the United States there had emerged greater opportunities for the young to pursue their educational goals independently from family resources. Besides financial support for education, in Vietnam the economic dependence of the young on their families had also been fostered in many cases by the expectation that the young would inherit the family business in the future. With migration to the United States, these familial economic resources were no longer as substantial or as crucial for children as before. This is by no means to suggest that familial economic support had become inconsequential to the educational and occupational achievements of young Vietnamese Americans. For example, financial support from kin could determine what type of college one attended and even whether or not one attended college, or completed high school. In fact, those young Vietnamese Americans who did not have the benefit of financial support from their families were often forced to drop out of high school before getting their diploma because welfare support was terminated at the age of nineteen—an age at which few young Vietnamese Americans managed to complete their high school studies because of disruptions in their schooling (Peters 1988, 53). Nonetheless, in comparison to the situation in Vietnam, the young generally had more financial independence from their families. This condition, coupled with a decline in the economic resources that families were actually able to offer to the young, had eroded the economic basis of parental authority.

For kin elders, the move to the United States had not only reduced the economic resources that they were able to offer to the young; it had also resulted in a decline in their social resources in comparison to the young, as exemplified by the greater difficulties experienced by many elders in effectively communicating and dealing with people and institutions of the "host" society. In many households, the English-language fluency of the children had clearly surpassed that of their parents. Thus some children had assumed an important role in dealing with institutions outside the ethnic community on behalf of the household—a situation that could result in an unprecedented degree of power for children. For example, in one household, twelve-year-old Danny interpreted and paid bills for his parents. Sometimes, he kept some of the money allocated to paying bills for himself. His mother was aware of his deception but seemed reconciled to it:

> I have difficulty reading English, so Danny reads all the letters that come to the house. He tells me how much to pay for the electric, the telephone. I give him the money and he takes it to the post office. I know Danny keeps money because he buys some things like this [points to a black leather jacket], and he doesn't work. I know it's not good. I asked him, why do you do like that? He doesn't say anything. If it was in Vietnam his father would beat him, but here it's different. We can't hit him because the police will come.

Rarely was the disregard of parental authority as blatant and extreme as in this situation. However, in many other households, too, the young's greater English-language fluency and familiarity with the procedures of bureaucracies in the United States had resulted in enhanced power and freedom for them. A fourteen-year-old girl, living with her older brother and his family, spoke at some length about the benefits she derived from being the most fluent in English and adept at dealing with persons outside the ethnic community:

> I learned English fast because when we first came here we lived in a place where there were no other Vietnamese people. Now I help my brother and sister with the landlord, and when my brother tried to get a loan from the bank, I helped him with that. It's weird, to be so important, because at home I was the baby in the family. I think I can get away with a lot more now, and my mother isn't here to tell me what to do. Before we came to Philadelphia, our school had a camp for a week out in the countryside. All my friends were going and I really wanted to go. But my brother and sister didn't understand. So I told them it was required, that my teacher said I had to go. It wasn't true, but they believed me because they didn't understand

151

the letter about it from the school. I don't like to lie, but my brother and sister are old; they don't understand about living in America, so when I want to do something I have to do that.

This loss of parental social and economic resources, coupled with a deepening cultural gap between the young and the old, was ripe ground for intergenerational conflict. I recorded many instances of overt discord between the young and the old in household settings. Not surprisingly, among teenagers, conflicts with family elders often revolved around dating and the freedom to "go out" when one chose. A seventeen-year-old girl spoke somewhat glumly about her parents' strictness:

I think my parents are more strict now than they were in Vietnam, because they see that the environment and the living conditions here are very different. Sometimes I feel that my parents are too strict; they don't give me enough independence. My parents won't let me associate with boys or have boyfriends. I just work, study, sometimes I go out with friends on the weekend. My parents don't want us to do something disgraceful so they don't have to disown us.

Some teenagers, particularly boys, were far less acquiescent of the rules set by parents than the girl quoted in the preceding. Khanh, who had been living in the United States with his father and brother for about five years, increasingly refused to accept his father's authority:

I'm eighteen years old, right? And he always looks after me like I'm a little boy. Every time I go out the door I have to ask him. That's not fair for an eighteen-year-old. Sometimes my girlfriends call me, and he just doesn't like it. He doesn't like me to have a girlfriend. Once here in America, he hit me with a stick. I didn't touch him but I said, "don't do that again or I'll call the police." He never hit me again.

One fourteen-year-old boy stunned household members when he began to deviate in his speech from Vietnamese norms regarding the proper forms of address and reference for older persons. The boy told me that he had stopped using the traditional forms because he felt that "everyone should be equal"—a sentiment that was not shared by his mother and uncle. While such explicit calls for greater equality among the young were rare, I did find many younger informants who wished for "more open communication" with older family members. This desire for more democratic communication patterns was coupled with complaints among the young about the absence of open expressions of affection among Vietnamese family members, such as hugging and kissing, in contrast to the behaviors that they had observed in "American families."

Such complaints suggested a growing generational divergence in conceptions of ideal family life among Vietnamese Americans. For parents and other family elders, this cultural divergence had many implications, not the least of which was a loss in their ability to exercise influence and authority over the young. But beyond this, the growing generation gaps also raised the prospect of the defection of the young from the collectivist household economy—a prospect that threatened the economic aspirations of family elders. Many family elders that I met pinned their hopes for acceptance and prosperity in their adopted society on the future occupational attainments of the young. For example, when I asked Suong, a woman in her late fifties, about her hopes for the future, she replied that so far as she and her adult children were concerned, her only hope was that they would have enough to eat and a warm place to sleep at night until her grandchildren had completed their education. She hoped and indeed expected that her grandchildren would do well at school and eventually become doctors, teachers, and engineers and support their parents in their old age. These hopes and expectations led her, like other family elders, to invest resources into the education of the young. However, not all young Vietnamese Americans were able to respond to this investment by doing well at school.

VALEDICTORIANS AND DELINQUENTS

Academic success was widely viewed by Vietnamese Americans as the central route by which the young could achieve acceptance and prosperity for their families in the future. Besides the frequently cited influence of Confucian tradition, which assigned high status and privilege to scholars, a number of other historical and structural circumstances had also contributed to the development of the emphasis on academic success. The ideology of education among Vietnamese Americans was one that emphasized the efficacy of education as an approach toward or vehicle for realizing life goals. Although in pre-1975 Vietnam academic achievement had been difficult because of the extremely competitive nature of the schooling system, for those who were able to succeed, the academic credentials they procured had been likely to secure them a middle- or high-ranking place in the government bureaucracy or military or in the professions. Thus, while schooling was seen as a difficult process, it was also understood to be an effective route for socioeconomic achievement. Formal education was valued not simply as an end in itself but as a process that carried specific, concrete rewards.[2] The vigor with which Vietnamese immigrants stressed education for the young in the United States reflected their view of education as an effective approach for realizing goals, as well as the difficulty that they had experienced in obtaining education in the past. In comparison to Vietnam, schooling opportunities in the United States seemed vast, as described by a male informant:

> In Vietnam, it was very difficult to get into the university. Not like here, where so many people go to college. In Vietnam, you had to pass many tests, and each one was more difficult than the one before. It was, I think, the same system the French had in their country. For most people, forget it, it was not possible to go to university. Here I would say that it's much easier. You have to do good at school, but it's not so difficult as in Vietnam! That's what I tell my younger brother; he's in high school now. I want him to go to college; it's good for him and good for us. Everyone, his brothers and sisters, will help him pay for college.

For many Vietnamese Americans educational opportunities had further contracted after 1975 when, because of familial association with the former regime, children had faced discrimination at school. In fact, providing education for the young was widely identified as a central goal of the migration process; many parents remarked to me that the only reason they were living in the United States was for the sake of providing education for their children. Similarly, school-aged Vietnamese refugees who had come to the United States alone talked of how the greater opportunities for education abroad had motivated their parents to grant them permission to leave Vietnam.

The value placed on the education of the young by family elders was coupled with the expectation that the kin group as a whole would reap certain rewards from the young's academic achievements. In the short run, the academic achievements of the young were a source of status and prestige for kin in the ethnic community. In the informal social gatherings that I attended, it was not unusual for parents or other family elders to pass around and compare the report cards of school-aged children. In the long run, family members expected to gain not only status privileges but also material rewards. In accordance with the prescriptions of the ide-

[2] This analysis draws on the work of John Ogbu (1978, 28), who suggests that historical experiences tend to lead immigrant minorities to anticipate rewards from education and thus emphasize educational attainment among children.

ology of family collectivism, the young were expected to pay back their families after completing their education. In fact, many parents explicitly identified the education of the young as an investment that they made for their future and for the collective future of the kin group. These expectations of payback were also shared, although not without ambivalence, by young Vietnamese Americans, who often focused their areas of study in high school or college in fields that would enable them to honor their financial obligations to their families more effectively. Thus a young Vietnamese American who was studying for a degree in pharmacy (although he would have preferred to study art) told me that he planned to buy a house for his sister and brother-in-law, with whom he was living, as soon as he completed college, in order to fulfill his obligations to them. Similarly, in a forthcoming study of Southeast Asian refugee youth conducted by Rubén Rumbaut and Kenji Ima, a young Vietnamese refugee spoke of how the children in his family were all expected to pay a money "tax" to their mother after completing college.

It was not only in their conception of the goals or ends of education that Vietnamese Americans approached education as a collective family affair. This familial orientation was also expressed and promoted by the manner in which homework and other academic activities tended to be organized in Vietnamese American households. Researchers have noted how studying is organized in Vietnamese refugee households as a collective rather than individual task or activity, with children sitting down together to study and assist one another with school-related problems (Caplan, Choy, and Whitmore 1992). Rumbaut and Ima further describe the Vietnamese refugee family as a "mini–school system," with older siblings playing a major role in mentoring and tutoring their younger brothers and sisters: "Each sibling needs to transmit schooling information to the next oldest and so on down the line, instructing them, socializing them into attitudes of academic achievement, and setting the tone. And all the while family reputation is established in the eyes of teachers who come to expect the younger ones to repeat a familiar, familial level of excellence."

The manner in which Vietnamese immigrants understood and approached education had important consequences for the academic experiences of the young. Perhaps most important, it created a context in which the stakes for doing well at school were extremely high. For the young, it was not only their own future that hinged on their ability to do well at school but also that of other family members. While some young Vietnamese Americans were able to meet these pressures successfully and perform well at school, others slipped into a pattern of academic failure. For the latter group, the general sense of failure that stemmed from their inability to do well at school was overwhelming; they felt that they had let their families down. One twelve-year-old Vietnamese American boy who was not doing well at school told me that his academic failure threatened his family's fundamental rationale or purpose for migrating to the United States. He, like many other children, felt that the burden of the migration process rested on his shoulders—and specifically on his ability to do well at school.

Such pressures were especially difficult given that young Vietnamese Americans faced many difficulties in the schooling process. In other words, whereas young Vietnamese refugees faced tremendous pressure to succeed, they also faced many barriers to academic success. The first of these was language difficulties, a problem that was easier to overcome for those arriving in the United States at a young age. There was also the problem of prior educational skills, since many had been out of school for years before arriving in the United States. These difficulties could be further aggravated by such school policies as age-grade matching (matching the ages and grades of the students as closely as possible) and mainstreaming (rapidly integrating students into regular classes regardless of their English-language skills) (Peters 1988, 50–53). Some young Vietnamese Americans also felt the school environment to be a significant barrier to academic success in that it was so threatening as to make them less inclined to attend classes regularly. A male high school student to whom I talked compared school to a "war zone" in which he and his peers were continually harassed by other students and called a variety of names such as "Yang," "Nip," "Chink," and "Jap." An Asian American teacher also talked at some length of the generally inhospitable character of the schools in the neighborhoods of study: "The high schools here are pretty scary places. When I was teaching at —— High School, all the Southeast Asian kids were getting their coats stolen regularly. They couldn't afford to go out and buy new coats every week! They were also getting mugged and beaten up. I told the principal and he said, 'it happens to everyone.'"

Those who were unable to do well at school sometimes joined the ranks of the *bui đời*, a term used by Vietnamese Americans to refer to those youth who belonged to gangs or engaged in criminal activities. Literally meaning the "dust of life," *bui đời* refers more generally to a person who is alone, without family, or to someone in a lowly position—"no better than dust." While *bui đời* included those who had become disenchanted with the pressures and demands posed by schools and families, it also included those youth who had arrived in the United States alone or under the guardianship of relatives such as brothers and cousins. Those who arrived alone, called "unaccompanied minors" by the social service bureaucracy, were usually placed in non-Vietnamese foster homes. But, as suggested by a Vietnamese American schoolteacher, the children often left these homes and moved to neighborhoods populated by Vietnamese Americans, where they became a highly visible and, to some, troublesome presence:

> The unaccompanied minors, they come into American foster homes here. Sometimes they are abused. Oh, the stories I've heard . . . of sexual abuse, of exploiting them by just keeping them there to work as servants. Eighty percent leave their foster homes. They live in the abandoned buildings in the city. They collect their welfare checks, which they automatically receive until they're eighteen, and they hardly go to school. They drink, take drugs, watch pornographic movies; that's how they spend their time.

Among the Vietnamese American teenagers who had abandoned their homes were those who had been sent to the United States with family members other than parents, such as siblings, cousins, and uncles. In some such households, relations between the teenager and appointed guardian(s) were harmonious. But in others, conflicts abounded and sometimes resulted in the teenager's moving out or running away from the home. In some cases, the high level of disharmony in such households stemmed from the fact that the young person perceived the authority of the guardian as less legitimate than that of his or her parents. In addition, it was not uncommon for relatives neither to expect nor to welcome the guardianship that had been assigned to them. A sixteen-year-old male teenager, who had left Vietnam with his married female cousin and her family, eventually left their home because of conflicts with the cousin's husband:

> I don't get along with my cousin's husband. When I arrived here with my cousin and her two little kids, he was already here, and he wasn't pleased to see me. He yells at me all the time, calls me stupid, and watches me to see if I make any mistake, so he can yell some more. In Vietnam, my parents yelled at me too, but that was different, and they never yelled at me like that. I got tired of that, so I left and now I live with some friends. I don't feel good here; I feel like a fish out of water.

Another case again illustrates the sometimes fragile and troubled quality of the relations between the young and their appointed guardians. Lien had arrived in the United States alone at the age of thirteen. She had

157

been sent by her parents to join her brother, who had been resettled in Philadelphia for a few years. Lien had never closely known her brother, who had been away from home since she was a small child. Soon after her arrival, as Lien put it, her brother began "beating me up every day, for no reason." Eventually, she moved into the home of a friend whose mother and siblings informally adopted her into their family.

As these cases suggest, young Vietnamese Americans responded to the changes wrought by the migration process on their family lives in a variety of ways. Although joining a gang was simply one in a whole range of responses I encountered, it was one that attracted much attention and was widely discussed by my informants. For older Vietnamese Americans, the highly visible presence of *bụi đời* in the United States was of tremendous concern. Among other things, these wayward youth generated a negative public image of Vietnamese in the United States. A Vietnamese American elementary school teacher spoke of these concerns, echoing the sentiments of many others in the community:

> More and more, when the Americans think about the Vietnamese, they think about the young men who come here without their families. The boys come here and because they're lonely they do bad things like steal and sell drugs. It's not so bad here, like in California. But the boys can affect us a lot because they are so many and this is a new country. The boys lose respect for people who are older. I think slowly all the Vietnamese will be like the boys because the young children see them and learn from them.

LIVING IN BETWEEN: THE YOUNG ADULTS

In the eyes of many older Vietnamese Americans, there was another subgroup of young Vietnamese refugees who also threatened Vietnamese identity in the United States. This subgroup was composed of the large numbers of young, single male adults with few or no family ties in the United States.[3] Some of these young single men, living and socializing primarily among themselves, had developed lifestyles that were viewed as

---

[3] This group dominated the flow out of Vietnam, particularly in the 1980s, for two reasons; first, because of their important status as sons, families were willing to invest the funds in them that were necessary to finance the departure. And second, for many of the younger male informants, escaping the military draft imposed by the Vietnamese government was a major reason for the departure.

unconventional or deviant by older Vietnamese Americans. There was some indication that many of these young unattached men were, on average, more Westernized than other Vietnamese Americans even prior to their arrival in the United States, because of the higher social class status of their fathers in Vietnam. Older Vietnamese Americans saw their apparent lack of attachment to family ties and their adoption of "American" ways of dress, speech, and public behavior as contributing to the erosion of Vietnamese familial values and cultural identity in the United States, in part by providing a dangerous and negative example for children.

Notwithstanding such concerns, I found much evidence to suggest that as a group, these young adults remained in many ways deeply tied to the traditional family system. This attachment undoubtedly had much to do with the age at which they had migrated—late teens or early twenties— well after core socialization processes had taken place. Michael Piore has suggested that among immigrants, adolescence is "the dividing line in terms of cultural affinity"(1979, 65–66). In other words, those who migrate in their late teens or early twenties retain their affinity for the native culture, whereas those who are younger absorb the "host" culture more fully and easily. In many cases, for example, those arriving in the United States during their teen years are unable to shed the "foreign" accents that accompany their English speech, in contrast to the more assimilated accents of those who arrive at a younger age.

There is little doubt that for young adult Vietnamese refugees, particularly those who had migrated alone, the move to the United States had been accompanied by many, often basic, changes in their experience of family life. In the following, a young male informant talked of how during the night before his departure from Vietnam, his previously difficult relationship with his father had transformed, signifying for him a movement into adulthood:

> My father was very strict; my mother was very easy with the children. So whenever I wanted something, I went to my mother first, not my father. My father was very critical of me all the time; whatever I did, he didn't like. I felt small with him; when I was in Vietnam I didn't like him, and sometimes I feel guilty about that now. But the night I left Vietnam, something changed between us. My father never hugged me in his life; the only time was before I left Vietnam, and that was the last time, too. I'll never forget the night I left home. I never drank and smoked in front of my father, but that night he told my sister, "go get him a drink and a cigarette." For the first time in my life, he treated me like a grown man.

159

For these young Vietnamese Americans, the physical separation from the force of familial authority and control that had been created by migration was one of the most important changes in their lives. Many of the young men with whom I spoke valued the freedom they had gained to adopt new behaviors and life-styles. For twenty-four-year-old Tang, the son of a former middle-ranking army officer in the South Vietnamese government, the distance from his father created by the move to the United States was especially welcomed:

My old man was very, very strict when I was in Vietnam. He was a military man, a very difficult person. I didn't get along with him; I had a lot of arguments. At that time I was young, also. We argued about everything, and he didn't like that I disagreed with him. He also beat me up many times because I didn't do well at school or something else. After the Communists came in 1975 I started to spend more and more time at school, in the activities organized by the Communists. I always wanted to get away from my father. That's why when he went to the reeducation camp in 1975, I only went to visit him there once. Here I smoke and drink; if I was in Vietnam maybe I wouldn't do that because of my family.

Others expressed a sense of apprehension about the increased freedoms:

If I was in Vietnam I would have a very different kind of life. Here I work where I want to, and if I want to go out with a girl, that's my business. In Vietnam my parents would decide many of these things. Maybe not decide, but they would influence my decision. Of course it's good to have freedom, but sometimes I worry about if I'm doing the right thing in my life, then I wish my family was here so they could give me advice.

Regardless of whether the changes were welcomed or shunned, for these young men, migration had fundamentally transformed their experience of family life by removing them from the immediate influence of familial authority. Greater independence from familial authority was also experienced by those young adults who had arrived in the United States with parents or other family elders. According to my informants, the shifts in generational power caused by the migration process had deeply affected relationships between adult children and their family elders. In the following, Thanh, a widow in her late fifties and the mother of five, bemoaned her growing lack of control over her adult children:

In Vietnam I had a lot of power. The children listened to me; that's the Vietnamese custom. They didn't do anything unless I said it was okay. Here, my sons have girlfriends and they don't ask me about them. Even my daughter, she goes out without my permission. Here my children, when they go out, they just call to report to me that they're going to be late, not to ask my permission. My son has an American girlfriend, and I don't like that. Still, I think that my children are better than others; they work hard and they work together. My family has good discipline.

While there is little doubt that migration had transformed the relationship of young adults to parents and other family elders, there was also an abundance of evidence to indicate the continued importance of familial ties for young adults. The continued importance of family ties found expression in the struggle of many young adults to send money to family members in Vietnam, often at considerable sacrifice to themselves. Some young adults informed me that sending money was a way for them to alleviate their guilt about leaving family members behind in Vietnam. Others reiterated to me the importance of obligations to the kin group over fulfillment of their own personal needs. In one case, a twenty-five-year-old man had recently begun a program in computer science at a local college. By working for a few years, he had saved enough money to pay for most of his tuition and living expenses. But shortly after beginning his studies, he received a letter from his mother requesting money to help with a family emergency—his sister had fallen deeply into debt and was being threatened by creditors. In response to his sister's emergency, the man sent her his savings and postponed his educational plans. He felt that this was the only reasonable course of action.

As this example suggests, for young adults, even those who were in the United States without kin, the connection to family, both moral and emotional, remained strong and powerful. As a result, despite the geographical distance, parental authority continued to exert influence in subtle but important ways. Man, who was in his midtwenties, had recently received a letter from his mother in Vietnam asking him to move from Philadelphia to Oklahoma, where his older brother lived. His mother wrote that she would feel better and worry less about her two sons in the United States if she knew that they were living together. The arrival of the letter sent Man into a state of panic because he did not want to leave Philadelphia, where he had lived for four years and had built up a large social circle. Man also did not get along with his older brother, who, after converting to Roman Catholicism in the refugee camp, had developed strong moral and religious convictions that Man found distasteful. Despite these misgivings, Man departed for Oklahoma six months after receiving his mother's letter. He felt obliged to honor the wishes of his mother.

In another case that illustrates in a similar fashion the continued pull of

161

parental wishes, Ba obeyed the request of his mother that he visit his uncle, against whom he bore a deep grudge:

> In September 1981 I left the refugee camp and came here. My uncle was supposed to receive me but he wasn't here. I got to the airport, I think about 9 P.M. . . . it was cold; I still remember that moment forever. My uncle had moved to Kentucky, so nobody came to pick me up. He didn't notify the agency that he moved. I waited for an hour, then I called the agency because they had a twenty-four-hour number. In the camp, they gave us that number and taught us how to use the pay phone. They [the agency workers] picked me up around 10:30. I was crying, I was kind of sad, it sucked. But that's what happened. The next day I called my uncle's number and the people there said he moved a long time ago. It was a difficult moment for me in my life. I thought before I had my uncle, so it would be all right; I felt safer.
>
> I went to visit my uncle in Kentucky in 1983 because of my mother. After that, forget it, forget it uncle, I don't have anything to do with you. Because of my mother, I went to visit him once, pay my respects, but that's all. My mother wrote and said, go visit him; it will make my life happy. So I did, but I don't have any relations with him.

In another situation in which a mother sent instructions from Vietnam, Lien received letters from her mother and sister in Vietnam shortly before the birth of her first child. The letters instructed her to observe the traditional Vietnamese postbirth restrictions: she was not to go out of the house for a month, not to eat seafood and certain vegetables, and not to wash her hair. Lien was extremely troubled by these restrictions, especially when she was unable to attend the wedding of a friend that was taking place that month. She told me that she did not believe in the taboos that aimed to ward off malevolent spirits and restore the health of the mother. But she obeyed the restrictions, out of respect for her mother and also out of fear of reprimands from her sister-in-law, who called her every hour to make sure that she had not left the apartment.

The continued importance of parental wishes for the young, unattached adults was also reflected in the significance attached to parental acknowledgment and approval of marriage decisions made in the United States. In the absence of older kin in the United States, couples first wrote to their parents or other family members in Vietnam, informing them of their desire to marry. In some cases, the parents of the couple met in Vietnam to discuss the marriage and assess the character of their children's future in-laws. Following this, they wrote back with their impressions and approval. In other cases, particularly when families lived in different areas of Vietnam, the meeting of the families occurred after the marriage had taken place in the United States. When they met, the families performed ancestral worship rites together, acknowledging their newly acquired kinship ties. Except in the case of proposed marriage to non-Vietnamese persons, I heard of no case in which parents forbade a child in the United States to marry, either before or after the meeting with the prospective in-laws. This was in contrast to Vietnam, where parental disapproval of proposed marriages was apparently a common predicament. In this sense, the involvement of the family in the marriage decisions of the young adults was far more superficial and symbolic in quality than it had been in Vietnam.

But the anticipation of family disapproval of marriage to non-Vietnamese persons strengthened the antipathy that existed among my young adult informants toward marrying across ethnic boundaries. The antipathy was somewhat surprising given the high sex ratio, which made the potential for intermarriage seem high. While conducting research, I heard of five intermarriages in the community.[4] In three of these, Vietnamese American men had married women of Asian (Chinese, Cambodian) origin. The other two involved marriages to whites—in one case a man, and in the other a woman. In general, ethnic intermarriages seemed to be somewhat less common among Vietnamese American women than men. This was no doubt related to the high sex ratio, which had enlarged rather than shrunk the pool of Vietnamese American male partners for women. Young Vietnamese American women who went out with whites tended to be seen as more promiscuous and more liberated in their relations with men, as these words of a female informant in her early twenties suggests: "Some Vietnamese boys in the high school go out with American girls because they're easy. But just a few girls go out with Americans. The ones who do are more Americanized, and they don't worry about having sex with their boyfriends. Those girls who go out with Americans say they have more freedom, to get a divorce, to decide things."

However, most young, adult Vietnamese Americans, both male and female, did not favor marrying a non-Vietnamese person, because of cultural differences between them. This attitude was present even among those young men who were dating non-Vietnamese women. As one young man told me, women of other ethnic backgrounds were "okay to

---

[4] According to Takaki, the rate of marriage to whites for Vietnamese in California in 1980 was 15 percent (1989, 473).

go out with, but not to marry."[5] For the men, perceived differences in attitudes about gender relations between themselves and non–Vietnamese American women were an important consideration: "Vietnamese women want to be good wives and mothers. I think that's not so important for American women. I want my wife to stay at home with the children, so I don't think I'll marry an American woman."

Long, a male informant, also spoke of cultural differences that had been highlighted for him by his experiences with non–Vietnamese American women. He especially objected to the "unfeminine" ways in which his "American girlfriends" behaved:

> I don't want that my girlfriends always listen to me, but sometimes they should. The American girls I went out with, they would drink a lot, and they wanted to go to bars all the time. I don't like that. I don't drink, and if I go to bars, I only go to the ones downtown, not the ones where people get drunk and then fight. So they wouldn't listen to me when I told them to cut down their drinking. And they would call me up at work and tell me to just leave to go to a party with them. And I couldn't, so they left. They say that's freedom in America.

In general, my young adult informants voiced aspirations for family life that were rather traditional in character. For example, in talking about how they would raise their future children, young adults, both men and women, spoke of how they would inculcate respect for the elderly and for parental authority in their children. A twenty-five-year-old Vietnamese man who had arrived in the United States alone at the age of twenty-one spoke with conviction about how he would work to instill such traditional familial values in his children. But what also emerges in his words is a recognition of the need to adopt a less rigid approach toward these values in light of the different social environment of the United States:

> I want to get married soon and have children. I hope my first child is a son; that's important to us because the son will remember the family and not the daughter. I will teach my children to obey and respect their parents, but I think I will be considerate of them. I understand that America is a very different place from Vietnam and my children will understand America more. But I don't want my children to live alone until they get married, and if I have a daughter I will be very careful that she doesn't have many boy-

[5] A similar finding is reported by Peters (1988, 83) in a study of Southeast Asian refugee youth in Philadelphia. She found that although male Vietnamese high school students "hung out" with Laotian and white girls and even considered an American girlfriend to be a status symbol, they wanted to marry only Vietnamese girls.

friends. We're in a new place and we have to change, but we also have to keep our customs.

The importance of preserving but also softening the traditional normative hierarchies of Vietnamese family life was also affirmed by another young informant, a female: "We're living in a different country that has very different customs. So I think Vietnamese people here should keep some of the traditions and should learn something new. I think children should listen to their parents, but the parents should know that they're living in a different country, so they should be considerate."

But there were other aspects of traditional Vietnamese family life, besides its age and gender hierarchies, that young Vietnamese Americans spoke of when I questioned them about their reasons for wanting to marry only others of Vietnamese origin. Families in the United States were invariably described in negative terms, as entities that were marked by selfish, distant, and uncaring relations among members. My young adult informants spoke of how Vietnamese families, in contrast, were cooperative and caring groups in which members were willing to sacrifice for one another. The desire to marry within ethnic boundaries arose in part from a sense that intermarriage threatened the possibility of maintaining such cooperative and caring family relations in the United States. The distinctive character of Vietnamese family life was also viewed with great pride, not only by young adults but also by Vietnamese Americans of all ages. Repeatedly I was told that what set Vietnamese apart from "Americans" was the more close-knit character of their family life:

> We're different from Americans because our families are much closer. I think that's the biggest difference between Americans and Vietnamese. For Vietnamese people their family is the most important thing in their lives; for an American it's not that important. I think that's why Americans have a lot of problems. [What kinds of problems?] A lot of Americans feel lonely, they live alone and they don't know their families, they don't care about them. I think that's why they feel sad and depressed a lot.

CONCLUSIONS

Migration to the United States had introduced more conflict and distance in the relations of young and old family members. However, both the extent and the character of the generation gap among Vietnamese Americans varied enormously, depending on the age and family circumstances of those involved. For family elders, besides signifying a loss of power and authority over the young, these generational schisms portended the defection of the young from their families, a prospect that in turn threatened their hopes of eventually attaining middle-class status via their children. But in addition to these concerns, older Vietnamese Americans also saw cultural rifts between the generations as a threat to the continued survival and integrity of Vietnamese culture and identity in the United States. Thus in speaking to me about the implications of cultural changes among the young for the cultural identity of Vietnamese in the United States, a local Vietnamese American community leader remarked that "the bamboo is dying but there are no shoots."

But the relationship of the young to their families and to the traditional Vietnamese family system was far more complex than kin elders often made it out to be. There is little doubt that many young Vietnamese Americans, particularly those who had arrived in the United States before their teen years, viewed the traditional family system as an outdated relic of the past. They chafed at the obligations and pressures imposed on them by this system and looked with favor and longing on the greater individual autonomy and egalitarianism of U.S. families. But this rebellious stance was rarely accompanied by a desire to reject Vietnamese family traditions completely. Even among the most rebellious Vietnamese American children and teenagers that I met, what I encountered was a struggle to come to terms with the traditional family system in ways that did not involve a complete rejection but a reworking, a "compromising" of these traditions.

This struggle to come to terms with the traditional Vietnamese family system in a manner that could be sustained in the context of life in the United States was particularly apparent among my young, single adult informants who were at a stage in their lives at which they expected to marry soon and have children. These informants voiced concerns about how to achieve a balance between the past and present, a family life that melded together the old and the new. In part, their attempts to create this ideological balance stemmed from the fact that they, like other young Vietnamese Americans, saw the distinctive features of Vietnamese family life as what set them apart as a group in the United States, what gave meaning to their ethnic identity as Vietnamese in the United States. Along with the traditional age and gender hierarchies of Vietnamese family life, they identified cooperative and caring relations between kin as distinctive core features of Vietnamese family life.

The Changing Contours of
Vietnamese American Family Life

AMONG THE MANY CHANGES in family life that had been generated by migration to the United States for Vietnamese Americans, perhaps the most basic one was that it had created new feelings of ambiguity and uncertainty about family arrangements. Doubts about what *family* means and what it should mean are, of course, not exclusive to Vietnamese Americans but are in fact endemic in contemporary U.S. society. According to Judith Stacey, this uncertainty about the concept of family is reflective of the current "postmodern" era of U.S. family life. This is an era in which there is no single dominant model of family life that has widespread legitimacy, and people are compelled to create their family lives from "a diverse, often incongruous array of cultural, political, economic and ideological resources" (1990, 60). In many ways this postmodern condition of uncertainty about family life is exemplified by the immigrant experience, which is one in which diverse family traditions from both the past and the present come together in powerful and concentrated ways. Immigrants are also experts at "recombinant family life" (ibid., 16), at fusing together old and new to create a family life in the wake of the personal upheavals that accompany the migration process.

The manner in which Vietnamese Americans constructed their family lives in the United States reflected the complex and contradictory set of challenges that had been posed to the group by the initial years of settlement in the United States. Faced with a precarious economic environment, Vietnamese Americans relied, much as they had in the past, on cooperative kin-based economic practices to survive and achieve economic stability in the United States. It was a response that both reflected and reinforced the power and relevance of traditional family arrangements for my informants. The cooperative household economy for example, was organized and legitimated by the traditional Vietnamese family system, which encouraged and enforced a collective, familial orientation toward economic resources. As Vietnamese Americans engaged in cooperative household economic practices, the economic salience of the traditional family system, and the importance of keeping this system alive and well in the United States, was highlighted for them. In the future, however, as the conditions of economic scarcity and uncertainty that motivated my informants to turn to the collective household economy perhaps dissipate, preserving the traditional family system may become a less pressing and significant concern for Vietnamese Americans. In other words, one can expect that economic mobility, by posing a new and different set of structural conditions and challenges for Vietnamese Americans, will alter the shape and character of Vietnamese American family life in the years to come.

Furthermore, while the conditions of Vietnamese American life in the early years of settlement in the United States had reinforced the traditional Vietnamese family system in certain respects, it had simultaneously challenged it in important ways. A central aspect of this challenge was the greater equality of family members in the United States, which had caused the fissures and conflicts of family life to become more visible and threatening. Migration had generated changes in the balance of power in families; men had lost some of their power over women, as had parents over children. The depth or extent of the shifts in the family balance of power that I observed reflected the recency of my informants' settlement in the United States. Over time, as men and parents become more acclimated to the social environment of the United States and gain more economic and social resources, it is likely that the balance of power in Vietnamese American families will more closely resemble their premigration levels. However, it seems improbable that the kinds of premigration advantages enjoyed by men over women and by parents over children, will ever be completely restored. One suspects, for example, that the relatively greater economic and social independence of the young from their family elders in comparison to the past will be a more-or-less permanent aspect of Vietnamese American family life. And although economic mobility into the middle class may restore the balance of economic power between men and women in favor of men, the shifts in gender relations that have been generated by the initial conditions of settlement in the United States are likely to have an enduring impact on Vietnamese American family life. For example, the negotiating skills acquired by women in the initial years, as they mediate between the household and key social institutions, may continue, in later years, to be a resource that women use in their familial relations with men.

Thus the period of time that I have described in this book—the initial years of settlement in the United States—is special in that the shifts in the established balance of power in families were exceptionally sharp at this time. The somewhat exaggerated character of this period did, however, provide an extremely sharp focus on processes of family change. It provided, among other things, a particularly good opportunity to explore the responses of women, men, and children to shifts in the family balance of power. Because of the shifts in power, more than ever before, women and children had the opportunity to raise their voices, to question previously hegemonic understandings of family. But neither of these previously disenfranchised groups within the family used this opportunity to reject completely the traditional Vietnamese family system. Instead, they strove to rework it, to alter it in ways such that it meshed with the new challenges and circumstances of life in the United States.

Vietnamese American women responded to the rise in their power vis-à-vis men in their families by working both to preserve the traditional family system and to enhance their power within the context of this system. One of the ways in which women tried to balance themselves on this ideological "tightrope" of change and continuity was by appropriating tradition, by taking elements of the traditional family system and using them to their advantage. For example, Vietnamese American women invoked the ideal of family solidarity, as well as traditional prescriptions regarding the obligation of men to provide economically for their families, in their efforts to sanction men who were acting against the interests of individual women. Women also used traditional Vietnamese notions of kinship to create households that contained members who supported their own interests.

Vietnamese American women's support of the traditional Vietnamese family system also reflected the multirelational quality of oppression and power within that system. Vietnamese refugee women were reluctant to relinquish the power that the patriarchal family system granted them over their children. No less important than this was the fact that women, like men, understood the traditional family system to be a vital part of the economic practices by which they survived and could potentially achieve mobility into the middle class, whether it was through buying a home, opening a small business, or investing in the education of their children. Thus Vietnamese American women saw little value in the demise of the traditional family system. For them, as for many other women in the United States, the fall of a family order that provided them with economic support was not something to hasten or even to welcome, given their economic vulnerability and dependence on family ties (Ehrenreich 1983; Klatch 1987; Stacey 1990; Zavella 1987).

On a related note, the efforts of Vietnamese American men and women to preserve the traditional Vietnamese family system also grew out of a sense that this was a way of life that had served them well in the past. It was a system that had helped them to survive and deal with social upheavals of various sorts, and thus it was not something to be casually discarded, either by them or by the young. Family elders felt that it was particularly important to preserve and to pass on Vietnamese family traditions to the young, given the marginal and precarious position that Vietnamese Americans held, as nonwhites, within the racial order of the United States. If and when U.S. society rejected them because of their Vietnamese origins, Vietnamese family traditions could provide them with a means of survival and of overcoming such obstacles.

Younger Vietnamese Americans (those in their early twenties or younger) were also engaged in a process of reworking Vietnamese family traditions. But their efforts to achieve a balance between the past and present had a more difficult and tortured quality to it, reflecting the deeper involvement of the young with U.S. majority culture and social institutions. Some young Vietnamese Americans that I met were striving to achieve family lives that were more "American," particularly more egalitarian in their parent-child relations. But even as among the young there was a growing discontent and distaste for the hierarchical aspects of the traditional Vietnamese family system, there was simultaneously a tremendous sense of pride in the cooperative dimensions or manifestations of this system. When attempting to define the fundamental characteristics of Vietnamese family life, young Vietnamese Americans spoke of close, cooperative, and selfless relations between family members. In fact, it was not just the young but Vietnamese Americans of all ages who spoke of these characteristics as what marked Vietnamese refugee families as special within the social milieu of the United States. Vietnamese American women, men, and children viewed the traditional Vietnamese family as embodying values that were antithetical to the materialism of U.S. culture and its denigration of nurturing and cooperative human relations (cf. Ginsburg 1989). In this implicit critique of capitalist culture, Vietnamese Americans spoke of the cold, impersonal, and instrumental quality of U.S. familial relations in contrast to Vietnamese ones. This contrast was a source of cultural pride for Vietnamese Americans.

These perceived contrasts also facilitated Vietnamese American attempts to perceive Vietnamese family traditions as an essential and defining ingredient of their ethnic identity in the United States. Contrary to the predictions of assimilation theory, which saw ethnicity as doomed to eventual obsolescence and death in "modern" society, in the contemporary United States ethnic groups are impelled in powerful ways, to maintain and cultivate their ethnic identity (Nagel and Olzak 1982; See and Wilson 1986). The compulsions to maintain ethnic identity are particularly sharp for nonwhite groups. In *Ethnic Options* (1990), Mary Waters describes how ethnic identities such as "Irish American" or "Italian American" have become largely a matter of choice for middle-class whites in U.S. society, who may claim such ethnic identities as a way of asserting their distinctiveness, as well as their membership in a community of fellow ethnics. But for Vietnamese Americans, ethnic identity is far less a matter of personal choice. In contemporary U.S. society, Vietnamese Americans are widely seen as nonwhite, and more specifically as "Asian," in their racial status; the option of simply becoming "invisible" by blending in with the majority society is not one that is available to them. The forces that support and generate ethnic identity are much stronger for them than they are for white immigrants.

But if Vietnamese Americans do not have the choice of melding into the majority group, they do have the option of creating a sense of cultural identity that is centered around the "Asian" racial label that is imposed on them. Since the 1960s, the "Asian" label has in fact become an important basis of political organization and solidarity among various Asian American groups. However, its ability to serve as a basis for ethnic identity for Vietnamese Americans as well as other Asian American groups is limited by the tremendous cultural diversity of the Asian American population (Lopez and Espiritu 1990). While a sense of solidarity and identity with other Asian Americans may become stronger among future generations of Vietnamese Americans, it was certainly the case that my Vietnamese American informants identified in only limited ways with other Asian American groups. It was their Vietnamese origins rather than their Asian racial status that provided them with a sense of unique cultural identity in the United States.

As I have mentioned, in their efforts to define the essence of their Vietnamese heritage, Vietnamese Americans often spoke of the unique character of Vietnamese family life. In recent years, Vietnamese American community leaders have also turned to Vietnamese family traditions as core symbols of Vietnamese identity and solidarity in the United States.[1]

[1] For examples of statements about Vietnamese American community leaders about family life see *Nguoi Viet*, vol. 12 (January 10, 1990) (speech by Nguyen Cao Thanh to The Vietnamese Lions Club in Houston) and *Nguoi Viet*, vol. 12 (Sunday, November 11, 1990) (speech by Dinh-Hoa Nguyen).

These traditions may well continue, in the future, to bind Vietnamese Americans together in important ways. But they are also likely to be re-negotiated and redefined as Vietnamese American women, men, and children continue to reconstruct their family lives in response to the shifting set of challenges posed by life in the United States.

Bibliography

Adams, Carolyn, David Bartelt, David Elesh, Ira Goldstein, Nancy Kleniewski, and William Yancey. 1991. *Philadelphia: Neighborhoods, Division, and Conflict in a Postindustrial City.* Philadelphia: Temple University Press.

Agarwal, Bina. 1992. "Gender Relations and Food Security: Coping with Seasonality, Drought, and Famine in South Asia." In *Unequal Burden: Economic Crises, Persistent Poverty, and Women's Work*, ed. Lourdes Benería and Shelley Feldman, pp. 181–219. Boulder, Colo.: Westview Press.

Amott, Teresa, and Julie Matthaei. 1991. *Race, Gender, and Work: A Multicultural Economic History of Women in the United States.* Boston: South End Press.

Angel, Ronald, and Marta Tienda. 1982. "Determinants of Extended Family Structure: Cultural Pattern or Economic Need?" *American Journal of Sociology* 87:1360–83.

Baker, Reginald P., and David S. North. 1984. *The 1975 Refugees: Their First Five Years in America.* Washington, D.C.: New Transcentury Foundation.

Benería, Lourdes, and Martha Roldán. 1987. *The Crossroads of Class and Gender.* Chicago: University of Chicago Press.

————, and Gita Sen. 1981. "Accumulation, Reproduction, and Women's Role in Economic Development: Boserup Revisited." *Signs* 7:279–98.

Beresford, Melanie. 1988. *Vietnam: Politics, Economics, Society.* London: Pinter Press.

Blood, Robert O., and D. M. Wolfe. 1960. *Husbands and Wives.* Glencoe, Ill.: Free Press.

Blumberg, Rae Lesser. 1991. "Income under Female versus Male Control: Hypotheses from a Theory of Gender Stratification and Data from the Third World." In *Gender, Family, and Economy: The Triple Overlap*, ed. Rae Lesser Blumberg, pp. 97–128. Newbury Park, Calif.: Sage Publications.

Bolles, A. Lynn. 1983. "Kitchens Hit by Priorities: Employed Working-Class Jamaican Women Confront the IMF." In *Women, Men, and the International Division of Labor*, ed. June Nash and M. Patricia Fernández-Kelly, pp. 138–60. Albany: State University of New York Press.

Brettell, B. Caroline, and Rita J. Simon. 1986. "Immigrant Women: An Introduction." In *International Migration: The Female Experience*, ed. R. J. Simon and C. B. Brettell, pp. 3–21. Totowa, N.J.: Rowman and Allenheld.

Brown, Clair. 1982. "Home Production for Use in a Market Economy." In *Rethinking the Family: Some Feminist Questions*, ed. Barrie Thorne and Marilyn Yalom, pp. 151–68. New York: Longman Press.

173

Buttinger, Joseph. 1958. *The Smaller Dragon: A Political History of Vietnam.* New York: Frederick Praeger.

———. 1966. *Vietnam: A Political History.* New York: Frederick Praeger.

Caplan, Nathan, Marcella Choy, and John Whitmore 1992. "Indochinese Refugee Families and Academic Achievement." *Scientific American* 266:36–42.

———, John K. Whitmore, and Marcella H. Choy. 1989. *The Boat People and Achievement in America: A Study of Family Life, Hard Work, and Cultural Values.* Ann Arbor: University of Michigan Press.

Caulfield, Minna D. 1974. "Imperialism, the Family, and Cultures of Resistance." *Socialist Review* 20:67–85.

Chafetz, Janet S. 1984. *Sex and Advantage: A Comparative, Macro-Structural Theory of Sex Stratification.* Totowa, N.J.: Rowman and Allenheld.

Coleman, James S. 1988. "Social Capital in the Creation of Human Capital." *American Journal of Sociology* 94:S95–S120.

Deutsch, Sarah. 1987. "Women and Intercultural Relations: The Case of Hispanic New Mexico and Colorado." *Signs* 12:19–740.

Dinerman, Ina. 1978. "Patterns of Adaptation among Households of U.S.-bound Migrants from Michoacan, Mexico." *International Migration Review* 12:485–501.

Doeringer, Peter B., and Michael J. Piore. 1971. *Internal Labor Markets and Manpower Analysis.* Lexington, Mass.: Heath Publishers.

Donoghue, John D. 1962. *Cam An: A Fishing Village in Central Vietnam.* Saigon, Vietnam: Michigan State University Vietnam Advisory Group.

———, and Vo Hung Phuc. 1961. *My-Thuan: The Study of a Delta Village in South Vietnam.* Saigon, Vietnam: Michigan State University Vietnam Advisory Group.

Dorais, Louis-Jacques, Lise Pilon-Le, and Nguyen Huy. 1987. *Exile in a Cold Land: A Vietnamese Community in Canada.* Lac-Viet Series no. 6, Yale Southeast Asia Studies. New Haven: Yale University Press.

Duiker, William J. 1980. "Vietnam since the Fall of Saigon." Southeast Asia Series no. 56, Papers in International Studies. Ohio University Center for International Studies, Athens, Ohio.

Ehrenreich, Barbara. 1983. *The Hearts of Men.* London: Pluto Press.

Ewen, Elizabeth. 1985. *Immigrant Women in the Land of Dollars: Life and Culture on the Lower East Side, 1890–1925.* New York: Monthly Review Press.

Fernández-Kelly, Maria Patricia. 1990. "Delicate Transactions: Gender, Home, and Employment among Hispanic Women." In *Uncertain Terms: Negotiating Gender in American Culture*, ed. Faye Ginsburg and Anna L. Tsing, pp. 183–95. Boston: Beacon Press.

———, and Anna Garcia. 1990. "Power Surrendered, Power Restored: The Politics of Home and Work among Hispanic Women in Southern California." In *Women and Politics in America*, ed. Louise Tilly and Patricia Guerin, pp. 130–49. New York: Russell Sage Foundation.

Finnan, Christine R., and Rhonda Cooperstein. 1983. *Southeast Asian Refugee Resettlement at the Local Level*. Menlo Park, Calif.: SRI International.

Folbre, Nancy. 1988. "Whither Families?" *Socialist Review* 18:57–75.

Freeman, James M. 1989. *Hearts of Sorrow: Vietnamese-American Lives*. Stanford: Stanford University Press.

Gardner, Robert W., Robey Bryant, and Peter Smith. 1985. "Asian-Americans: Growth, Change, and Diversity." Population Reference Bureau, *Population Bulletin*, vol. 40.

Geschwender, James A. 1992. "Ethgender, Women's Waged Labor, and Economic Mobility." *Social Problems* 39:1–16.

Ginsburg, Faye D. 1989. *Contested Lives: The Abortion Debate in an American Community*. Berkeley and Los Angeles: University of California Press.

Glenn, Evelyn Nakano. 1983. "Split Household, Small Producer, Dual Wage-Earner: An Analysis of Chinese-American Family Strategies." *Journal of Marriage and the Family* 45:35–46.

———. 1986. *Issei, Nissei, War Bride*. Philadelphia: Temple University Press.

———. 1990. "The Dialectics of Wage Work: Japanese-American Women and Domestic Service, 1905–1940." In *Unequal Sisters: A Multicultural Reader in U.S. Women's History*, ed. Ellen Carol DuBois and Vicki L. Ruiz, pp. 345–72. New York: Routledge.

———. 1991. "Racial Ethnic Women's Labor: The Intersection of Race, Class, and Gender Oppression." In *Gender, Family, and Economy: The Triple Overlap*, ed. Rae Lesser Blumberg, pp. 173–201. Newbury Park, Calif.: Sage Publications.

Gold, Steve. 1992. *Refugee Communities: A Comparative Field Study*. Beverly Hills, Calif.: Sage Publications.

Goode, William J. 1963. *World Revolution and Family Patterns*. New York: Free Press.

———. 1982. *The Family*. Englewood Cliffs, N.J.: Prentice Hall.

Gordon, Linda. 1990. "Family Violence, Feminism, and Social Control." In *Women, the State, and Welfare*, ed. Linda Gordon, pp. 178–98. Madison: University of Wisconsin Press.

———. 1990. "The New Feminist Scholarship on the Welfare State." In *Women, the State, and Welfare*, ed. Linda Gordon, pp. 9–36. Madison: University of Wisconsin Press.

Gordon, Milton. 1964. *Assimilation in American Life*. New York: Oxford University Press.

Grant, Bruce. 1979. *The Boat People*. New York: Penguin.

Grasmuck, Sherri, and Patricia Pessar. 1991. *Between Two Islands: Dominican International Migration*. Berkeley and Los Angeles: University of California Press.

Gutman, Herbert. 1976. *The Black Family in Slavery and Freedom, 1750–1925*. New York: Pantheon Press.

175

Guttentag, Marcia, and Paul F. Secord. 1983. *Too Many Women? The Sex Ratio Question*. Beverly Hills, Calif.: Sage Publications.

Haines, David W. 1989. "Introduction." In *Refugees as Immigrants: Cambodians, Laotians, and Vietnamese in America*, ed. David W. Haines, pp. 1–24. Totowa, N.J.: Rowman and Littlefield.

Hamamoto, Darrell. 1992. "The Contemporary Asian American Family on Television." *Amerasia Journal* 18:35–55.

Handlin, Oscar. 1952. *The Uprooted*. Boston: Little, Brown.

Harevan, Tamara. 1982. *Family Time and Industrial Time*. New York: Cambridge University Press.

———. 1987. "Historical Analysis of the Family." In *Handbook of Marriage and the Family*, ed. Marvin Sussman and Suzanne K. Steinmetz, pp. 37–57. New York: Plenum Press.

Hein, Jeremy. 1988. "State Incorporation of Migrants and the Reproduction of a Middleman Minority among Indochinese Refugees." *Sociological Quarterly* 29:463–78.

Hendry, James B. 1954. *The Small World of Khanh Hau*. Chicago: Aldine Publishing.

Hickey, Gerald C. 1964. *Village in Vietnam*. New Haven: Yale University Press.

Hirschman, Charles. 1983. "America's Melting Pot Reconsidered." *Annual Review of Sociology* 9:397–423.

Hondagneu-Sotelo, Pierrette. 1992. "Overcoming Patriarchal Constraints: The Reconstruction of Gender Relations among Mexican Immigrant Women and Men." *Gender and Society* 6:393–415.

Hume, Ellen. 1985. "Vietnam's Legacy." *Wall Street Journal* (Thursday, March 21).

Johnson, Kay A. 1983. *Women, the Family, and Peasant Revolution in China*. Chicago: University of Chicago Press.

Kandiyoti, Deniz. 1988. "Bargaining with Patriarchy." *Gender and Society* 2:274–91.

Keyes, Charles F. 1979. *The Golden Peninsula*. New York: MacMillan Publishing.

King, Deborah H. 1988. "Multiple Jeopardy, Multiple Consciousness: The Context of a Black Feminist Ideology." *Signs* 4:42–72.

Kivisto, Peter. 1990. "The Transplanted Then and Now: The Reorientation of Immigration Studies from the Chicago School to the New Social History." *Ethnic and Racial Studies* 13:455–81.

Klatch, Rebecca. 1987. *Women of the New Right*. Philadelphia: Temple University Press.

Kolko, Gabriel. 1985. *Anatomy of a War, 1960–1975*. New York: Pantheon Books.

Lal, Barbara Ballis. 1986. "The Chicago School of American Sociology, Symbolic Interactionism, and Race Relations Theory." In *Theories of Race and Ethnic*

Relations, ed. John Rex and David Mason, pp. 280–99. New York: Cambridge University Press.

Le Thanh Khoi. 1955. *Le Viet-Nam; histoire et civilisation. Le milieu et l'histoire.* Paris: Les Editions de Minuit.

Lieberson, Stanley. 1980. *A Piece of the Pie: Blacks and White Immigrants since 1880.* Berkeley and Los Angeles: University of California Press.

Lee, Gary. 1987. "Comparative Perspectives." In *Handbook of Marriage and the Family* ed. Marvin B. Sussman and Suzanne K. Steinmetz, pp. 59–80. New York: Plenum Press.

Lindholm, Richard W., ed. 1959. *Viet-Nam: The First Five Years.* East Lansing: Michigan State University Press.

Lopez, David, and Yen Espiritu. 1990. "Panethnicity in the United States: A Theoretical Framework." *Ethnic and Racial Studies* 13:198–224.

Luong, Hy Van. 1984. "'Brother' and 'Uncle': An Analysis of Rules, Structural Contradictions, and Meaning in Vietnamese Kinship." *American Anthropologist* 86:290–313.

Mai Thi Tu. 1966. "The Vietnamese Woman, Yesterday and Today." *Vietnamese Studies* 10:7–59.

Marr, David G. 1971. *Vietnamese Anticolonialism: 1885–1925.* Berkeley and Los Angeles: University of California Press.

———. 1976. "The 1920s Women's Rights Debates in Vietnam." *Journal of Asian Studies* 35:371–89.

Massey, Douglas S. 1981. "Dimensions of the New Immigration to the U.S. and the Prospects for Assimilation." *Annual Review of Sociology* 7:57–85.

———, R. Alarcon, J. Durand, and H. Gonzalez. 1987. *Return to Aztlan.* Berkeley and Los Angeles: University of California Press.

Min, Pyong Gap. 1988. *Ethnic Business Enterprise: Korean Small Business in Atlanta.* Staten Island, N.Y.: Center for Migration Studies.

Morawska, Ewa. 1985. *For Bread with Butter.* New York: Cambridge University Press.

Mus, Paul. 1950. *Viêt-Nam: Sociologie d'une guerre.* Paris: Editions du Seuil.

Nagel, Joanne, and Susan Olzak. 1982. "Ethnic Mobilization in New and Old States: An Extension of the Competition Model." *Social Problems* 30:127–43.

Ngo Vinh Long. 1973. *Before the Revolution: The Vietnamese Peasants under the French.* Cambridge: MIT Press.

Nguyen Long. 1981. *After Saigon Fell: Daily Life under the Vietnamese Communists.* Berkeley: Institute of East Asian Studies, University of California.

Nguyen Ngoc Huy and Ta Van Tai. 1987. *The Le Code: Law in Traditional Vietnam.* Athens: Ohio University Press.

Nguyen Van Canh. 1983. *Vietnam under Communism, 1975–1982.* Stanford: Hoover Institute Press, Stanford University.

Nguyen Van Vinh. 1949. "Savings and Mutual Lending Societies (*ho*)." Southeast Asia Studies, Yale University. Mimeograph.

Nguyen Xuan Dao. 1958. Village Government in Viet Nam. Saigon, Vietnam: Michigan State University Vietnam Advisory Group.

Nyland, Chris. 1981. "Vietnam: The Plan/Market Contradiction and the Transition to Socialism." *Journal of Contemporary Asia* 1:426–28.

Office of Refugee Resettlement. 1983. "A Short-Term Evaluation of the Changes in Federal Refugee Assistance Policy on State and Local Governments and on Refugees." Prepared by Urban Systems Research and Engineering.

———. 1983. Report to the Congress: Refugee Resettlement Programs.

———. 1988. Report to the Congress: Refugee Resettlement Programs.

———. 1989. Report to the Congress: Refugee Resettlement Programs.

Ogbu, John U. 1978. *Minority Education and Caste*. New York: Academic Press.

Okamura, Jonathan. 1981. "Situational Ethnicity." *Ethnic and Racial Studies* 4:452–65.

Omi, Michael, and Howard Winant. 1986. *Racial Formation in the United States*. New York: Routledge.

Paddock, Richard C., and Lily Dizon. 1991. "Three Vietnamese Brothers in Shoot-Out Led Troubled Lives." *Los Angeles Times* (April 15).

———, and Carl Ingram. 1991. "Priest Calls Youths in Store Siege Obedient." *Los Angeles Times* (April 7).

Park, Robert, and E. Burgess. 1969. *Introduction to the Science of Society*. Student ed. abridged by M. Janowitz. Chicago: University of Chicago Press.

Palmer, John, and Isabel Sawhill, eds. 1984. *The Reagan Record*. Washington, D.C.: Urban Institute.

Pedraza-Bailey, Silvia. 1985. *Political and Economic Migrants in America: Cubans and Mexicans*. Austin: University of Texas Press.

Perez, Lisandro. 1986. "Immigrant Economic Adjustment and Family Organization: The Cuban Success Story Reexamined." *International Migration Review* 20:4–20.

Perez-Aleman, Paola. 1992. "Economic Crisis and Women in Nicaragua." In *Unequal Burden: Economic Crises, Persistent Poverty, and Women's Work*, ed. Lourdes Benería and Shelley Feldman, pp. 239–52. Boulder, Colo.: Westview Press.

Peters, Heather, Bambi Schieffelin, Lorraine Sexton, and David A. Feingold. 1983. Who Are the Sino-Vietnamese? Culture, Ethnicity, and Social Categories. Philadelphia: Institute for the Study of Human Issues.

Philadelphia City Planning Commission. 1984. Socioeconomic Characteristics for Philadelphia Census Tracts: 1980 and 1970. Technical information paper.

Piore, Michael J. 1979. *Birds of Passage: Migrant Labor and Industrial Societies*. Cambridge: Cambridge University Press.

Pleck, Elizabeth H. 1984. "Challenges to Traditional Authority in Immigrant Families." In *The American Family in Social-Historical Perspective*, ed. Michael Gordon, pp. 504–17. New York: St. Martin's Press.

Portes, Alejandro, and Robert L. Bach. 1985. *Latin Journey: Cubans and Mexi-*

can Immigrants in the United States. Berkeley and Los Angeles: University of California Press.

———, and Rubén G. Rumbaut. 1990. *Immigrant America: A Portrait*. Berkeley and Los Angeles: University of California Press.

Philadelphia Commission on Human Relations. 1984. Asians and Their Neighbors: A Public Investigatory Hearing.

Race, Jeffrey. 1972. *War Comes to Long An*. Berkeley and Los Angeles: University of California Press.

Rumbaut, Rubén G. 1989a. "The Structure of Refuge: Southeast Asian Refugees in the U.S., 1975–85." *International Review of Comparative Public Policy* 1:97–129.

———. 1989b. "Portraits, Patterns and Predictors of the Refugee Adaptation Process: Results and Reflections from the IHARP Panel Study." In *Refugees as Immigrants: Cambodians, Laotians, and Vietnamese in America*, ed. David W. Haines, pp. 138–83. Totowa, N.J.: Rowman and Littlefield.

———, and Kenji Ima. Forthcoming. *Between Two Worlds: Southeast Asian Youth in America*. Boulder, Colo.: Westview Press.

———, and John R. Weeks. 1986. "Fertility and Adaptation: Indochinese Refugees in the United States." *International Migration Review* 20, no. 2: 428–66.

See, Katherine O' Sullivan, and William J. Wilson. 1988. "Race and Ethnicity." In *Handbook of Sociology*, ed. Neil J. Smelser, pp. 223–43. Newbury Park, Calif.: Sage Publications.

Stacey, Judith. 1990. *Brave New Families*. New York: Basic Books.

Stack, Carol. 1974. *All Our Kin*. New York: Harper and Row.

Stern, Lewis M. 1981. "Responses to Vietnamese Refugees." *Social Work* 26:306–11.

Stoecker, Randy. 1991. "Evaluating and Rethinking the Case Study." *Sociological Review* 39:88–112.

Sully, Francois, ed. 1971. *We the Vietnamese*. New York: Praeger Press.

Tai, Hue-Tam Ho. 1983. *Millenarianism and Peasant Politics in Vietnam*. Cambridge: Harvard University Press.

Takaki, Ronald. 1989. *Strangers from a Different Shore: A History of Asian Americans*. New York: Penguin.

Thorne, Barrie. 1982. "Feminist Rethinking of the Family: An Overview." In *Rethinking the Family: Some Feminist Questions*, ed. Barrie Thorne and Marilyn Yalom, pp. 1–25. New York: Longman Press.

Thornton Dill, Bonnie. 1988. "Our Mothers' Grief: Racial Ethnic Women and the Maintenance of Families." *Journal of Family History* 13:415–31.

Thrift, Nigel, and Dean Forbes. 1986. *The Price of War: Urbanization in Vietnam, 1954–1985*. London: Allen and Unwin.

Trullinger, James Walker, Jr. 1980. *Village at War: An Account of Revolution in Vietnam*. New York: Longman Press.

179

Truong Ngoc Giau and Lloyd W. Woodruff. 1962. *The Delta Village of My Thuan*. Saigon, Vietnam: Michigan State University Vietnam Advisory Group.

Wain, Barry. 1981. *The Refused: The Agony of the Indochinese Refugees*. New York: Simon and Schuster.

Wallerstein, Immanuel, and Joan Smith. 1991. "Households as an Institution of the World-Economy." In *Gender, Family, and Economy: The Triple Overlap*, ed. Rae Lesser Blumberg, pp. 225–45. Newbury Park, Calif.: Sage Publications.

Warner, W. Lloyd, and Leo Srole. 1945. *The Social Systems of American Ethnic Groups*. New Haven: Yale University Press.

Waters, Mary. 1990. *Ethnic Options: Choosing Identities in America*. Berkeley and Los Angeles: University of California Press.

Werner, Jayne S. 1981. *Peasant Politics and Religious Sectarianism*. New Haven: Yale University Southeast Asia Studies, Monograph Series no. 23.

Wilson, William Julius. 1987. *The Truly Disadvantaged*. Chicago: University of Chicago Press.

Wolf, Diane. 1990. "Daughters, Decisions, and Domination: An Empirical and Conceptual Critique of Household Strategies." *Development and Change* 21:43–74.

———. 1992. *Factory Daughters: Gender, Household Dynamics, and Rural Industrialization in Java*. Berkeley and Los Angeles: University of California Press.

Wolf, Margery. 1972. *Women and the Family in Rural Taiwan*. Palo Alto: Stanford University Press.

———. 1974. "Chinese Women: Old Skills in a New Context." In *Women, Culture, and Society*, ed. M. Rosaldo and L. Lamphere, pp. 157–73. Palo Alto: Stanford University Press.

Woodruff, Lloyd W. 1961. Local Administration in Vietnam: The Number of Local Units. Saigon, Vietnam: Michigan State University Vietnam Advisory Group.

Woodside, Alexander B. 1976. *Community and Revolution in Modern Vietnam*. Boston: Houghton Mifflin.

———. 1971. *Vietnam and the Chinese Model*. Cambridge: Harvard University Press.

Yancey, William, Eugene Ericksen, and Richard Juliani. 1976. "Emergent Ethnicity: A Review and Reformulation." *American Sociological Review* 41:391–403.

Zavella, Patricia. 1987. *Women's Work and Chicano Families*. Ithaca: Cornell University Press.

Zhou, Min, and John R. Logan. 1989. "Returns on Human Capital in Ethnic Enclaves: New York City's Chinatown." *American Sociological Review* 54:809–20

Zinn, Maxine Baca. 1990. "Family, Feminism, and Race in America." *Gender and Society* 4:68–83.

Index

academic failure, 156. *See also* education
Adams, Carolyn, 80
African American families, 22
Aid to Families with Dependent Children, 12, 83, 85, 92, 94, 106, 127
Amott, Teresa, 9
Ancestral worship, 43, 99–100, 163
Angel, Ronald, 78
Asian American families, 21
Asian American identity, 171
assimilation theory, 15; immigrant families and, 16; critique of, 17

Bach, Robert, 18, 82
Bangladeshi, 30
Benería, Lourdes, 19, 21, 107
Beresford, Melanie, 51, 52, 53
Blood, Robert, 23
Blumberg, Rae Lesser, 23
Bolles, A. Lynn, 77, 106
breadwinner, 57, 90, 111, 131, 142
Brettell, Caroline, 20
Brown, Clair, 78
Bryant, Robey, 70
Buttinger, Joseph, 40

Caplan, Nathan, 105, 155
case study, 28
Catholic, 27, 49, 147
Caulfield, Minna, 20
Chafetz, Janet, 111
Chicago School of Sociology, 15
Chinese family, 48
Chinese in Vietnam, 33, 38–39, 55, 65, 91
Choy, Marcella, 155
Communist takeover of Vietnam, 64–67; family life and, 67–70
Confucianism, 39; commerce and, 47; family and, 43–44, 49, 99; women and, 45, 48

consumer items, 75–76
Cooperstein, Rhonda, 26
Council of Notables, 41
cultural assimilation of young, 146–47

Deutsch, Sara, 16, 19
Dinerman, Ina, 19
Doeringer, Peter, 80
domestic violence. *See* police intervention and wife beating
Donoghue, John, 41
Dorais, Louis-Jacques, 62, 63, 68, 150
Duiker, William, 65, 91

economic assistance from kin, 41, 55, 89, 90. *See also* Vietnamese American families
economic recession of 1980s, 13
education: emphasis on, 153–56; South Vietnamese system of, 62, 150; U.S. system of, 85, 150. *See also* academic failure and school environment
Ehrenreich, Barbara, 142, 169
Ericksen, Eugene, 21
escape from Vietnam, 70
Espiritu, Yen, 171
ethnic economic enclaves, 18, 81–82
ethnicity, 18–19, 21
Ewen, Elizabeth, 146

family businesses, 46, 55, 58, 62, 91–93, 140
family life in Vietnam. *See* Vietnamese kinship system
family life of Vietnamese Americans. *See* Vietnamese American families
Fernandez-Kelly, Maria Patricia, 139, 142
Finnan, Christine, 26
Food stamps, 13, 83
Freeman, James, 56, 62, 64, 70, 71
French colonization of Vietnam, 40, 42, 50

181

Gallup polls, 13
gangs, 145, 148, 156, 158
Garcia, Anna, 142
Gardner, Robert, 70
gender relations in Vietnam. *See* women in
 Vietnam
Geneva Treaty, 49
Ginsburg, Faye, 170
Glenn, Evelyn Nakano, 20, 21, 77, 140,
 141
Gold, Steven, 11–12, 14, 26–27, 76, 113
Goode, William, 16–17
Gordon, Linda, 125, 133, 145
Gordon, Milton, 15
Grant, Bruce, 70
Grasmuck, Sherri, 75, 99, 142
Gutman, Herbert, 22
Guttentag, Marcia, 112, 113

Haines, David, 57
Hamamoto, Darrell, 7
Handlin, Oscar, 16
Harevan, Tamara, 18, 107
health care, 127
Hein, Jeremy, 85
Hendry, James, 41
Hickey, Gerald, 41, 48
Hirschman, Charles, 17
home ownership, 76–77, 89–90
Hondagneu-Sotelo, Pierrette, 142
household composition, 34–35. *See also*
 patchworking
household strategies, 19, 21
housework, 125, 138–39
Hume, Ellen, 7

Ima, Kenji, 155
immigrant adaptation, 18
immigrant families, 21–23
immigrant women, 19–20
Immigration Act of 1965, 11–12
Indian, 30–31
informal economy, 80–81, 91–92, 138–
 39
Ingram, Carl, 145
intermarriage, 163–64

job conditions, 74, 79, 80–82, 88–89, 91–
 93, 96–97; women's, 137–41
Johnson, Kay, 48
Juliani, Richard, 21

Keyes, Charles, 40, 51–52, 55
King, Deborah, 20
Kivisto, Peter, 18
Klatch, Rebecca, 142, 169
Kolko, Gabriel, 51, 53

Lal, Barbara Ballis, 15
landlords, 128
Le Code, 45
Lee, Gary, 17
Lopez, David, 171
Luong, Hy Van, 44

Mai Thi Tu, 46, 48
male desertion, 59
Marr, David, 40, 45, 47
marriage decisions, 63, 162–63
Massey, Douglas, 12, 19, 107
Matthaei, Julie, 9
Medicaid, 13, 83
middle class of South Vietnam. *See* South
 Vietnamese middle class
Min, Pyong Gap, 18
"model minority" image, 7, 14
Morawska, Ewa, 17–18

Nagel, Joanne, 21, 171
nationalization of businesses, 65–66
neoconservatives, 7
New Economic Zones, 64
Ngo Vinh Long, 40
Nguyen Huy, 62, 63, 68, 150
Nguyen Ngoc Huy, 46
Nguyen Trai, 38
Nguyen Van Canh, 64
Nguyen Van Vinh, 42
Nguyen Vinh Long, 40
Nguyen Xuan Dao, 39

Office of Refugee Resettlement, 11, 14, 84,
 112

Ogbu, John, 154
Okamura, Jonathan, 19
Olzak, Susan, 21, 171
Omi, Michael, 13, 17

Paddock, Richard, 145
Palmer, John, 13
Park, Robert, 15
patchworking, 77, 86; effects of household
    composition on, 78, 94, 98; family ideol-
    ogies and, 99–100; household conflict
    and, 87, 93
Pedraza-Bailey, Silvia
Perez, Lisandro, 19
Pessar, Patricia, 75, 99, 142
Peters, Heather, 150, 156, 164
Philadelphia: Commission on Human Re-
    lations of, 25; economic conditions in,
    25, 79–80; racial-ethnic tensions in, 25;
    Vietnamese ethnic associations in, 26–
    27; Vietnamese refugees in, 25
Pilon-Le, Lise, 62, 63, 68, 150
Piore, Michael, 159
Pleck, Elizabeth, 132
police intervention, 123–24, 133, 147–48
Portes, Alejandro, 12, 18, 82
postmodern family, 167

Race, Jeffrey, 43
racial-ethnic tensions, 14
Reagan, Ronald, 13
reeducation camps, 64, 67, 68, 87
Refugee Act of 1980, 12–13. See also
    refugee aid programs
refugee aid programs, 82–85, 106
refugee camps, 70–71
Roldan, Martha, 21, 107
rotating credit clubs, 42
Rumbaut, Rubén, 12, 14, 18, 82, 106,
    112, 155

Sawhill, Isabel, 13
school environment, 146–47, 156
schooling. See education
Secord, Paul, 112–13
See, Katherine O'Sullivan, 171

Sen, Gita, 19
service sector jobs, 80, 138
sex ratios. See Vietnamese American gen-
    der relations
Simon, Rita, 20
small variety stores, 58, 88
small-scale trading, 57–58, 68
Smith, Joan, 78, 106
Smith, Peter, 70
social capital, 83
social networks, 27; economic adaptation
    and, 78–79, 94, 98–99; Vietnamese
    women's, 48; Vietnamese American
    women's, 128–29, 133–36
social service agencies, 26, 82, 83, 85
South Vietnamese middle class, 54–55. See
    also urbanization of South Vietnam
Southeast Asians in the United States, 11,
    13; Philadelphia settlement of, 25; social
    science research on, 11
Srole, Leo, 16
Stacey, Judith, 142, 167, 169
Stack, Carol, 22, 77, 79, 106
Stern, Lewis, 13
Stoecker, Randy, 28
Sully, Francois, 60
Supplemental Security Income, 12–13, 83,
    92, 94

Ta Van Tai, 46
Takaki, Ronald, 163
Tai, Hue-Tam Ho, 39
Thorne, Barrie, 21
Thornton Dill, Bonnie, 20
Tienda, Marta, 78
Time magazine, 7
Trung sisters, 39

unaccompanied minors, 157
United States refugee policies, 10, 12–13.
    See also Refugee Act of 1980
United States in Vietnam, 40–41, 52, 64
urbanization of South Vietnam, 51; kin-
    ship system and, 55–56, 61–64; war
    and, 52–54; women and, 56–60;
utility companies, 126

Viet Cong, 40

Viet Minh, 40, 49–50

Vietnamese American families: children's obligations in, 131–32; ideology of, 99–100, 103–4; parental authority in, 132–33, 146–53; rebuilding of, 100–103; women and, 130–37; young adults and, 158–65. *See also* Vietnamese American gender relations

Vietnamese American gender relations: cultural challenges and, 121–25; expansion of women's roles and, 125–30; greater equality of, 108–12; sex ratios and, 112–21. *See also* Vietnamese American families and job conditions

Vietnamese Americans, 10–11; economic status of, 14; ethnic associations of, 26

Vietnamese kinship system, 43–44. *See also* urbanization of South Vietnam and Communist takeover of Vietnam

VOLAGS. *See* social service agencies

Wain, Barry, 70

Wallerstein, Immanuel, 78, 106

war in Vietnam, 40–41, 50–56

Warner, W. Lloyd, 16

Waters, Mary, 171

Werner, Jayne, 42

Whitmore, John, 155

wife beating, 60–61, 123–24, 132–34, 148. *See also* police intervention

Wilson, William Julius, 13, 80, 171

Winant, Howard, 13, 17

Wolf, Diane, 21, 77, 99, 107

Wolf, Margery, 48

Women in Vietnam, 45–49. *See also* urbanization of South Vietnam and Communist takeover of Vietnam

Yancey, William, 21

Zavella, Patricia, 169

Zinn, Maxine Baca, 21